Taking Care of Our Own

The Black American's Guide
to Family Medicine

George Edmond Smith, M.D., M.Ed.

Hilton Publishing Company   Roscoe, IL

Hilton Publishing Company
Roscoe, IL
Published by Hilton Publishing Company, Inc.
PO Box 737, Roscoe, IL 61073
815-885-1070
www.hiltonpub.com

Publisher's Cataloging-in-Publication
(Provided by Quality Books, Inc.)

Smith, George Edmond.
    Taking care of our own : the black American's guide to family medicine /
George Edmond Smith.
    p. cm.
    Includes index.
    ISBN 0-9675258-6-1

    1. African Americans—Health and hygiene. 2. Family medicine—Popular
works. 3. African Americans—Medical care. I. Title.

RA778.4.A36S45 2004   610'.8996073
                                                                 QBI04-200154

Printed and bound in the United States of America

I dedicate this book to the millions of Black Americans who are ill or who have died from common diseases that could have been prevented if they had the information I offer here.

Thank you to my partner in life, Brenda Ford, who contributed to the research and writing of this book. Your dedication to medically underserved populations is most admirable. I love you more than you know.

—George Edmond Smith, M D

Special thanks to Dr. Mercy Obeime and Susan Yard Harris for skilled editing that made this good book better still.

Contents

Preface

Many textbooks and health guides are available for people who want to learn more about their health and well-being, but few are culturally sensitive to the health of Black Americans. *Taking Care of Our Own* addresses that gap by bringing good health closer to home, and by showing how Black culture can be a starting point for taking charge of your own health care.

This guide aims to be informative, and it provides information in a straightforward, honest, and, I hope, lively way. True stories, based on actual doctor/patient encounters, are included so that you, the reader, can relate to the health information, which can sometimes be complicated. Easy-to-understand facts will assist you in making well-informed decisions about your health. Knowledge of basic medical facts also prepares you to talk with your doctor with conviction and confidence.

As you read, you will start to understand the medical facts you need in order to make good decisions about your family's health and your own. Believe it or not, as you read, you will find yourself becoming healthier and wiser, and you will also add quality to your life.

Taking Care of Our Own argues that you do best to work with a family physician. Family physicians are trained to have a "patient-centered" relationship with the people who trust them with their health. Once you have such a doctor, you and the doctor can make decisions as a team. This book will train you in your part of the conversation, and, at the same time, help you understand how a doctor thinks. Best of all, it will show you how your body works, in sickness and health—along with what makes it stronger and what makes it weaker.

While *Taking Care of Our Own* was written with Black Americans in mind, the information provided here is invaluable for all people. Diseases presented within this book's pages are thoroughly explored.

At the end of the book, you will find a glossary to help you with some basic medical terms, and a list of resources to guide you toward further information and assistance.

Please use this guide with the knowledge that it was written because Black Americans—and *all* people—deserve to be healthy, happy, and disease-free. This book aims, above all, to instill that message in every African American individual and every African American community.

Introduction

MRS. DEARBORN

Mrs. Dearborn arrived early for her first doctor's appointment. She was a pleasant, well-groomed, lively, forty-six-year-old African–American woman. But I saw at a glance that Mrs. Dearborn's health was at great risk.

At 5' 3", she weighed over two hundred and sixty pounds. After I checked her blood sugar with the standard finger-stick technique, I found that her blood pressure too was high—well over 300, a cause for serious concern. Additional tests indicated that Mrs. Dearborn was at severe risk for cardiovascular disease.

When I completed her physical exam, we moved into my office for the customary doctor/patient conference. This one wasn't easy for Mrs. Dearborn. I saw her eyebrows furrow when I explained the urgent need for her to change her diet and begin an exercise routine. She listened, nervously, as I educated her about the risks that went with her high blood pressure and high blood sugar.

What I'd done wasn't very pretty. Mrs. Dearborn had come into my office in an upbeat and pleasant mood, but by the time I'd finished my little speech, her liveliness had vanished, to be replaced with a confused and defensive scowl.

When I finished, I saw that I might as well have been talking a foreign language. Mrs. Dearborn's face showed me she was not receptive. It was as if she'd heard it all before. But I knew that wasn't the end of the road for our conversation. Change is difficult. Of course people resist it.

I encouraged Mrs. Dearborn to tell me all the reasons why she couldn't act on the truth I was telling her, truth that could add years to her life. She had plenty. The fact is that as an unwed mother struggling to make a living, she had a lot of things to worry about, and I was adding still another one.

In each case, I tried to suggest some solution that would take down the roadblock. I knew we were making progress when she finally asked me, with a resigned sigh: "Doctor, how can I change my lifestyle at my age?"

"Mrs. Dearborn," I responded, "I'm glad you asked that question," and I began to explain what I'll explain to you a little later in this book.

MR. JOHNSON

Mr. Johnson was a fifty-five-year-old, barrel-chested Black man who worked in a factory. He was scheduled with me for the annual physical exam required by his employer. At a glance, you wouldn't think Mr. Johnson had much to worry about. His big arms and vice-like handshake made you think: "power-lifter." But except for his arms, his body was flabby, and he had a belly like a Sumo wrestler's. I could see that Mr. Johnson had a high percentage of body fat.

Surprisingly, Mr. Johnson's routine lab tests were normal. But there was still one test I needed to perform, as I do on all male patients: a prostate exam, known in medical terms as the "digital rectal exam." When I told Mr. Johnson that I needed to examine his prostate and rectum, he focused on my latex-gloved right hand.

I took the time to explain to him that Black American males in his age group were more susceptible to cancer than White males of the same age. I explained that the digital rectal exam could rule out the presence of the life-threatening disease, or help to catch it early, when it best responds to treatment.

Maybe I didn't put this argument together as well as I might have. Mr. Johnson snatched up his clothes and simply declared, "I don't have prostate cancer!" The fear in his voice was evident and there was nothing I could say to convince him to have the exam. He nervously got dressed.

As a last resort I soothingly said, "Mr. Johnson, let's go into my office so that I can give you more information." Mr. Johnson, bless his heart, sat there and listened, even though he was still reluctant and fairly unreceptive. This time I patiently explained the details of prostate cancer to him. I also explained that countless Black Americans needlessly die of prostate cancer, when a simple screening exam could have let them live. I told him we could change statistics by taking that exam, and we'd be doing something not only for ourselves but also for the health of our people.

But nothing I said could shake Mr. Johnson's conviction that real men don't get cancer and real men don't submit to the digital examination, even when it is to determine whether there is a problem or not.

MS. SAMUEL

Ms. Samuel was a single, twenty-two-year-old Black American woman with two young boys, one seven-months-old and the other seven-years-old. She seemed stressed as she ushered her sons into the examining room. I greeted the older boy, made a face at the baby, and cheerily said hello to her with a smile. But she returned my greeting with angry, narrow eyes, and belted out, "The nerve of that school, sending my son home just because he missed some of his shots! On top of all that, I'm missing a half day's work to bring him in."

Once we were in the examination room, Ms. Samuel tried to keep the younger child quiet as I looked over the older one's chart. I said, "You have missed several scheduled appointments for your son's immunizations." She shifted in her chair and didn't look at me. As my nurse prepared the injections, I explained to Ms. Samuel the importance of immunizations for her children, and told her which diseases vaccines can prevent. But Ms. Samuel wasn't an easy sell. Before I'd finished explaining, she was tapping her foot, and finally she said, sourly, "Can you hurry? I have a bus to catch."

But it wasn't quite over. The kids got their shots and the nurse rewarded them with stickers. Ms. Samuel already was turning the knob and getting ready to lead the children out when I said: "You haven't followed up on your abnormal Pap smear, either."

"That's just foolishness," she replied. "I'm the one who knows how I feel, and I feel just fine." A real struggle was going on, and I could appreciate how stressed Mrs. Samuel felt, and how hard she worked to meet all her obligations. But I knew I had things to say to her that would make her life easier and healthier, and maybe even happier.

I invited her back into my office, shut the door, and then sat down in the chair next to her to explain my concerns for her health. I focused on the reason children need immunizations, and on the reasons she needed a Pap smear. Little by little she began to get it. "You're saying some sicknesses can be prevented by shots, and that other ones can be spotted early with tests that you do."

"Exactly," I said.

As our conversations continued, the two of us came up with a good medical plan for her and the children. "Finally," I thought, "this story has a happy ending."

THE KEY TO GOOD HEALTH

Educating yourself is absolutely the key to good health. The three stories you've just read show that patients who don't have much knowledge of health issues tend to be fearful and confused, or even downright stubborn. Such attitudes can cause a person to avoid full participation in his or her treatment plans. Doctors know that a good treatment plan works best when the patient participates actively and knowingly. That's why we need to know all we can about the body and diseases that can hurt it, especially diseases such as diabetes, high blood pressure, and cancer—diseases that occur more often in our African American culture than in other population groups.

The language used in this book is designed for the layperson. The chapters are laid out in a way

> Educating yourself is absolutely the key to good health.

that makes it easy to find what you are looking for, and I have avoided medical jargon insofar as possible. The glossary at the end of the book will assist you with unfamiliar terms.

A thorough discussion follows each real-life story, highlighting and exploring the main issues of that story. Illustrations and annotations in the margins emphasize key points, allowing you to find additional information quickly. Each doctor/patient relationship is outlined in detail with an easy-to-understand question and answer section following each subject.

Based on questions people most commonly ask me and other doctors, this book concentrates primarily on medical issues specific to adults, but it also offers general information on infant, child, and adolescent health. In addition, along with discussions of diseases that primarily affect Black Americans, there are discussions of medical problems and diseases that affect the general population.

OBESITY AND ILLNESS

One of the many health issues especially threatening to the Black community is obesity. Mrs. Dearborn represents many African Americans, living in both rural and urban America, for whom a high-fat diet is part of an ongoing tradition and physical fitness is not a priority. The figures for the general population are bad enough: thirty percent of the general American population is obese. But the same studies show that among Black Americans obesity runs to over fifty percent. Worse, these trends suggest that in the future even more Black Americans will be obese and unhealthy.

Specialists have known for a long time that obesity goes hand in

Obesity goes hand in hand with a many serious illnesses, including cardiovascular disease, diabetes, high blood pressure, and cancer. The prevalence of these diseases in the African American population is staggering.

hand with a many serious illnesses, including cardiovascular disease, diabetes, high blood pressure, and cancer. The prevalence of these diseases in the African American population is staggering.

Mrs. Dearborn didn't understand that her obesity and other risk factors could be reduced if she would just enter a partnership with me, for the purpose of her good health and long life. Too many patients still don't understand that. Sure, people are willing to control obesity by taking some "cure-all pill." We live in a culture where you can make a buck by telling people such hokum. But in the long run these pills don't work. You are the one who has to do the work—by changing your lifestyle and habits.

It's only common sense that health/wellness is a way of life and should be approached as such. Too often, doctors themselves are at fault—by treating a symptom too narrowly. Say a patient can't sleep, so the doctor prescribes a sleeping pill. But by doing so, such doctors miss the larger picture. You can start to change that by learning more about your body and illnesses. Knowledge is the power to make yourself healthy and strong, by understanding your own body and why the doctor makes certain recommendations.

PROSTATE CANCER AND EARLY DIAGNOSIS

A disease that hits men hard in our community is prostate cancer. In our second story, Mr. Johnson had some false ideas about prostate cancer. He believed he couldn't have it because he was big and strong. He also believed he would be humiliated by the examination. These beliefs, unfortunately, are common to Black men of all social classes—and to many Whites as well.

The incidence of invasive prostate cancer is thirty percent higher for African American men than for the general population. A major reason is that Black men don't get properly diagnosed until later stages of the disease, so they are more likely to die of it. Forty-two thousand Black men died of prostate cancer in 1995, the date of the latest statistics. That rate has presumably risen since then. Black American men with low incomes, poor educational backgrounds, and little or no access to medical care are at the highest risk.

EMOTIONAL ILLNESS

Ms. Samuel had to grow up very quickly. She became a mother in her mid-teens after growing up with an alcoholic mother and a father who was in jail. She received little support and guidance during her adolescence. By then, her grandmother had become the primary caregiver. The grandmother's intentions were good, but the gap between her and the growing girl was too wide.

Like many teenage mothers, Mrs. Samuel was poorly equipped for motherhood, and knew little about how to care adequately for her infant and the seven-year-old boy. She was often stressed-out and, as time went on, she became depressed.

Ms. Samuel's reactions and behavior during her visit to me were common for her. She had been coming to my office for several years when she or one of the kids was sick, and each time she seemed more hostile than the last. When I suggested that she could get free emotional counseling that would make her feel better, she said "Absolutely no!" When I tried to explain a few basic principles of proper health care for her children, she was too overwhelmed to take it in. She felt that I was just laying one more burden on her.

Ms. Samuel's story ends happily. She finally opened herself to the social support necessary to help her make the changes she and I agreed were necessary. Before long, she was preaching to her friends about the importance of getting their children vaccinated. She even knew the statistics. And she herself was eating better and making sure the children did. She was even beginning to talk about an exercise program.

Depression and mood disorders are more common among young Black Americans than is often realized. Sometimes, as in Ms. Samuel's case, stress, and the fear and anxiety that go with it, get in the way of good parenting.

Making sure your child gets the proper inoculation is an important part of good parenting. Too many children are going without inoculations, and the result is that certain diseases are more common than they should be. In 1994, there were only 958 cases of measles

> Making sure your child gets the proper inoculation is an important part of good parenting.

in the U.S., but over one million people worldwide died from this disease. Vaccines for measles, tetanus, whooping cough, and polio could prevent much childhood mortality.

MAKING CHANGES

Too many of us are getting sick and dying of ailments that, with proper knowledge, we could have prevented or, at least, have had treated earlier. For many diseases, early detection and treatment can make all the difference, because the most effective time to treat a disease is in its early stages.

I write this book out of the belief that knowledge can make you free. I will explain to you as I explain to my patients:

- How your body works
- What sickness is, both physical and mental
- How sickness can be prevented and treated
- How you can get the best help available from health care providers and other community resources
- Special health issues of children, women, and men
- The ABCs of nutrition and exercise
- Reasons why African Americans need to know more about organ transplants, and explanations of how the process works
- An extensive guide to the health resources available to you, whatever your income

Along the way, you'll find that I've tried to keep this book sensitive to women's health issues, and to the issues of good diet and exercise that are so important for all African Americans to understand. You'll also find information about how Hospice can help people die with dignity. In short, you'll find information on the health issues important to all of us, from cradle to grave.

Read and be well.

Part I
ABCs of Good Health
for Black Americans

Chapter 1

The Doctor-Patient Relationship

The people who stay healthiest are usually the people who stay in regular touch with their doctors, going in for annual checkups, and maybe seeing their doctors at other times because of an injury or condition.

Knowing how to find and work with a good doctor isn't easy, nor is it easy to learn how to manage your own medications and doing the other things you need to do to help control a condition or disease. But once you have information and understanding you can manage those tasks.

PARTNERING WITH YOUR DOCTOR

Doctors want to help you, but you have to help them in return. Quality care can happen only when you and your doctor explore your medical situation together, face-to-face. Sure, often you're busy or the doctor's busy and you just call in for a prescription over the phone. This is the "age of convenience." But fast medicine can be as dangerous as fast food, and, at best, neither can do you much good.

The right kind of medicine is a partnership between you and your doctor. The doctor's part is to guide and encourage you to good

health, whatever your condition is, and to treat you when you are ill. The doctor's part is also to help you understand that good health is crucial to your effectiveness and happiness in this world.

Your part is to make and keep appointments, consult with your doctor personally about your health issues, and carry out treatment programs to which you have agreed. By being an active team player with your doctor, you'll get the very best medical services, the services that all of us deserve and to which we are entitled.

QUESTIONS TO ASK YOUR DOCTOR

Like all freedoms, the freedom to have good health care carries responsibilities. But these responsibilities are simple enough. Clear communication with your doctor is basic. Here's a guide to that communication, questions you can ask, lists of medications to prepare in advance, and cues on to how best remember what your doctor tells you in the office. If you write down what the doctor or other health care providers tell you, you'll remember it better. Those who have a hard time reading or writing can get help from a family member, or bring a tape recorder, or ask the doctor to help work out the problem.

Doctors have people on their staffs, or can refer you to people, who can help you understand and write down information you need to remember. These people can be interpreters between you and the doctor. During your visit to your doctor, listen carefully when he or she discusses your disease and instructs you on how the team, including you, can get you well again. Don't let your worry keep you from listening. Most people worry when they're in a doctor's office or examination room. But you can learn to deal with this worry. If at any time you don't understand what the doctor is saying, ask him or her to repeat it. Be sure to let your doctor do the talking when it's his turn. That way, if you listen carefully and even take notes, you'll come away with answers to your questions.

Some of the things you'll want your doctor to explain:

- Your disease or condition
- The kinds of treatment available
- What can happen if the disease isn't treated at all, or not treated properly
- What you need to do in order to stay healthy or return to good health

You'll also want to talk over with the doctor:

- The reason why you are to take the medicine
- How the medicine will work in your body
- Possible side effects and how to deal with them

AFTER YOU LEAVE THE DOCTOR'S OFFICE

Sticking to your doctor's instructions may be difficult, especially if you're not used to working with schedules. But once you've agreed to a treatment plan, it's most important you keep up your end. What the doctor is telling you can make the difference between good health and bad, even between life and death.

In spite of that, people get careless. Say, the doctor tells Mrs. R. to take a specific antibiotic for ten days, but she stops after five days because she's starting to feel better. The danger here is that the medicine hasn't yet gotten to the organism that caused the disease, and that, when Mrs. R. falls ill again, the medicine is less likely to work.

Talk to your doctor if you have questions or problems about your treatment plan at any stage. That's what the doctor is there for. Between the two of you, you can stay on the path of good medical treatment.

KEEPING YOUR OWN MEDICAL RECORDS

- Keep a list of all the medicines, prescription and over-the-counter, you are taking. If you have trouble making such a list, bring the bottles in and the doctor can talk to you about the medicines, and explain which he or she wants you to continue, and which not. But your best bet is to keep that list. It makes life simpler for everyone.
- Write down any diseases or conditions that you know you now have or were treated for in the past.
- Write down in your own terms the state of your health, and what you have to do to keep it up or improve it.

If you have a serious chronic disease, such as seizures or angina (chest pain) or asthma, ask your doctor or staff how to get an identification card or bracelet that identifies you and your disease. This could help save your life if you are unable to speak for yourself.

TYPES OF DOCTORS IN MEDICAL CARE

In order to understand what doctors do, you must understand their basic job descriptions. There are two types of doctors:

Allopathic Physicians (MD)

These are physicians who hold a doctorate in medicine (MD). *Allopathic* doctors treat patients with remedies, or medicines, in order to prevent, treat, or cure a disease or illness. For example,

MDs may give you injections so your body can strengthen its immune system in its fight against a disease.

Osteopathic Physicians (DO)

Doctors of Osteopathy (DO), like MDs, hold a doctorate in medicine. They also use the same methods of treatment, including drugs and surgery. However, Doctors of Osteopathy place a special emphasis on the body's musculoskeletal system. They believe that good health requires proper alignment of bones, muscles, ligaments, and nerves.

MDS AND D.O.S IN PRIMARY CARE

Another way of understanding what doctors do is to look at the difference between primary care doctors and specialists. A primary care doctor is the one whom most patients see first and, usually, more frequently. Primary care doctors tend to see the same patients on a regular basis to do checkups, treat specific ailments, or recommend or provide preventative treatments.

Most primary care doctors are pediatricians, general and family practitioners, and general internists. Like all doctors, primary care doctors have completed a one-year internship and specialized training (residency) after they graduate from medical school, and they have passed an exam given by the National Board of Medical Examiners (N.B.M.E.). All doctors who practice medicine in the United States must pass this exam.

> A primary care doctor is the one whom most patients see first and more frequently.

After residency, doctors take another exam for board certification given by the American Board of Medical Specialists (A.B.M.S.) or the American Osteopathic Association (A.O.A.). There are certifications in twenty-three specialties.

Some primary care doctors are both primary care physicians *and* specialists in a particular field of medicine. Others practice only in the field of their specialty. A kidney specialist sees only kidney patients. A

Key to abbreviations

MD—Medical Doctor
DO—Doctor of Osteopathic Medicine
N.B.M.E.—National Board of Medical Examiners
A.B.M.S.—American Board of Medical Specialists
A.A.F.P.—American Academy of Family Practice Physicians
A.O.A.—American Osteopathic Association
Fellow—Fellowship in a specialty
PC—a Primary Care business corporation

heart surgeon only does heart surgery. A primary care doctor will recommend you to a specialist if your illness or condition requires.

CHOOSING THE RIGHT DOCTOR

If you're looking for a doctor or want to know how good your doctor is, call the medical board office in your state, or go to the data banks with the help of your local librarian or the Internet. In this way you can find out if the doctor's license is in good standing and also get other information about the doctor's professional standing.

If negative information turns up, you have the right to question the doctor about the details. Doctors with integrity are more than willing to explain any and all circumstances. If this doctor *isn't* willing, look for another.

When you are getting ready to select a doctor, set up an appointment to meet him or her *before* any medical exam. Ask such questions as:

- Are you board certified?
- In what area of medicine (for example, internal, pediatric, or family medicine) did you specialize?
- If I need to call you to answer a question, how do I best do so?
- If I need to call you because of a medical emergency, how do I best do so?

The doctor's answers to such questions can tell you whether this doctor is likely to suit your personal medical needs.

Besides finding out about the doctor's professional competence and availability to meet your needs, you'll want a doctor you feel comfortable with. Some things you may notice as soon as you enter the office, like whether the office itself is clean and tidy, and how the doctor interacts with his or her staff.

During the interview, notice if the doctor's manner is rushed, or comforting and calm, as it should be. You may discover whether the doctor's value system harmonizes with yours. Pay attention also to whether this doctor strikes you as sensitive to your state of mind and emotions because that sensitivity is where the healing ultimately begins.

Your doctor's job goes beyond simply having completed medical school and a specialized residency program. For a great many doctors medicine is a calling, not a part-time endeavor. The doctor you choose should be a role model for both you and the community. He will practice and teach nutrition and good exercise, staying clean of nicotine and drugs or excessive drinking. In other words, he'll teach good health by his example as well as his instruction.

> Pay attention also to whether this doctor strikes you as sensitive to your state of mind and emotions because that sensitivity is where the healing ultimately begins.

EDUCATION, PREVENTION, AND REFERRAL PROGRAMS

Good doctors care about patients. They don't just write out prescriptions and send you on your way. They educate you about your condition and treatment, they recommend programs that will keep you in good health, and they connect you with agencies or groups that may help you in your efforts to remain healthy or regain health. Good doctors talk directly to their patients, and they take time to explain the disease process and how to prevent or treat it.

Keep in mind that "doctor" also means "teacher." Try to find a doctor who takes the extra time to educate and counsel, and who encourages a healthy lifestyle and gives you the tools you need to make necessary changes.

Because of the HMO and managed care systems, many Blacks (and many patients of other races as well) are either assigned to a doctor or have limited choices. But often if you ask the right questions, patiently but determinedly, you'll discover that you have the right to choose. Don't be intimidated. Exercise your rights wisely. If you aren't pleased with the doctor you are assigned to or choose, insist on another.

MANAGED CARE

No health care issue spurs more debate and controversy than managed care. At the same time, many people don't clearly understand how managed care works. Here are the ABCs you need to make this system work for you most effectively.

Black Americans, like many Americans, need to participate more actively in the managed care system. Active participation is based on knowledge. There are probably several reasons why Black Americans are more likely than the general population to experience major illnesses like cardiovascular disease, diabetes, and stroke, and more likely to die of them. But often the heart of the trouble is that they don't get medical care as early as they should. They don't get the benefits of the medical system because they don't know how it works.

You don't have to be rich to get the medical care you need and deserve. There are welfare HMOs that can give you good medical attention, even if you can't pay for it. But to get it, you must understand how these systems work.

What is Managed Care?

The term "Managed Care" refers to a system for health care in which an organization, such as an HMO, some other type of doctor-hospital network, or an insurance company, acts an intermediary, or "middleman," between the patient and the doctor. At their best, managed

Some Terms Used in Managed Care

Capitation The fixed amount of money paid on a monthly basis to an HMO or individual health provider (such as your doctor) for the full medical care of a patient.

Case Manager A health professional, (e.g., nurse, doctor, social worker) affiliated with a health plan, who is responsible for coordinating the medical care of a patient enrolled in a managed care plan.

Co-insurance The amount of money paid out of pocket by plan members for medical services. Co-insurance payments are usually a fixed percentage of the total cost of a medical service covered by the plan. For example, if a health plan pays eighty percent of a physician's bill, the remaining twenty percent that the member pays is referred to as co-insurance.

Co-payment The amount of money (always a flat fee) paid by plan members up front and out-of-pocket for specific medical services at the time they are rendered. Most managed care co-payments are between $0–$20 per visit or per prescription.

Formulary A health plan's list of approved prescription medications for which it will reimburse members or pay directly.

Gatekeeper physician The primary care physician who directs the medical care of HMO members. HMOs require that each enrollee be assigned to a primary care physician. This physician is referred to as the "gatekeeper."

Health Plan An HMO or traditional health insurance plan that covers a set range of health services.

Medicaid The federal and state health insurance program for low-income Americans. Medicaid also foots the bill for nursing home care for the indigent elderly.

Medicare The federal health insurance program for older and disabled Americans.

Preventative Care An approach to health care that emphasizes preventative measures such as routine physical exams, diagnostic tests (e.g., Pap smears), immunizations, and more.

care systems provide an organized approach to health care, by providing opportunities for annual checkups, diagnosis, and treatment. But because these systems are big and, often, profit-driven, they can also be intimidating and frustrating.

Managed care is designed to control high costs. This means that the system sets specific, and sometimes rigid, controls on what medical services (tests, surgical procedures, and other treatments) are to be provided and how much they should cost. The system can sometimes decline to pay for a service that your doctor recommends.

Managed Care and the Doctor/Patient Relationship

One hundred million Americans now get their medical services through managed care plans, and this number will probably keep rising. Some people are satisfied with their plans. They get the examinations and treatment they need, and sometimes the medical education they also need.

But many other patients, and doctors as well, are worried about the effect of managed care on the patient/physician relationship. We've all read stories, sometimes sensationalized, about patients in managed care systems who are refused treatment that their doctors believe they need. Such conflicts of interest *do* happen, and when they do, they can be damaging to the patient's health, not to mention the doctor's professional authority.

Both doctors and patients also argue that the mere size of these organizations makes them bureaucratic and unresponsive to the patient's needs. A patient can be subjected to a long wait in the emergency room while the hospital waits for his or her HMO to authorize a visit with a physician. Sometimes, a patient must wait several weeks to see a specialist for a condition that may be urgent. Such delays can mean unnecessary suffering.

Another issue that worries patients and doctors is that doctors in HMOs usually have to see a certain number of patients each day to meet the HMO's criteria for payment. That means your doctor is less likely to have time to chat and build a trusting relationship with you. In some cases, time pressures may even mean that your doctor provides poorer treatment than he'd prescribe if he had more time for you.

Of course, like most big issues, this one has two sides. Supporters of managed care argue that HMOs work to correct a problem caused by doctors themselves. In the old days, they say, when doctors made all the decisions, tests were ordered without regard to their cost, and sometimes, even to whether they were useful or not. Because there was no quality control, there was also no cost control.

Managed care, its defenders say, cuts high medical costs by monitoring both the cost and the quality of treatment. Further, many HMOs realize that preventing disease is cheaper and far better for the patient than having to treat it. People who eat a healthy diet and exercise regularly are less likely to fall ill from serious and sometimes life-threatening illnesses. For that reason, HMOs encourage good health habits in their patients.

This debate will go on. The important thing is that, for the time being, most Americans will get their medical care as managed care. For that reason, you need to know how to use the system. (See the glossary at the end of this book for a list of terms used in managed care.)

African Americans and Managed Care

A large number of African Americans who are not covered by private health care insurance are covered under Medicaid or Medicare. They want and deserve a doctor or other health care provider who has the cultural sensitivity to understand them. They also deserve a doctor who can explain in clear terms what wellness and illness are and, if they are ill, the path to recovery.

> People who ask questions and who are politely assertive about their needs are people who will get the best care.

But cultural sensitivity requires work on both sides. Yes, doctors need to be able to present information so that it's understandable to people who haven't been to medical school, or even to college. At the same time, patients who belong to plans such as Medicaid need to learn everything they can about their plans. People who ask questions and who are politely assertive about their needs are people who will get the best care.

Calling Your Doctor and Planning Ahead

Through your HMO, you will work with one person responsible for your primary care. Primary care includes checkups, treatment, follow-up on treatment, and good information on how to keep your body in the best shape possible, whatever your condition of health or illness.

Your responsibility to your primary care provider includes showing up for your pre-scheduled meetings, and taking medications that you and your doctor agree are necessary. If you listen, and the doctor is clear, such cooperation comes easy. If for some unavoidable reason, like an accident or some other emergency, you can't keep an appointment, be sure to call the provider to say why you can't make it and to arrange for a later appointment.

Under certain circumstances, you may need to contact or see your primary care provider immediately. Here are some of those circumstances:

Call if you have an accident or are ill enough to require immediate medical attention. If your call is at night, you may talk to another doctor who isn't familiar with your condition. Be ready to describe your condition and the immediate problem. The doctor may also ask you what medications you are taking, so have your list handy.

Here are some typical reasons why people call their doctors:

- A fever not reduced by Tylenol® or aspirin
- Feeling so ill you cannot eat or drink fluids
- A sore throat with swollen tonsils and glands, and not being able to eat or drink
- A cough that cough syrups don't help and that worsens over time
- A cough with chest pain
- A sinus cold that does not respond to decongestants and is accompanied by severe headache, dizziness, or vomiting

- Ear pain with fever, ringing in the ear, nausea and vomiting, fever with weight loss
- A problem with urination accompanied by pain or fever
- A fever with rash
- An infant with fever, irritability, and poor feeding and drinking

Pain can also be a reason to call your provider. Call if you have:

- Sudden pain with no apparent cause
- Pain caused by trauma
- Pain with mental status changes, including seizures
- Excessive pain
- Pain that suddenly keeps you from moving
- Pain connected with nausea and vomiting
- Pain with fever

Sometimes you need to call your doctor about chronic conditions—that is, about diseases you must learn to live with. In such a case, call if you have:

- Any bad effect from taking medicines
- Any change in mental status, including loss of consciousness
- Worsening of your chronic illness (for example, a patient with asthma who begins to have more wheezing or shortness of breath)

Preparing for Medical Emergencies

One way to be prepared is to keep a first aid kit at home. Any box will do, as long as it is clearly marked, and kept in a place where everyone in the household can easily find it. A basic first aid kit should contain:

- Band-Aids®, sterile gauze, antiseptics and hydrogen peroxide for wound cleansing
- Antibiotic gels such as Neosporin® and something for pain such as ibuprofen or Tylenol®

- A thermometer to check for fever, particularly if you have young children
- Medicines for fever, such as Children's Tylenol Elixir® (I have purposely excluded aspirin for children because of its link to a deadly disease called Reyes Syndrome. This disease often follows a viral illness. Some studies have reported that babies who are given aspirin for fever have had liver failure and brain edema, symptoms of Reyes Syndrome. This syndrome occurs most commonly among children between the ages of one and fifteen years, although cases have been reported in teenagers and even adults.)
- Two aspirin, dissolved in water, as excellent first aid in the case of heart attack
- Decongestant cough syrup and Benadryl® for relief of symptoms of the common cold and runny nose
- Pediacare®, special water that contains electrolytes, commonly used by mothers to help relieve the symptoms of the common cold in infants and to ensure that dehydration does not occur (Read instructions carefully to use the correct dosages. If you are unsure, call your doctor or a pharmacist for assistance.)
- Fluids such as Pedialyte®, spring water, Gatorade®, and nutritional liquids like Ensure®, basic supplies for every household
- Hydrocortisone cream, to relieve itching from a rash. (However, for a rash of unknown origin, see a doctor.

When you need to call your doctor or nurse in the case of an emergency, be prepared. One good way is to keep a list of medical conditions and symptoms for yourself and other members of your family. If you can't make up this list on your own, ask the doctor or one of his staff to help you. They'll be glad to.

Before you go in to see your doctor for a visit, think about what you want to ask and write the questions down. There are no bad questions, only bad answers. If you've called when your doctor is off duty, be ready to tell the doctor why you need help now, not during regular hours.

Be ready to write down the doctor's instructions. Even if you are calling because you can't remember instructions he gave in the office, that's okay. But write them down now or have someone else do so.

Avoid having to make last-minute calls because you've run out of some medicine that is critical for your well-being. If you do delay, you'll probably get an on-call doctor, who may not want to call in a prescription for you because your medical record won't be handy. That's why it's so important for you to keep track of your medications and call your doctor at least a week before you need a new prescription filled.

Keep your pharmacy phone number handy. The doctor doesn't have such numbers handy and won't be happy if you call at 2:00 A.M. asking him or her to look up the number of your pharmacy.

In an emergency, when you or a family member experiences an accident or medical crisis that threatens life, like a severe asthma or heart attack, call 911 or go directly to the emergency room of the nearest hospital. Staff there will notify your doctor and your insurance carrier.

Be totally prepared when you call your doctor.

To sum up, be totally prepared when you call your doctor. Be ready to describe your symptoms and your specific needs. Be ready to ask questions about whatever is bothering you. There are *no* bad questions. You want a doctor who treats all your questions seriously.

Chapter 2

Visiting Your Doctor to Keep Yourself in Good Health

W e've been talking about one kind of doctor's visit, the kind you make when you're sick or hurt. But there is another kind of visit, the kind you make because you want to stay well. Prevention is the key to good health.

Here are some guidelines for preventative office visits:

- Make an appointment once yearly for a physical exam.
- Women should make an appointment once yearly for a gynecological exam, in addition to the annual physical exam.
- If your doctor hasn't told you already, ask about diet, exercise, and relaxation techniques. All three are crucial to staying in good health if you are healthy, or, if you are not healthy now, becoming healthy.

> Prevention is the key to good health.

YOUR FIRST VISIT

Your first visit to your doctor can be the most important one. This is when you and your doctor start to communicate. As part of that communication, the doctor needs to know something about your medical history, including the medical histories of your parents, grandparents, brothers, and sisters. If the doctor is a family physician, he or she will also ask about the health of your children.

The doctor will want to know about your present state of health, past illnesses or surgeries, and drugs you may be taking. The doctor will also talk with you about your body's major systems and sometimes find symptoms you aren't aware of. Symptoms that may seem unimportant to you can sometimes help the doctor focus in on your particular medical complaint and diagnose the problem.

The reason the doctor explores your family background is that some diseases run in families—in medical language, they have a genetic background. For example, if a middle-aged Black man complains of low back pain and difficulty urinating, *and* his father had prostate cancer, the doctor will suspect prostate cancer and have tests performed to prove or disprove the hypothesis.

During your first medical exam, your doctor will diagnose illness and disease mainly by observing and considering your symptoms and outward signs. "Symptoms" are the complaints you have; "signs" are what your doctor finds when he or she examines you. These, along with your medical history, help your doctor determine why you are having certain symptoms.

In a nutshell, your doctor does the detective work by:

- Asking questions about your current illness (chief complaint)
- Asking questions about your past medical history and medications
- Reviewing your symptoms
- Exploring your family history

The current illness is the reason for most office visits, and the chief complaint is what you describe when you feel pain or some other symptom.

Still another way your doctor seeks to detect illness and explore your health behavior is through your social history. Some of the information that may come up in such a conversation is:

- Whether or not you smoke or drink alcohol
- Your educational background
- Your financial status
- Your employment record
- Your marital status

Each of these factors may have an impact on your health.

Give the doctor as much information as you can, knowing that he or she is using it to help you stay healthy or become healthy. That way you help the doctor to help you.

The Physical Examination

If you are in the examination room because you have a physical ailment, the doctor will form a general impression of your physical characteristics. Are you:

- Overweight or underweight?
- Older or younger?
- Nervous or calm?
- Bright-eyed or sullen?

During the physical exam, the doctor will measure and observe:

- Your height and weight
- Your skeletal proportion and posture
- Your sexual development
- Your fat and muscle distribution
- Your skin characteristics

Each of these factors can tell the doctor something that will help him or her understand your condition.

Your physique can also provide medical clues to your doctor. For example, the body of an abnormally tall person may make too much growth hormone. That may be fine if you are a basketball player, but there are also risks. A person who is "too tall" may have thyroid problems, or problems caused by high levels of the male hormone called "androgen." Chromosome and heart abnormalities are other serious problems that can go along with extreme height.

Other kinds of physiques may point to potential health problems of still other kinds. If you are overweight, the doctor will consider nutritional problems, and will also want to find out if you have an under-active thyroid. If you are short and heavy, sex hormone abnormalities can be a cause.

Distribution of Body Fat

The distribution of body fat is important to your doctor, too. Men who have a lot of fat in their lower abdomen are at risk for heart disease. Abnormal fat build-ups in other parts of the body can result from diseases. Fat deposits in the chest, stomach, and face, while the limbs remain skinny, may point to a disorder of the adrenal glands called *Cushing's Disease*. Patients with asthma who take oral steroid medication can have the same distribution of fat.

Your doctor will use all available resources—observation and tests—to find out the state of your physical health. But your mental health is also important. Nervousness and excitability, or unresponsiveness and lethargy, can be signs of depression or anxiety. I've known some Black American patients who feel that their lives are at a standstill. They appear to have little motivation. Sometimes, they stare at the floor, refuse to make eye contact, or even to answer questions. Many of these people I've been able to treat with medication and counseling.

What it boils down to is that your doctor's job is to help you feel better, in body and mind. *Your* job is to be open and honest with your doctor. Between the two of you, in open communication, you'll work out the best possible treatment plan if you're ill, or the best plan to keep you healthy if you're already there.

Vital Signs

Your doctor will monitor, during your first visit and all later visits:

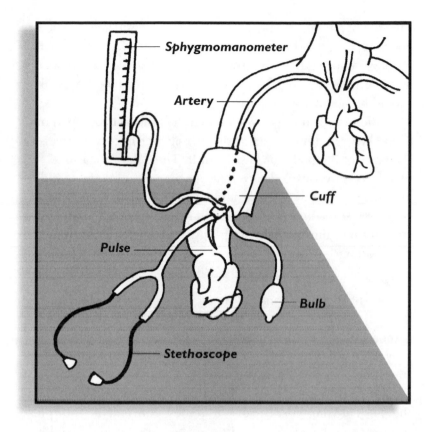

How blood pressure is measured

- **Blood Pressure**

  This is the force of blood on the blood vessel's wall. Blood pressure changes each time the heart, a muscle, squeezes and then relaxes. The higher pressure occurs during the tightening cycle, when blood is pushed out from the heart into your arteries. This is called *systolic pressure*—the top number in your blood pressure reading. A normal systolic pressure is approximately 120.

  The lowest point of the cycle is when your heart is at the relaxed stage. Then the *diastolic* pressure (the bottom number in your blood pressure reading) should be in the neighborhood of 70. A normal blood pressure reading, then, is 120/70. According to national guidelines, any blood pressure registering 140/90 or above is considered to be high and dangerous. In fact, new studies have reported that for African Americans who have diabetes and heart disease, high cholesterol and obesity, blood pressure should be below 130/80.

Blood pressure measures how much blood is pumped out of the heart and how much resistance it runs into as it travels to the parts of the body furthest from it. The doctor measures blood pressure with a device that consists of an inflatable bulb, an inflatable bag with a cuff, and a meter that shows the numbers for the reading. Your doctor may take your blood pressure several times during one visit, because that gives the most accurate reading.

- **Pulse**

In ancient times, healers and medicine men checked the pulse to determine how sick their patients were. Today, as then, doctors gather a wealth of information from your arterial pulse. By carefully combing through that information, your doctor can understand the rate, rhythm, and strength of your heartbeat.

Normal pulse rate is 72 beats per minute. The doctor feels the pulse at your wrist because it is most convenient. Your pulse occurs when the *aortic valve* in your heart opens and blood is pushed out from the heart. Patients with an irregular heartbeat (*arrhythmia*) will have an irregular pulse. Your doctor will carefully investigate an irregular heart rhythm.

- **Temperature**

Another ancient clinical tool is measurement of the body's temperature. A fever (the elevation of body temperature) often results from disease. When germs (viruses or bacteria) enter your body, your body works harder, creating more heat. Fever is one way your body manages the extra heat.

The doctor will take your temperature at all office visits to be sure you don't have a fever. If you do, that might help detect a disease before you even know you have it. Normal body temperature is 98.6 degrees.

- **Respiration**

  When you take in a deep breath, it is called *inspiration*. The respiration rate is the number of inspirations per minute. Doctors are interested in the rate and volume of your respiration. The normal adult resting respiratory rate is 14 to 18 per minute. A faster respiratory rate is termed "tachypnea," and a slower rate is called "bradypnea."

  Fast or slow respiratory rates may be the symptoms of particular diseases and may be the result of inhaling certain poisons or toxins that cause the rate and depth of the breaths to increase. Asthma and other respiratory ailments, on the other hand, cause slow, shallow breaths.

  Slow, shallow breathing is called "hypoventilation." It often occurs in obese patients and can cause sleep apnea (a disorder where low oxygen levels in the blood can lead to chronic headache, sleep disturbances, and depression). Sleep apnea can occur for several reasons, but most commonly it results from obstructed upper airways caused by obesity.

Skin

Dermatology" is the study of the skin. When doctors examine the skin, they focus on:

- **Pain**

  Are there lesions? Lesions are any abnormality of the skin, such as a bump, wart, mole, or rash. If you have lesions, the doctor will want to know if they are painful or not, because that too will help the diagnosis.

- **Dysfunction**

  Are there areas of the skin that don't function normally? Some dysfunctions, like scaling, or not being able to sweat, may be signs of skin abnormality.

- **Change**

  Having a thorough history of a lesion helps the doctor determine, for example, whether a lesion on the skin is a birth mole or points to cancer.

- *Skin turgor*

  Turgor refers to the consistency and state of hydration of the skin—that is, whether it feels well hydrated or like dry velvet. Healthy skin will bounce back when pulled by fingers, indicating that the capillary blood flow is good and the skin is getting nutrients and water.

  In the case of elderly patients who are dehydrated, the skin will remain "tented" when pinched. This response indicates the need to drink more water.

- *Skin texture*

  Roughened skin with long, deep "crow's feet" at the corners of a patient's eyes could indicate heavy cigarette smoking.

- *Skin color*

  Liver failure can turn the skin yellow. Substance abuse or low saturation of oxygen in the blood can cause the skin to take on a dull grayish hue.

- *Distribution of skin lesions*

  Red spots on the palms of hands may indicate syphilis. Painful rash or blisters on one side of the face could indicate shingles (*herpes zoster*), an infection caused by the same virus that causes chicken pox.

Eyes

A wealth of information can be obtained by examining eyes. The eye exam can tell the doctor if a patient has anemia, diabetes, or high blood pressure and cardiovascular disease. Bulging eyes could indicate abnormalities of the thyroid gland. Eye pain is taken seriously, as is a sudden loss of sight.

Patients with eye problems should receive care from an ophthalmologist, who is an MD specializing in eye disorders. Optometrists specialize in eyesight, and in selling and fitting glasses to improve sight. They do examine the eye, but this exam is minimal compared to the thorough exam done by an ophthalmologist.

When examining the eyes, the doctor focuses on:

Orbit and Surrounding Structures

- **The eye bulb**
  rests on the bony socket called the orbit. Disorders of any of the muscles attached to the eyeball can cause it to shift its position. For example, a weak lateral muscle (the muscle closest to your ear) will cause the eye to shift toward the nose. This is called "strabismus."

  - *The eyebrows* are important also. Sudden loss of hair in the eyebrows could indicate a hormonal disease.
  - *Drooping of the eyelids* can indicate problems with the nervous system.
  - *Blockage of the tear ducts* can cause pain and swelling of lids.

- **Cornea**
  The cornea is the clear covering of the eye. Damage to the cornea, such as a scratch, is very serious. Your doctor will usually examine this part of your eye with an *ophthalmoscope*. Your doctor may also use a blue light with a fluorescent strip of paper to stain the eye. The strip, which shows any breaks in the cornea membrane, is easily seen under a blue light.

- **Conjunctiva and Sclera**
  It is important to consult your doctor if your eyes are red.
  The conjunctiva is the pink part of the eye. When this area is inflamed, it is called pink eye (conjunctivitis). Many children come in to the doctor with this disorder, their eyes red and puffy. Conjunctivitis can be caused by bacteria or viruses, and can be treated with oral antibiotic medication or antibiotic drops.
  The white part of the eye, the sclera, can become inflamed and red as well. This is called "scleritis," which is more serious than conjunctivitis.

- **Retina**
  The retina is the back of the eye, referred to as the "eyeground." The doctor looks at this area with his ophthalmoscope as well.
  The nerves and small arteries of the eye are located in the retina. So is the optic disc, where nerves and arteries converge at

the back of the eye to send impulses to the brain that allow vision to occur.

Changes in the vessels or surface area of the retina can indicate diseases such as diabetes and arteriosclerosis.

Other Eye Diseases

Other eye diseases and problems that deserve mention are glaucoma, papilledema (a bulging eye disc caused by increased pressure in the brain), cataracts, and poor vision, all of which can be determined by your doctor.

Ears

Usually a person's family or friends will recognize your hearing loss first.

The doctor will examine the outside of the ear carefully for any type of lesion that could have diagnostic importance. The doctor will then examine the middle ear with what is called an "otoscope," carefully inspecting the eardrum for disease and functioning. The inner ear, which contains the nerves that transport sound to the brain, is also assessed during the ear exam, usually with a tuning fork and good neurologic examination.

Keep in mind how important it is for all people, and especially for children, that eyes and ears perform normally. Both systems are crucial for learning. Parents can minimize learning loss by making sure that their children's eye and ear problems are diagnosed early.

Your doctor will perform both hearing and eye screenings for all school-age children. Be sure to take advantage of this screening.

The Nose

Problems of the nose will affect your sense of smell. The nose filters or cleanses the air and helps to humidify the air you breathe in.

A runny nose is called "rhinorrhea." The doctor may use an "otoscope" (the same instrument used to examine the ear) to look in the nose. The membrane in the nose can become inflamed. Polyps (a stalked, pea-shaped bump in the sinus cavity) can also cause discomfort and be a problem.

Nosebleeds are pretty common. The two most common causes of nosebleeds are polyps and dry, swollen nasal membranes.

Snoring can be a sign of a blocked nose and should not automatically be dismissed as unimportant or untreatable, especially when it occurs in children.

Perforation of the septum (the membrane that separates each nostril) is a serious medical condition and can be caused by infectious disorders such as syphilis or substance abuse (e.g., inhaling nonprescribed drugs).

Mouth and Throat

Poor oral health can compromise your immune system. Some sore throats result from poor oral hygiene.

Painful swallowing implies a mechanical problem with the throat and esophagus, the tube that takes food from your mouth to your stomach.

In an examination of your mouth and throat, your doctor will look for:

- Masses or lesions
- Infections
- Hoarseness
- Halitosis (bad breath)
- Abnormalities of the tongue
- Abnormalities of the hard and soft palates (the roof and floor of your mouth)

There is also a direct link between cigarette smoking in the home and inflamed tonsils in children who live in that home. Some children who inhale secondhand smoke will develop an allergy to cigarette smoke, and sore throats will result.

The Neck

Examination of the neck can serve several purposes. The thyroid gland, located here, needs the doctor's special attention. The thyroid gland controls metabolism and iodine in the body.

Other areas in the neck that can become diseased:

- Lymph nodes
- Blood vessels sending blood to the brain
- Esophagus
- Trachea
- Cervical spine

The muscles in the neck are important, and a strain or spasm can cause a stiff neck, a common patient complaint. Your doctor may use his stethoscope to listen for turbulence or roaring of blood flow on each side of your neck, indicating a narrowing or blockage of the blood vessel.

Breasts and Axilla (see Breast Cancer Chapter also)

Thousands of women die from breast cancer each year. Women are most alarmed when they suddenly discover a lump or tender mass while doing a self-exam. If this happens to you, consult with your doctor immediately. Denial plays a significant role in the death rate of all women from breast cancer. Black women should have a mammogram at the age of forty. If you have a family history of breast cancer, it is important to get a mammogram before you reach age forty. The emphasis here is that early detection is the best weapon against breast cancer.

Cancer travels through the body by using the blood and lymphatic system or lymph nodes. It usually affects the nodes under the armpit (axilla), so it is important for women to always feel for tenderness or lumps in this area.

When a woman comes to her doctor with a breast mass, the doctor will ask these questions:

- How long have you had the problem?
- Is there pain or absence of pain?
- Is the mass enlarging or constant?
- Are there other symptoms such as fever or weight loss?
- Is there nipple discharge, and if so, what type? (Milk, blood, fluid, etc.)

Your doctor will examine your breasts while you are disrobed to the waist and sitting with your back straight. He or she may also have you lie on your back with your arm behind your head and examine the sides of your breasts and under your armpit.

A woman should examine her breasts once a month, right after her menstrual period. This examination can be done in the shower with wet fingers in a circular fashion starting at the nipple and slowly radiating over the entire breast. Feel under your armpit (axilla) and end your self-exam with a nipple squeeze. If a bloody or waxy black substance is extruded from the nipple, consult your doctor immediately. When you examine your breasts each month, you will not only familiarize yourself with the architecture of your own breasts, but you will also be able to detect any sudden changes that may develop.

The Thorax

The thorax is the upper part of the body between the neck and abdomen. The term refers to a large portion of the body's mass and houses many organs, including the heart and lungs. So when a patient comes in with a pain or other complaint in the area of the thorax, the doctor must sort out which organ is at fault and arrive at a proper diagnosis. The doctor's knowledge of your medical history will help him or her in this time-consuming process.

Two main complaints of the thorax are chest pain or cough. To most people, chest pain means heart disease or possible heart attack. While that possibility must be uppermost in the doctor's mind, patients must understand that there can also be pain in other structures in the thorax, and the doctor must check out these possibilities, too.

The two most common types of pain are pain that feels like an uncomfortable pressure or weight in your chest, which suggests *heart trouble*; or a sharp pain when you breathe in deeply, which suggests *pleurisy*. The pleura is the membrane that surrounds the lungs and helps lubricate them. When it is inflamed, the membranes rub against each other, causing the pain. Pleurisy is commonly caused by pneumonia. As with cardiac pain, this illness may result in shortness of breath.

In order to learn which illness you may have, your doctor will look for answers to the following questions:

- Is your pain a pressure sensation in your chest, or a sharp pain in the chest when you breathe in deeply?
- Do you have a cough that causes pain?
- Does the pain occur when you are exerting yourself? Such pain may suggest angina.
- What color is the sputum you cough up? Green sputum may indicate infections like bronchitis or pneumonia (which may result in pleurisy).
- Do you have a fever?
- Do you cough up blood? Coughing up blood can be caused by serious illness like tuberculosis, cancer, or severe lung infection. In rare cases, a patient can develop a blood clot in a major vessel that sends blood through the lungs. This often-fatal occurrence is called *pulmonary embolism*.

The Heart

The heart is something like the engine of the body. It sets everything in motion. For that reason, doctors, along with health organizations and insurance companies, give special attention to diseases of the heart. Most doctors carry stethoscopes around their necks. In an emergency, the first thing the doctor does is to listen to the patient's heart.

Chest pain related to a heart problem results from disease of the blood vessels that send blood to the heart ("coronary arteries") or of the heart valves. Chest pain that feels like pressure and radiates down the arm is called "angina." When your doctor listens to your heart, he or she listens to the sound the valves make as they open and close. The doctor also listens for murmurs. Murmurs are sounds that resemble a "roaring of the ocean." They are the sound the blood makes as it rushes through the heart.

The doctor will already have asked you questions about whether you have shortness of breath, palpitations, fatigue, sweating, or fainting (syncope) fainting. All of these signs can result from coronary disease.

Congestive heart failure (CHF) is a heart disease that plagues a good number of my patients. CHF occurs when the heart is not strong enough to pump blood to the outer, or peripheral, parts of the body. The blood leaves the heart by way of the left ventricle. Often, this chamber of the heart is unable to squeeze down strongly enough to drive out all the blood that has accumulated in it during the heart's rest period. The backup of blood and fluid that results can cause lungs to become congested. (See more under *Cardiovascular Illness.*)

A patient who is middle-aged or older, and who has fatigue, shortness of breath on exertion, and swollen ankles toward the end of the day is a candidate for CHF. In addition, if you are unable to sleep flat on your back, you need several pillows in order to breathe properly, and have to get up during the night to urinate, you and your doctor must be thinking about CHF.

Several tests help determine if a person has heart disease. These include the EKG (electrocardiogram), the Echo (Echocardiogram), and cardiac stress testing.

The Abdomen

Adults and children often complain of abdominal pain. The doctor investigates the pain first by determining your medical history, and looking for specific symptoms. The doctor will also explore whether symptoms go together—for example, vomiting or diarrhea that happen after eating.

In an examination of your abdomen, the doctor divides the area into four sections. Pain in the right upper section can occur from the gallbladder, liver, or intestines. In the left upper section, ulcer disease must be investigated. Right lower quadrant pain can originate from an inflamed appendix. Left lower abdominal pain points to possible disease of the colon.

Diseases of the abdomen, which may involve problems with the liver, can cause:

- Jaundice
- Anemia
- Hematemesis (vomiting blood)

- Inability to eat without vomiting or diarrhea
- Abnormal bowel movements
- Ascites (pooling of fluid in the abdomen)

The doctor uses his stethoscope and hands to examine the abdomen. There are also several technical tests used to survey the abdomen. Most useful are the ultrasound and CAT scan, which show internal images more clearly than an X-ray.

An Explanation of Some Lab Tests

If the physical exam points to a problem, your doctor may want you to have lab tests that provide information necessary for a firm diagnosis. I always give my patients a brief description of the tests I've ordered, so they won't be surprised. Here is what I tell them.

Blood Tests

Doctors can determine if you have a disease, or can confirm their initial diagnosis, by obtaining a blood specimen from you. Your blood sample is sent to a laboratory for analysis. Whatever is present in your blood is measured by its concentration, blood cell counts, or enzyme activity. The lab report will also give the doctor a reference range that would be expected for healthy adults. Normal or abnormal is determined by whether the test value falls inside or outside the reference range. These reference ranges have been questioned lately, since they are based on studies of healthy White males. African American men and women may have a unique reference range not the same as healthy White males.

Other common blood tests include:

- ***Chemzyme Plus Test***
  An enzyme is a protein substance that causes beneficial metabolic changes in cells and organs. Enzymes are usually produced and housed inside cells, and when the cell is damaged, the enzyme will move into the blood, where high levels can be measured.

  This test puts together several organ studies and provides a blood profile. The doctor wants it in your medical file in order to

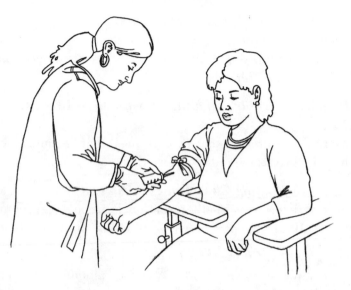

note changes later if any occur. That's why the doctor will probably ask you to have this test during your first visit, or shortly after.

- ***Glucose test***
This test measures blood sugar. The normal range is around 100. Glucose is the substance needed for energy in the cells of the body. A high glucose level may indicate diabetes.

- ***Glucose Hemoglobin A1C test***
This test helps determine the presence of diabetes by monitoring levels of glucose over a period of several weeks. This test is relatively new.

- ***Blood Urea Nitrogen test***
This test indicates how your kidneys are functioning.

- ***Creatinine test***
This test measures kidney functions.

- ***Sodium, Potassium, Chloride, Magnesium, Calcium, Phosphorous test***
This test measures particles in the blood that maintain body balance. Many of these particles are electrically charged (without

electricity the body would not be able to function properly). Potassium, in particular, is needed for electrical balance and healthy heart function. When you take diuretics, potassium in the body is often diminished.

- **Albumin, Bilirubin, Alkaline Phosphatase, LDH, GGT, AST, ALT test**
  This test measures substances (enzymes) that become elevated when the liver is injured or diseased.

- **Iron, Iron-Binding Capacity, Ferritin test**
  This test determines whether iron levels are low and anemia is present. If it is, the patient will need to take iron supplements.

- **Triglycerides, Cholesterol test**
  This test measures fats (lipids). A certain amount of fat is needed for cellular structure. But high fat levels are dangerous and can cause heart disease as well as other diseases.

- **Complete Blood Count (CBC) test**
  Low blood counts indicate anemia. High counts can signify diseases such as leukemia.

Other Tests

Besides blood tests, your doctor may also order the following tests:

- **Urinalysis**
  A urine sample tells your doctor much about kidney and liver function, kidney stones, diabetes, and infections.

- **Rapid Plasma Reagin (RPR)**
  This test determines if such diseases as arthritis, inflammation, or syphilis are present.

Routine Procedures

As medicine has evolved, so have the many medical procedures that doctors use to find answers to puzzling health problems. While blood testing is the most common form of testing, other procedures use a hands-on approach to find information that cannot be determined through the blood test.

Pelvic Exams

The American Cancer Society recommends that a pelvic exam with a Pap smear begin at age eighteen or at the onset of sexual activity. Most women will require only an annual exam. More frequent pelvic exams are necessary if you have an infection or an abnormal Pap smear. The pelvic exam can also determine cervical and ovarian cancer and various viral and bacterial infections.

Colposcopy is a pelvic exam performed by a doctor using a microscope that allows close visual examination of the cervix. This test is performed when cells of the cervix are abnormal or cancerous. If portions of the cervix must be surgically removed, the doctor can do so during colposcopy.

Rectal Exam

Patients often want to avoid this procedure because they see it as uncomfortable and unnecessary. But the rectal exam is the doctor's surest way to find out if you have cancer and/or GI bleeding. The doctor uses a latex glove and special lubricant to administer the procedure. The digital (finger) rectal exam is invaluable for screening for prostate cancer in men.

- **Upper Gastrointestinal (GI) and Endoscopy Studies**
  Many patients complain of abdominal discomfort. Many of these symptoms are relieved with antacids. But when symptoms persist even with medications, ulcers or cancer may be present. The upper GI and endoscopy are then used to examine the stomach lining and better diagnose an illness.

  Before you have an upper GI study done, you will swallow a liquid that will show up as a contrast in the X-ray. The lining of the stomach and intestines are then visualized on film, and ulcers and other possible illnesses are easily detected.

  An "upper endoscopy" is a procedure in which small camera is passed down the esophagus into the stomach. The patient is sedated and is not uncomfortable. Using this procedure, the doctor can see the lining of the GI tract first-hand to determine any abnormalities. With a device attached to the endoscope, the doctor can also sample fluid in the stomach to determine its properties. Some stomach problems are caused by high secretions of acid that damage the lining of the intestine.

- ***Sigmoidoscopy and Colonoscopy***
  These tests allow the doctor to detect pathologies of the colon. The tests are used for patients with complaints of colon pain and bleeding. After the patient gets an enema, a scope is passed into the rectum to look for problems such as polyps or cancer. This test can also detect colitis (inflammation of the colon).

  The sigmoidoscope is passed into the rectum only up to the descending colon. The colonoscope is a longer scope that is passed through the entire colon (cecum). If you are over fifty years of age, it is a good idea to have sigmoidoscopy screening for preventative purposes. Some doctors prefer the colonoscopy procedure for patients in this age group.

- ***Ultrasound Studies***
  Ultrasound is a procedure that passes sound waves into the body in order to get images of internal structures. Gallstones, uterine fibroids, fluid-filled lesions, pancreatic abnormalities, and much more can be detected by the use of the ultrasound.

- ***CAT Scan and MRI***
  Both these high-tech, high-resolution X-rays are invaluable for viewing internal structures and any pathologies that may be present, such as brain tumors, bone cancers, soft tissue abnormalities, and others.

  Other useful procedures are EKGs, echocardiograms, cardiac stress tests, and mammograms, all covered in detail in later chapters.

Part II

Illnesses Common
to Black Americans

Chapter 3

The ABCs of Hypertension

Heart disease and cardiovascular illness are the major causes of death in the United States today, and more African Americans suffer from heart disease and cardiovascular illness than any other group of people. High cholesterol, hypertension, obesity, diabetes, and cardiovascular disease are conditions that commonly lead to stroke and heart attack.

Cholesterol causes deposits to form inside blood vessels. These deposits, called "plaque," are made of fats deposited from the bloodstream. If the deposits get large enough, blood vessels may become clogged, thus decreasing blood flow to vital organs. These deposits result in fat deposits in the arteries (atherosclerosis), which can cause the formation of blood clots that totally stop blood flow. When vessels become blocked, vital tissues suffer and die because of a lack of oxygen-rich blood. If this blockage occurs in the arteries supplying the heart, a heart attack will result. If blockage occurs in the brain, a portion of brain tissue dies and a stroke will result. Atherosclerosis causes more deaths from heart disease than any other single condition.

BASIC TERMS

High Cholesterol

(Also known as hypercholesterolemia)

Description: Cholesterol is a waxy substance found mostly in the fatty foods that come from animals. The body also manufactures it. You need small amounts of cholesterol to make and maintain nerve cells and to manufacture hormones. When you have too much, your blood vessels can become blocked.

For every one percent reduction in cholesterol level, the risk of heart disease is reduced by two percent. It is also possible, by lowering cholesterol levels with diet and medications, to partially reverse atherosclerosis.

Incidence: Common (higher among African Americans)

Predominant Gender: Cholesterol increases from birth to adulthood, particularly in men before the age of fifty. However, after the age of fifty, both men and women are at equal risk for developing high cholesterol levels.

Signs and Symptoms: Hypercholesterolemia is a silent disease. There are no symptoms until the resulting atherosclerosis causes complications, such as the chest pain of a heart attack or a stroke with subsequent paralysis.

Risk Factors: The most common risk factor for high cholesterol is eating foods that are high in saturated fat and/or cholesterol. High cholesterol can be inherited.

An underlying disease that raises the cholesterol level (for example, diabetes mellitus, kidney disease, liver disease, or hypothyroidism) can be a risk factor. Obesity itself leads the body to produce excessive amounts of cholesterol.

Diagnosis: High cholesterol is diagnosed by taking a blood specimen after the patient has not eaten or drunk anything (except water) for twelve hours. Generally agreed upon acceptable limits for LDL cholesterol ("bad cholesterol") are 130 mg/dl and under 200 mg/dl for total cholesterol. (Mg/dl is a system for determining molecular counts.) If your cholesterol is elevated, discuss your situation with your physician to determine if treatment is appropriate.

Usual Treatment: Initial treatment for high cholesterol requires changing your diet by:
- Reducing your intake of total fat, saturated fat, and cholesterol
- Increasing your intake of soluble fiber (for example, bran, whole grains, and other sources of fiber)
- Losing weight, if necessary
- If a diet low in saturated fats and in cholesterol itself doesn't substantially reduce your cholesterol level, you may need medication.

Special Concerns: Recent research hints at the possibility that some antioxidant vitamins (for example, vitamin C, vitamin E, and selenium) can help rid the body of free oxygen. Free oxygen not bound by another element, like hydrogen, can cause damage to cells.

Recovery Time: High cholesterol is often a chronic condition that can be managed throughout a person's lifetime with proper diet, exercise, and/or medication.

Prevention and Spiritual Considerations:
- Maintain a normal weight; reduce your weight if you are overweight.
- Reduce the amount of fat and cholesterol you consume.
- Avoid smoking.
- Add fiber to your diet (whole grains, beans, raw fruits, and vegetables).
- Exercise regularly (especially aerobic exercise).
- Become personally centered on making yourself the healthiest you can possibly be. Use prayer, meditation, and yoga to lead you toward your personal goals.

Resources:
American Heart Association
7272 Greenville Avenue
Dallas, TX 75231
1–800–AHA-USA1
http://www.americanheart.org

Hypertension

(Commonly Known as High Blood Pressure)

Description: Sustained blood pressure above "normal." The American Heart Association defines high blood pressure as 140/90 and above for those under sixty-five years of age, 160/90 and above for those over sixty-five years of age.

The higher (systolic) number represents the pressure when the heart is beating. The lower (diastolic) number represents the pressure when the heart is resting between beats.

Incidence: Common (about fifty million Americans; twenty percent of the U.S. population); over thirty percent in the African American population

Predominant Gender: Men more than women

Signs and Symptoms: Sometimes referred to as "the silent killer" because there are usually no symptoms until the disease becomes a significant problem. At that point, these symptoms can occur:
- Headaches
- Dizziness
- Visual problems
- Chest pain (if chest pain and high blood pressure occur together, consult your doctor immediately)
- Shortness of breath
- Changes in mental status (slurred speech, inability to concentrate)
- Calf pain
- Sweating

- Tremors

Risk Factors:
   (Primary)
- Obesity
- Smoking
- Family history of hypertension
- High cholesterol
- High-salt diet
- Stress
- Alcohol
- Sedentary lifestyle
- Overactive hormone production

(Secondary)
- High propensity of body to hold water
- Kidney disease
- Adrenal gland disease
- Pregnancy
- Neurological disorders
- Lead poisoning
- Use of steroids
- Use of NSAIDs (Nonsteroidal anti-inflammatory drugs)
  Vitamin deficiency

Diagnosis: A doctor will:
- Take your blood pressure
- Investigate your medical and family history
- Give you a complete physical exam
- Order laboratory tests, including an X-ray

Usual Treatment: Medication (diuretics, angiotensins, calcium channel blockers, etc.)
- Dietary changes and restrictions
- Salt-restricted diet
- Lifestyle changes (weight loss, smoking cessation, exercise)
- Stress reduction
- Education

Recovery Time: Often a chronic problem, but can be controlled. Prevention and Spiritual Considerations:
- Use prayer, meditation, and yoga to help reduce stress levels.
- Take a personal inventory of changes and make them one at a time.
- Maintain a normal weight; reduce your weight if overweight.
- Reduce the amount of fat and cholesterol you consume.
- Avoid smoking.
- Add fiber to your diet (whole grains, beans, raw fruits and vegetables).
- Exercise regularly (especially aerobic exercise).
- Comply with treatment to reduce risk of stroke and heart attack.

Resources:
American Heart Association
7272 Greenville Avenue
Dallas, TX 75231
1–800–AHA–USA1
http://www.americanheart.org

If you are diagnosed as suffering from hypertension, you have a disease that can lead to heart attack or stroke. Yet you feel perfectly healthy, if you are like most patients at the time they are diagnosed. That's why you need to see your doctor at least once a year for a physical examination that can diagnose this condition *before* you know you have it.

The Story of Gil

One morning my tennis opponent, Gil, a distinguished African–American lawyer, seemed especially unhappy that he could not return my serves during a match. As our game came to an end and we shook hands, my satisfaction over winning turned to concern. Gil looked not defeated but confused, so I asked him if he had something on his mind. "It must be that darn medicine," Gil replied.

Gil had just started taking pills his doctor had prescribed to control his high blood pressure. But Gil didn't like the way the pills made him feel. "Why should I take this medicine if it makes me tired and slow? I felt fine before. The doctor even told me that because I was an African–American man, I was more prone to having hypertension. Is it true?" I stepped back, swallowed hard, and proceeded to give him the truth that many African Americans may not fully understand.

HYPERTENSION IN AFRICAN AMERICANS

Data from the Centers for Disease Control (CDC) suggest that roughly twenty percent of the general population has hypertension. But over thirty percent of African Americans have high blood pressure; that's one in three—over ten million—people.

Of those people who have high blood pressure, 31.6 percent don't know they have it. This woeful statistic is even more alarming when coupled with the fact that hypertension is one of the major risk factors contributing to heart attack and stroke.

Some social scientists believe that African Americans are more likely to suffer from high blood pressure because they are under more social stress. Others trace it to heredity and the high salt content in the diets of African-American slaves. A diet high in sodium, the main ingredient in salt, causes the body to retain fluid, which increases blood volume and pressure. Sodium acts like a sponge and promotes water retention.

Whatever the reason, African Americans, more than other populations, tend to retain water and salt in their bodies and, thus, to suffer high blood pressure. Doctors often must prescribe diuretics to African Americans to help eliminate water and salt from their bodies, thereby helping to reduce blood pressure. Some patients, like Gil may be affected by uncomfortable side effects when they first start taking these drugs. These side effects usually disappear in a short time.

Organ Damage from Hypertension

Hypertension, if not controlled, can affect various organs of the body, reduce your quality of life, and even shorten your life span. Obesity, high sodium intake, genetics, and stress contribute to high blood pressure. Organs most commonly damaged by the effects of hypertension are the following:

Kidneys

When vessels that supply the kidneys constrict, "nephrosclerosis" results. This means that blood flow to the kidneys is decreased and the kidneys shrink and harden. Doctors determine kidney disease by the amount of protein found in urine through a routine analysis. An ultrasound and CAT scan will show small-sized kidneys.

Heart and Blood Vessels

A thickened, stiff heart muscle results when the heart must pump too hard, in order to force blood flow to peripheral systems. The left ventricle may enlarge because of the hypertension. If a segment of the artery wall is weakened, the vessel may balloon out. Where such widening occurs, the wall of the artery is weakened and can burst, creating serious internal bleeding. The condition in which an artery swells and is weakened is called an "aneurysm."

Sustained high blood pressure can also cause blood vessels to leak or rupture. In arteriosclerosis, the high pressure can cause a shearing effect on the inner walls of vessels, causing them to split. This roughened surface then becomes a medium on which plaque (fat deposit) can accumulate.

Brain

Hemorrhagic stroke, a common killer, can occur when increased pressure in vessels that supply the brain rupture and blood extrudes onto brain tissue, impairing cerebral functioning. This event is considered a "brain attack."

Eyes

Foremost damage occurs in the retina and the vessels that supply blood, oxygen, and nutrients to this vital tissue. Retinal damage and blindness can result.

Depending on your personal circumstances and how well you follow your doctor's treatment plan, hypertension does not have to control your life. In fact, you are in total control!

Chapter 4

Coronary Artery Disease

C oronary artery disease continues to be the number one killer in the United States. But we need to fix our attention not only on the deaths that are the result but also on such causes as high blood pressure, from which many millions of Americans suffer.

Coronary artery and related diseases of the heart and circulatory system kill far more African Americans than White Americans. Some studies show that deaths from cardiovascular disease are almost fifty percent higher for African–American men and seventy percent higher for African–American women.

As health care costs continue to rise and lives are needlessly destroyed in our community, we all need to know the ABCs of this often-preventable disease.

WHAT IS CORONARY ARTERY DISEASE?

Coronary artery disease is a life-threatening condition that involves the heart and its vessels. The blood vessels that feed oxygen to the heart can be narrowed by plaque, a hard, fatty, crusty substance that sticks to vessel walls. High blood pressure can also limit the flow of oxygen and blood to the heart. High blood pressure can not only constrict coronary arteries that supply blood to the heart, but can also cause damage to the lining of the inner surface of vessels and thus cause narrowing or blockage of blood flow to the heart. Here, in a nutshell, are some more facts you need to know.

Coronary Heart Disease (CHD)

(Also Known as Cardiovascular Disease)

Description: Coronary heart disease is caused by a fatty buildup that causes narrowing of the coronary arteries (atherosclerosis). It is likely to produce angina pectoris (chest pain), heart attack, or both.

Incidence: Cardiovascular illness is the leading cause of death among African Americans: 7.1 percent of African–American men have coronary heart disease, and 9.0 percent of African–American women have coronary heart disease.

Prevalence: Each year, 41.4 percent of African–American women and 34.2 percent of African–American men die from CHD.

Signs and Symptoms:
- Shortness of breath
- Tiredness or weakness
- Cough or coughing up blood
- Pallor or paleness (caused by lack of oxygen in the blood)
- Chest pain
- Palpitations
- Dizziness
- Fainting
- Swollen legs or ankles
- Calf pain

Risk Factors:
- Family history of heart attack or stroke
- Increasing age
- Smoking
- High cholesterol

- High blood pressure
- Physical inactivity
- Obesity or being overweight
- Diabetes
- High stress
- Drinking too much alcohol

Diagnosis: Specific tests depend upon your particular problem(s) and an overall physical assessment. Your doctor may refer you to a cardiologist who may perform additional tests. Normally, a doctor will:

- Take your family and medical history
- Give a complete physical exam
- Take your blood pressure
- Do blood tests to detect any abnormal levels of certain enzymes in the bloodstream
- Use an electrocardiogram (EKG) to detect any abnormalities caused by damage to your heart
- Take a chest X-ray
- Do a cardiac stress test
- Possibly do a cardiac catheterization

Specific tests depend upon your particular problem(s) and an overall physical assessment. Your doctor may also refer you to a cardiologist who may perform additional tests.

Usual Treatment:
- Behavioral modification (stop smoking, eat better)
- Nutritional counseling and diet restructuring
- Medication (nitrates, aspirin)
- Exercise
- Education (learning to read food labels, counting calories, self-monitoring, meal planning)
- Support groups
- Surgery (catheterization, angioplasty)
- Treatment of underlying disease (diabetes, high blood pressure)

Recovery Time and Complications: Heart disease cannot be cured, but it can be controlled, and the risk can be reduced by appropriate exercise, good diet, and medications. Without proper treatment of heart disease, you can have a heart attack or stroke.

Preventative and Spiritual Considerations:
- Become more personally centered, by making yourself the healthiest you can possibly be. Use prayer, meditation, and yoga to lead you toward your personal goals.
- Maintain a normal weight; reduce your weight if overweight.
- Reduce the amount of fat and cholesterol you consume.
- Avoid smoking.
- Add fiber to your diet (whole grains, beans, raw fruits and vegetables).
- Exercise regularly (especially aerobic exercise).
- Educate yourself about heart disease and its consequences.

Resources:
American Heart Association
7272 Greenville Avenue
Dallas, TX 75231
1–800–AHA-USA1
http://www.americanheart.org

The Consequences of Coronary Artery Disease

Heart Attack

1.5 million Americans a year suffer heart attacks. Unfortunately, it is common for a person who is having a heart attack to wait several hours, or even days, before seeking medical assistance. Effective treatment of a heart attack requires prompt diagnosis. By understanding the early warning signs of heart attack and the appropriate action to take at the onset of an attack, you can reduce your risk of death.

A heart attack results when your coronary artery is completely blocked. Simply put, a heart attack means the death of heart muscle and is a result of coronary heart disease. A heart attack is sudden but the causes are not. Unhealthy living habits over time can lead to high cholesterol, obesity, diabetes, and coronary artery disease, all of which can lead to a heart attack or stroke.

A heart attack may feel like the chest is being crushed, squeezed, or strangled. Some people have described it as a burning-like indigestion. It may also feel as if the chest is being ripped apart from the breastbone. Other descriptions include tearing, gripping pain, fullness, numbness or tingling, or a pointed stabbing pain. Dizziness, weakness, shortness of breath, and nausea may often occur along with the chest pain. The symptoms of a heart attack aren't always this intense. Some people describe the sensation as merely a discomfort.

Surgery can remove the blockage. In another procedure, called *angioplasty,* a balloon catheter is inserted into the blocked vessel to remove the plaque and reopen the artery so the blood can flow freely again. Angioplasty has enabled cardiologists to successfully treat the effects of cholesterol and its complications. Angioplasty can be helpful both in prevention and treatment of heart attacks. Obviously, however, what we all *most* want is to prevent them.

Chest Pain or Angina

Unlike a heart attack, which results when coronary arteries are blocked completely, angina or *angina pectoris* is chest pain resulting from an insufficient supply of blood to the heart caused by plaque that *partially* blocks the coronary arteries.

The coronary arteries, even with a seventy percent blockage, can supply the heart with adequate oxygen and nutrients while "at rest"—that is, at its normal heart rate of about sixty to seventy beats per minute. During physical activity or stress, the heart rate may increase to over 200 beats per minute. Blood pressure also increases, creating more work for the heart.

When the heart does more work, it requires more blood for nourishment. But a partially blocked artery will not allow the extra blood to get to the heart. (This insufficient blood supply to the heart is called "ischemia.") When any working muscle is deprived of its blood supply, it develops a cramp-like pain. In the heart, this pain is called "angina."

Angina quickly subsides as activity is stopped. Since the heart no longer has to work hard, the reduced blood supply is again adequate for the heart's needs.

Activities that can cause angina include:
- Running (especially when you're running because you're late and stressed)
- Walking up an incline or steep hill
- Walking against a strong wind
- Exertion to which you are unaccustomed
- Walking fast after eating a meal
- Surprise, a scare, rage, or bad news
- Excitement

The pain from angina is similar to the pain from heart attack in location and character, but heart attack pain lasts longer and is often more severe.

The pain from angina and heart attack is usually felt in the chest, over the breastbone (sternum). It usually covers an area the size of a fist. The pain may also move or radiate from the chest to the throat, jaw, arms, and hands. Left arm discomfort is more common than right, and the inner area of the arm is more often involved. The pain may also start in the arm and not until shortly afterwards be felt in the chest. Pain rarely extends through to the back. If pain does extend to the back, it usually strikes at the area between the left shoulder blade and the spine.

Stroke

Just as a heart attack (myocardial infarction) is the result of an interruption of blood flow to the heart, a stroke (ischemic attack) is the result of the interruption of blood flow to the brain. It is an emergency condition that needs immediate medical attention.

In some instances, the fat deposits (plaques) on the lining walls of vessels can be dislodged and a chunk of fat can move through arteries, causing damage along its path. Eventually, it will flow upstream toward the brain and become lodged in smaller vessels causing ischemia (blocked blood flow).

Every stroke is different, and recovery from a stroke depends on which part, and how much, of the brain has been damaged. Some people suffer a mild stroke, which means that there is very little injury to the brain. Those people usually recover fully or have few problems. In more severe cases, it may take a long time for stroke survivors to regain even partial use of their arms, legs, speech, or whatever has been affected.

Signs of Stroke
- *Weakness:* Sudden weakness, numbness or tingling in the face, arm, or leg
- *Trouble Speaking:* Sudden temporary loss of speech or trouble understanding speech
- *Vision Problems:* Sudden loss of vision, particularly in one eye, or double vision
- *Headache:* Sudden severe and unusual headache
- *Dizziness:* Sudden loss of balance, especially with any of the above signs

Immediate action is required if you or someone you know has any of the above signs. New treatments are becoming available for use in the minutes and hours immediately after a stroke. If they are able to act soon enough, doctors can now do a great deal to minimize the damage strokes can cause.

After a Stroke
A major stroke will change your life. While some people become severely disabled, many stroke survivors recover and lead meaningful lives. Recovery can be accomplished by natural body healing and/or through stroke rehabilitation programs. Families, friends, and relatives can also give valuable support. Every stroke is different. Although stroke does not affect any two people in exactly the same way, it often brings similar challenges.

Chapter 5

Obesity

The more weight the body frame carries, the harder the body organs and circulatory system must work. Being overweight is often the result of diet and lack of exercise. The American Heart Association tells us that nearly fifty percent of African Americans are "sedentary"—that is, they get no exercise at all.

Excess weight caused by fat deposits strangles vital organs and reduces their performance. Joints suffer because they are carrying more weight than they were designed for. When you put on extra weight, the body works harder and wears out faster. Long-term obesity will take years off your life and create health problems you could have avoided.

> When you put on extra weight, the body works harder and wears out faster.

The most effective weight-loss programs combine diet, behavior modification (lifestyle change), nutritional education, exercise, medication (where appropriate), and long-term maintenance support. Weight loss itself is only the beginning of a successful weight management program. Obesity is a chronic medical disorder. Keeping the weight off and avoiding the "roller coaster" effect of weight loss

Keeping the weight off and avoiding the "roller coaster" effect of weight loss and gain is the most difficult, yet most important, part of any program. Talk to your family doctor about the best treatment.

and gain is the most difficult, yet most important, part of any program. Talk to your family doctor about the best treatment.

OBESITY

(Also Known as Morbidly Obese, Overweight, Heavy)

Description: Obesity is an excess of body fat, frequently resulting in significant health impairment. Obesity results when the size or number of fat cells in a person's body increases. A normal-sized person has between thirty and thirty-five billion fat cells. When a person gains weight, these fat cells increase first in size and later in number.

Incidence: African Americans have a higher propensity towards obesity than any other group of people. Obesity results when there is an imbalance between energy intake and energy expenditure. In other words, you consume more calories than you expend in your daily activities.

Prevalence: New data (www.surgeongenral.gov) indicate that sixty-one percent of adults are overweight or obese. Obesity is more common among women and in the poor; the prevalence in children is also rising at a worrisome rate. 37% of African-American women are obese; as compared with 33% of Mexican-American Women and 24% of Caucasian women.

Signs and Symptoms:
Excessive weight gain
Body Mass Index (BMI) over 35 is considered severely obese
Back pain and/or joint pain
Gastrointestinal problems
Difficulty breathing or shortness of breath
Inability to walk
Fatigue
Lack of energy
Low self-esteem

Risk Factors
Age: As you grow older, your metabolic rate slows down and you do not require as many calories to maintain your weight. People frequently tell me that they eat the same and do the same activities as when they were twenty-years-old, but, at forty, they are gaining weight.

Gender: Men have a higher resting metabolic rate than women, so men require more calories to maintain their body weight. When women become postmenopausal, their metabolic rate decreases significantly, part of the reason that many women start gaining weight after menopause.

Activity Level: Active individuals require more calories than less active individuals. Activity tends to reduce appetite in obese individuals while increasing the body's ability to preferentially metabolize fat as an energy source.

Body Weight: Heavier people require more calories to maintain their body weight. For example, a 250–pound woman doing minimal amounts of physical activity may require 2700 calories to maintain her body weight. If she goes on a 2000 calorie-per-day diet, she will lose weight. Eventually, however, even if she stays with a 2000 calorie per day diet, her weight will stabilize, since her metabolic rate will gradually decrease. When this woman reaches approximately 200 pounds, she will require only about 2000 calories per day to maintain her new weight. This is a normal process and takes place in all individuals.

Heredity: Heredity is associated not only with obesity but also with thinness. A person's weight is most closely correlated with his or her biological mother's weight and metabolic process. If the biological mother is heavy as an adult, there is an approximately seventy-five percent chance that her children will be heavy. If the biological mother is thin, there is a sixty-five percent chance that her children will be thin.

Complications:
- Hypertension
- Diabetes
- Cancer
- Degenerative arthritis
- Elevated cholesterol
- Gallstones
- Heart attack
- Stroke
- Sleep disorders
- Depression

Recovery: Cannot be cured, only treated

Diagnosis: A doctor will:
- Determine your body mass index (BMI). BMI is a formula calculation that uses weight and height to determine mild, moderate, and severe obesity
- Take a complete family and medical history
- Perform lab tests (complete blood count, thyroid levels, anemia, diabetes, and cholesterol)
- Order an EKG (electrocardiogram)

Usual Treatment:
- Behavioral modification

- Medication (appetite suppressants, antidepressants)
- Restricted diet
- Exercise
- Education (learning to read food labels, counting calories, self-monitoring, meal planning)
- Support groups

As a last resort:
Surgery (gastric bypass or stomach stapling)

Prevention and Spiritual Considerations:
- Make your own good health a top priority.
- Eat a healthy diet and talk to a doctor who is culturally sensitive to your personal needs.
- See a psychologist for underlying emotional problems.
- Use prayer, meditation, and yoga to become more spiritually centered.
- Take a personal inventory of changes and make them one at a time.
- Reduce the amount of fat and cholesterol you consume.
- Avoid smoking.
- Add fiber to your diet (whole grains, beans, raw fruits and vegetables).
- Exercise regularly (especially aerobic exercise).
- Comply with treatment to reduce risk of stroke and heart attack.

Resources:
American Heart Association
7272 Greenville Avenue
Dallas, TX 75231
1–800–AHA-USA1
http://www.americanheart.org

Book Recommendation:
Smith, G. Edmond, MD, MEd.: *Weight Loss for African–American Women: Eight Weeks to Better Health.* Roscoe, IL: Hilton Publishing, 2001

Smoking and Obesity

When people stop smoking, they commonly gain weight. Most people think that they are substituting food for cigarettes, which is partially correct. Smoking is a form of oral gratification that does not involve the consumption of calories. But, also, people who smoke require approximately ten percent more calories to maintain their body weight than when they are not smoking. Therefore, if people stop smoking and eat the same amount as they did before, their body weight is likely to increase between five and ten percent.

An excellent way to avoid weight gain when you quit smoking is to exercise regularly. For example, start walking thirty minutes a day three to four times a week—a very easy goal. Another approach is to record your food intake. By writing down everything you eat before you eat it, you will become much more aware of what you are eating. This helps you make better food choices, thereby helping you maintain your weight.

It is more important to stop smoking than to worry about weight gain. The harmful effects of smoking far outweigh the effects of putting on the extra pounds. Some people think that when they stop smoking it is also a good time to go on a strict diet, but I don't recommend making two major changes at once. Both changes can be stressful, and it is difficult to do both effectively. Stop smoking first. Then you can deal with your weight.

Chapter 6

Diabetes

AFRICAN AMERICANS AND DIABETES

Throughout the nineteenth century, African Americans did not appear to be affected by diabetes. This disease was not recognized in the African American population until urbanization, when the incidence of diabetes increased. Changes in lifestyle that occurred during this period are the most likely cause for the spread of diabetes.

After slavery was abolished, African Americans adopted western lifestyle patterns (dietary behavior, changes in physical activity, and attitudes toward body size and weight) that caused obesity and contributed directly to the higher incidence and prevalence of diabetes in the African American population. As more people gained weight, the incidence of diabetes increased. Today, diabetes is one of the most common diseases that affect African Americans.

Diabetes is often referred to as "having sugar." It affects African Americans at a disproportionately high rate. African Americans are fifty-five percent more likely than White Americans to have the disease. Diabetes is the leading cause of blindness, amputation, and heart and kidney failure for African Americans. In order to take charge of your diabetes, you must become knowledgeable about the disease, so that you can participate in your doctor's treatment plan. You do not have to let diabetes ruin your life.

DIABETES

(Also Known as High Sugars)

Description: Diabetes is a disorder originating in the pancreas. It occurs when there is not enough insulin production or none at all. Insulin is the hormone needed to control blood sugar.

There are Two Types of Diabetes:

Type I Diabetes Mellitus: Type I is also known as "insulin-dependent diabetes." It occurs when the insulin-producing cells in the pancreas have been damaged or destroyed, usually by either a viral infection or by an autoimmune disorder in which the body attacks itself. This type of diabetes usually develops in childhood or early adolescence and always requires injections of the hormone insulin.

Type II Diabetes Mellitus: Type II is referred to as "noninsulin dependent diabetes." Eighty-five percent of diabetics have Type II diabetes. It mostly occurs in adults over age forty who are also overweight or obese. In type II diabetes, the body produces more than the normal amount of insulin because of extra fat tissue: obesity makes the insulin receptor cells on the outside of each of your cells less effective, and your body becomes resistant to insulin.

Type II diabetes has a strong hereditary link: if your parents have diabetes, your child has a greater chance of having the disease during his or her lifetime. Therefore, as more adults get the disease, more children will also. As children become more obese, more children will develop diabetes.

Incidence: Sixteen million people in the United States have diabetes. African Americans are fifty to seventy percent more likely to develop diabetes. An estimated 2.3 million African Americans, or 10.8 percent, have diabetes. African Americans are 1.7 times more likely to have Type II diabetes than the general population.

Prevalence: In the United States, twelve percent of the population has diabetes, approximately 7.5 million men and approximately 8.1 million women. Ninety percent of diabetics have type II disease. More than one third of people with diabetes do not know they have this disease.

Signs and Symptoms: Diabetes may show few symptoms, or symptoms may include:
- Fatigue and/or lightheadedness
- Sudden loss of weight
- Increased urination
- Excessive thirst
- Weight loss
- Blurred vision
- Skin infections
- Bladder or vaginal infections
- Pins and needles sensation in fingers and toes
- Nonspecific causes of itching
- Abdominal pain
- Nausea, vomiting, mood changes
- Slow to heal cuts or bruises
- Becoming comatose, especially in people with undiagnosed diabetes

Risk Factors:
- Obesity
- Family history of diabetes
- Excessive weight gain during pregnancy
- Diagnosis of cardiovascular disease (CAD)
- Being over the age of forty-five and not exercising regularly
- Low HDL cholesterol or high triglycerides

Diagnosis: A doctor will:
- Perform a complete physical exam and take your personal and family medical histories
- Order blood tests to evaluate your kidneys, liver, and thyroid
- Order a urine test

- Order a finger-stick blood test
- Order a hemoglobin A1c blood test
- Ask you questions about your nutrition and exercise habits

Usual Treatment: Treatment will depend on several factors:

Type I Diabetes: Type I diabetes requires lifelong insulin injections, which are necessary because the body is not producing insulin. There is no way to repair the damage to the insulin-producing cells.

Type II Diabetes: Type II diabetes is treated very differently. The body needs help so that it can best use the insulin that it does produce. Dietary changes are usually the first course of action because weight reduction helps control diabetes in the majority of people who have Type II diabetes. If weight reduction is a problem, your doctor will probably put you on medication that increases the amount of insulin your body produces. If this course of treatment doesn't get results, you may be placed on additional medications that cause your liver to produce less glucose (sugar), or on medications that make your body more responsive to the insulin that it does produce. If these approaches fail, you may be placed on insulin injections to control your blood sugars.

Recovery Time: Diabetes is a chronic condition that cannot be cured. However, you can usually prevent the disease or keep it under control by maintaining normal weight, eating nutritious foods, avoiding excessive alcohol intake, and exercising regularly.

Special Considerations: Untreated or uncontrolled diabetes can lead to:
- Blindness
- Kidney disease
- Nerve disease
- Amputation
- Heart disease and stroke

Spiritual Considerations:
- Start putting yourself first.
- Talk to a doctor who is culturally sensitive to your personal

needs and shares your concerns about being diagnosed with diabetes.

- Use prayer, meditation, and yoga to become more spiritually centered.
- Take a personal inventory of changes and make them one at a time.
- Reduce the amount of fat and cholesterol you consume.
- See a diabetic nutritionist to become more educated about the foods you need to eat to stay in control of your diabetes.
- Avoid smoking.
- Add fiber to your diet (whole grains, beans, raw fruits and vegetables).
- Exercise regularly (especially aerobic exercise).
- Comply with treatment to reduce risk of stroke and heart attack.

Resources:

American Diabetes Association
1701 North Beauregard Street
Alexandria, VA 22311
1–800–DIABETES (1–800–342–2383)
www.diabetes.org

How Diabetes Works in Your Body

Diabetes is a defect in carbohydrate metabolism. Carbohydrates are a major nutrient in every person's diet. (Protein and fats are the other two nutrients that make up the foods we eat.) When we eat food with carbohydrates (that is, starch and sugars) the digestive process breaks them down into much smaller parts called "glucose," which the body needs for energy and to replenish cells.

Glucose travels through the digestive tract, where it is absorbed through the small intestine and enters the blood stream to feed the cells. Insulin, a hormone that comes from the pancreas, is secreted and helps the glucose enter the cells from the bloodstream. When not enough insulin is produced by the pancreas, glucose can't enter the cells. An increase of glucose in the blood (hyperglycemia) results, and the blood thickens with glucose. Normally, the body produces other hormones that also help control the levels of glucose in the blood, but in the diabetic person hormone production does not work properly either.

The thickened blood caused by excess glucose affects body organs. Kidneys try to help by removing excess glucose but are often overworked or damaged. As the body works to remove the excess glucose, water is also removed. As a result, diabetics are often thirsty and urinate a great deal.

The thickened blood causes damage to blood vessels and injures organs such as the eyes and heart. Small blood vessels can't filter the blood. As a result, limited quantities of blood are delivered to the far regions of the body, like the feet and hands. For this reason, diabetics often have poor circulation and may have problems with their feet, even lose their legs to amputation.

Laboratory Tests

If diabetes is suspected, your doctor will test your urine. In ancient times, medicine men would taste urine and note its sweetness. In fact, diabetes mellitus means "sweet like honey." Today's physicians do not taste the urine. Instead, they perform what is called a *urinalysis*. Glucose and other substances called "ketones" show up on the tests of diabetics as strongly positive.

Doctors also do "finger stick" and serum glucose level tests. A level greater than 140 mg/dl usually indicates diabetes. These readings can be influenced by whether or not you eat before the test. Thus, it is important to follow your physician's instructions prior to taking the test. A more comprehensive test is called the Hemoglobin A1c, which tests your blood. This test allows the doctor to determine your glucose levels over a forty-five to sixty-day period. This test is often preferred by physicians and is an invaluable, objective measure of your glucose control.

Treatment

Pills and insulin injection therapy are used to eliminate symptoms of diabetes and assist in preventing major metabolic problems. Insulin therapy, first introduced in 1921, is utilized if pills are not successful. Several new medicines, such as Glucophage®, and chromium can assist the uptake of insulin into the cells. It is important that you ask your doctor about the newest drug therapies available.

Diet

Fewer African Americans know about good nutrition and proper diet than people from other groups in the American population. Over thirty percent of African Americans are obese, compared to twenty-five percent of White Americans. Some studies suggest that as many as sixty percent of African American women in the inner cities are obese and have a high rate of diabetes. Many of these people don't get exercise, which can cause additional health complications.

Diabetics must eat properly and exercise regularly. If you have been diagnosed with diabetes, and especially if you are taking insulin or oral medications for glucose control, you must eat every four hours so that you maintain an even level of glucose. Patients who do not eat regularly and take these drugs develop low glucose or "low sugar" (hypoglycemia), and they also have severe problems that can even cause death. Eating the right foods on a regular basis also helps the body's metabolism speed up and burns off excess body fat.

Patients with diabetes often tell me they only eat one or two meals a day, often big meals with lots of calories and fat. In diabetics, when the body is fed only one or two large meals a day, the metabolism begins to slow down, almost to a state of starvation. It attempts to compensate by holding onto nutrients, so, on such a diet, it actually stores fat, which only compounds the diabetic's inability to metabolize glucose.

Counting calories is very important for controlling glucose. In order to count calories, the first step is to read and understand food labels.

Knowing how much fat, cholesterol, and carbohydrates each meal contains will help you take control of your diet. If you don't understand the ingredients of your meals, you can't take an active role in your overall disease management.

Nutrition Facts

Serving Size 2 oz. (56g/2/3 cup) Dry
Servings Per Container 8

Amount Per Serving

Calories 210   Calories From Fat 10

% Daily Value*

Total Fat 1g	**2%**
Saturated Fat 0g	**0%**
Polyunsaturated Fat 0.5g	
Monounsaturated Fat 0g	
Cholesterol 0mg	**0%**
Sodium 0mg**	**0%**
Total Carbohydrate 42g	**14%**
Dietary Fiber 2g	**8%**
Sugars 3g	
Protein 7g	

Vitamin A 0%	•	Vitamin C	0%
Calcium 0%	•	Iron	10%
Thiamin 30%	•	Riboflavin	10%
Niacin 15%	•	Folate	30%

*Percent Daily Values are based on a 2,000 calorie diet. Your daily values may be higher or lower depending on your calorie needs.

	Calories	2,000	2,500
Total Fat	Less Than	65g	80g
Saturated Fat	Less Than	20g	25g
Cholesterol	Less Than	300mg	300mg
Sodium	Less Than	2400mg	2400mg
Total Carbohydrate		300g	375g
Dietary Fiber		25g	30g

Calories per gram Fat 9 • Carbohydrate 4 • Protein 4

Nutrition Label

Activity

Regular aerobic exercise for thirty to sixty minutes, three to five times a week is critical to good health. Exercise also keeps you from gaining weight, reduces your risk of cardiovascular problems, and helps control blood glucose. Ask your doctor about an activity regimen that is geared specifically for you.

Patient Education

Through formal diabetic education, you, as a Black American, can begin to take charge of your diabetes. In classes, you will learn about the warning signs of hypoglycemia, how to give up smoking, how to care for your feet, how to give yourself insulin injections, how to avoid coronary artery disease(a major complication of diabetes), and much more. Support groups are also available through local hospitals and clinics. In a support group, you meet other diabetics and share your experiences with, and information about, diabetes, so that you do not feel alone.

Finally, through education, you can better manage your glucose. You will do better when you are given direction and specific information geared to your personal situation. Your self-esteem will rise to new heights when you take an active role in your battle against diabetes, meet and share with other people, and attend diabetic education classes. People who take diabetes education classes often become "partners" with their doctors in managing their diabetes. Such partnerships make for the best kind of medicine.

Chapter 7

Cancer

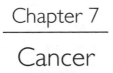

The American Cancer Society defines cancer as "involving out of control growth and spread of abnormal cells." To understand the growth of abnormal cells, you must first know that normal body cells grow, divide, and die in a predictable way. But cancer cells are not regulated by the body and are unpredictable. Instead of dying naturally, they continue to grow and divide, spreading to other parts of the body.

The abnormal cells eventually form "colonies" that become lumpy. These lumps are called "tumors." The tumors compress and invade healthy tissue, even breaking off and entering the bloodstream through the lymphatic system (a system that filters the blood). In that way the cancer spreads, by a process known as "metastasis," and can invade different parts of the body. A cancer is named for the part of the body in which it originates. For example, if breast cancer spreads to the kidneys, it is still called breast cancer.

Cancers vary in the way they grow, spread, and respond to treatment. Not all tumors are cancerous. Some tumors do not metastasize and are normally not life-threatening. If you are diagnosed with cancer, your treatment will be aimed at your specific form of cancer. Many doctors and researchers are working toward better management and treatment of cancer, but we still have much to learn, and the research continues.

AFRICAN AMERICANS AND CANCER

The American Cancer Society estimates that there will be nearly 140,000 new cases of cancer diagnosed among African Americans in the next year. The most common form of cancer found in African American men is prostate cancer; the most common form of cancer found in African–American women is breast cancer. Both forms of cancer are discussed later in this chapter.

RISK FACTORS FOR DEVELOPING CANCER

> If you smoke, your chances of developing lung cancer are much higher than if you do not smoke.

Having risk factors for developing cancer does not necessarily mean you will develop the disease. However, doctors know that certain unhealthy behaviors put you at a greater risk for developing cancer. For example, if you smoke, your chances of developing lung cancer are much higher than if you do not smoke. Some of the known risk factors are the following:

- Family history of cancer
- Poor nutritional habits (for example, eating high-fat and low-fiber foods)
- Smoking
- Exposure to environmental toxins
- Alcohol abuse
- Risky sexual behavior

EARLY CANCER DETECTION

The good news is that many cancers can be prevented or detected early with screening methods. Early detection means effective treatment. That's why, during your annual visit, your doctor will probably use screening examinations for prostate and testicular cancers, as well as breast, colon, rectal, cervical, and skin cancers. If your doctor fails to provide screening, you should request it or change doctors. The truth is, your life may depend on it.

Recommendations for Early Detection of Cancer

The American Cancer Society recommends a cancer-related checkup every three years for people twenty to forty years old, and every year for people over forty. This exam should include health counseling and, depending on a person's age, might include examinations for cancers of the thyroid, oral cavity, skin, lymph nodes, testes, and ovaries, as well as for some nonmalignant diseases.

The American Cancer Society makes these special recommendations depending on the site of detection:

Screening Guidelines for Some Other Types of Cancer

Colorectal Cancer

- Annual digital rectal exam and PSA test for men over the age of forty
- Sigmoidoscopy every three to five years after the age of fifty
- Colonoscopy every ten years after age of fifty.

Endometrial Cancer (cancer of the lining of the uterus)

- Menopausal women who are over age forty and who are going to have hormone replacement therapy should have an endometrial biopsy.

Ovarian Cancer

- Annual pelvic exam beginning at age eighteen and pelvic ultrasound or blood test for cancer markers for high-risk patients with a family history of ovarian cancer

Site of Detection

Breasts • Women age forty and older should have an annual mammogram, an annual clinical breast examination (CBE) by a health care professional, and should perform monthly breast self-examination (BSE). The CBE should be conducted close to the scheduled mammogram. Women ages twenty to thirty-nine should have a clinical breast examination by a health care professional every three years and should perform monthly breast self-examination.

Colon and Rectum • Beginning at age fifty, men and women should follow one of the examination schedules below:

- A fecal occult blood test every year and a flexible sigmoidoscopy every five years.
- A colonoscopy every ten years.
- A double-contrast barium enema every five to ten years.

A digital rectal exam should be done at the same time as sigmoidoscopy, colonoscopy, or double-contrast barium enema. People who are at moderate or high risk for colorectal cancer should talk with a doctor about more frequent tests.

Prostate • Both the prostate-specific antigen (PSA) blood test and the digital rectal examination should be offered annually, beginning at age fifty, to men who have a life expectancy of at least ten years and to younger men who are at high risk. Men in high-risk groups—who have two or more affected first-degree relatives or who are African Americans—may begin at age forty-five.

Uterus Cervix • All women who are or have been sexually active or who are aged eighteen and older should have an annual Pap test and pelvic examination. After three or more consecutive satisfactory examinations with normal findings, the Pap test may be performed less frequently. Discuss the matter with your physician.

Endometrium • Women at high risk for cancer of the uterus should have a sample of endometrial tissue examined when menopause begins.

(Source: American Cancer Society, 2000)

Testicular Cancer

- Monthly testicular self-examination beginning at age thirteen
- Annual professional testicular exam beginning at age fifteen

Skin Cancer

- Monthly skin self-examination
- Annual professional skin examination (It is important to inform African-American patients that they, too, can get skin cancer.)

TREATMENT FOR CANCER

The more a patient knows about and understands treatment options the better the treatment is likely to go. Some treatments involve longer periods of uncertainty than others, so your choice may be determined by your temperament. Here are the options:

Surgery

Removal of the cancerous cells and surrounding tissues is the oldest and most common medical treatment for cancer and offers the greatest chance of survival.

Radiation Therapy

Radiation is often used to destroy cancerous cells or to damage them so that they cannot continue to proliferate. It is a form of X-ray and is non-invasive. Sometimes surgery and radiation therapy are used in combination to treat cancer.

Chemotherapy

Anticancer drugs are given intravenously or by mouth, and the medication travels through the blood stream to reach cancerous cells. This type of treatment is most often used when the cancer has spread to other parts of the body.

Hormone Therapy

Some cancer relies on the body's own hormone production to grow and spread. Treatment with hormones or drugs that interfere with hormone production can slow or stop the growth of cancer cells.

Immunotherapy

Immunotherapy uses drugs to increase the body's natural defense mechanisms in order to combat cancer. It is often used in conjunction with other courses of cancer treatment.

If you have been diagnosed with cancer, discuss treatment options with your doctor. For more information about cancer treatment, contact:

The American Cancer Society
1–800–ACS-2345
(1–800–227–2345)
http://www.cancer.org

Prostate Cancer

Had my own father known even the most limited information about prostate cancer, he might not have died at the young age of forty-seven. Our family was poor, and I'm sure that he had no idea what cancer was. In fact, at that time (the 1960's) information about cancer was still limited. My father did not have a doctor explain prostate cancer to him and screen him properly. In fact, he never even saw a doctor unless he had symptoms that were more than he could handle. Prevention was not even in his vocabulary. Unfortunately, at that time, it was not in the vocabulary of many doctors, either.

Today, though the information is there, African–American men are still reluctant to seek preventative measures for their health. The following story illustrates this point.

The Story of Mr. James

Mr. James, a forty-two-year-old man who worked for a manufacturing company, came in for a complete physical exam required by his employer. He was broad chested, had huge, muscular arms, and a vice-like handshake. Aside from his imposing stature, he also carried roughly twenty pounds of excess weight, which he jokingly referred to as his "beer belly." Otherwise, he appeared to be in excellent health. Routine blood tests showed no evidence of high blood pressure and revealed normal sugar levels.

After going through the steps of Mr. James's physical, the time came for the routine rectal examination, an important part of the screening for African American men in his age group. However, the moment I put on my latex glove and reached for the tube of KY Jelly, he became agitated and aggressive. "No way, Doc!" he animatedly said to me. "You keep that glove away from me!" He immediately started putting on his clothes. I removed the glove and asked him to sit for a moment so that I could re-explain the importance of a prostate exam.

But after I explained to Mr. James that screening for prostate cancer is vital for early detection and treatment of prostate cancer, he told me firmly, "I'm fine. You won't find any cancer in me." I went on to tell him that African American men in his age group are particularly susceptible and again asked him to please let me examine him. It was only after I told him the story of my father, and other men just like him who had died from prostate cancer, that Mr. James relented and had the exam. What the exam showed was that he had prostate cancer in its early stage. We were both thankful that we'd caught it in time.

Mr. James, like a lot of men, preferred the risk of having undiagnosed prostate cancer to having a simple test. Two specific issues came into play with Mr. James that kept him from exercising a common-sense approach to prevention of the disease: his own aversion to a test he considered humiliating and uncomfortable and his fear of the unknown. Both themes are familiar among African–American men. Indeed, many African–American men are not so fortunate as

Mr. James. If prostate cancer progresses undetected, seventy-five percent of untreated men are likely to die.

With early detection and treatment, ninety-five percent of men, like Mr. James, survive prostate cancer. Today, Mr. James encourages all of his friends to take prostate screening seriously and to insist on receiving the health care that could save their lives.

What is the Prostate?

The prostate, found only in men, is a walnut-sized gland located in front of the rectum, at the outlet of the bladder. It contains cells that produce some of the seminal fluid, which protects and nourishes sperm cells in semen. Just behind the prostate gland are the seminal vesicles that produce most of the fluid for semen. The prostate surrounds the first part of the urethra, the tube that carries urine and semen through the penis. Male hormones stimulate the prostate gland to develop in the fetus. The prostate doesn't reach its full growth until adulthood and maintains that size throughout the life of a man as long as male hormones are produced.

Although several other cell types are found in the prostate, over ninety-nine percent of prostate cancers develop from the glandular cells. Most prostate cancers grow very slowly. Autopsy studies show that many elderly men who died of other diseases also had prostate cancer that neither they nor their doctors were aware of. Some prostate cancers, however, grow and spread quickly.

Many doctors believe that prostate cancer begins with a condition called "prostatic intraepithelial neoplasia" (PIN). In this condition there are precancerous changes in the microscopic appearance (the size, shape, or the rate at which they multiply) of prostate gland cells. This precancerous condition begins to appear in men in their twenties, and by the time they reach fifty, almost fifty percent of men have PIN. Cancer may occur about ten to twenty years after PIN develops.

PIN can be either low-grade or high-grade. If you have high-grade PIN, cancer is likely to develop, and your condition should be carefully watched. PIN can be diagnosed by biopsy of tissue from the prostate gland. If the diagnosis is made, future biopsies are performed annually or every two years, depending on the degree of tissue disease.

Early Screening for Prostate Cancer

Proportionately more African American men die of prostate cancer because they are not screened early enough. African American men should take the following screening measures:

- Annual digital rectal exam at forty years of age (sooner if there is a family history of prostate cancer). Because your prostate gland lies just in front of your rectum, the doctor can feel if there are any nodules or areas of abnormal hardness in your prostate. Nodules or areas of abnormal hardness often indicate the presence of cancer.
- Annual blood test called prostate-specific antigen (PSA) level at age forty. PSA, a protein enzyme (serine proteinase), is localized in prostate tissue. Its function is not known, but in diseases of the prostate, serum levels of PSA are almost always elevated. Prostate cancer can often be found early by testing the amount of prostate-specific antigen (PSA) in your blood.
- Trans-rectal ultrasound (TRUS) is used if the digital rectal exam is abnormal. This radiological test allows doctors to see the prostate gland.

Symptoms of Prostate Cancer

Prostate cancer may not cause symptoms for many years. By the time symptoms *do* appear, the disease may have spread beyond the prostate.

When symptoms occur, they may include:

- Frequent urination, especially at night
- Inability to urinate
- Trouble starting or holding back urination
- A weak or interrupted flow of urine
- Painful or burning urination

- Blood in the urine or semen (the fluid that is released through the penis during orgasm, made up of sperm from the testicles and fluid from the prostate and other sex glands)
- Painful ejaculation (the release of semen through the penis during orgasm)
- Frequent pain or stiffness in the lower back, hips, or upper thighs

These symptoms can indicate cancer, but more often they indicate a noncancerous enlargement of the prostate. It is important to check with a doctor.

Risk Factors for Prostate Cancer

- *Age and Race*
  The older you are the greater your risk; African Americans have a higher death rate from the disease than the general population.

- *Family History*
  You are at a higher risk for prostate cancer if a family member has had it.

- *Exposure to Cadmium*
  Although a variety of other potential risk factors have been examined—sexual activity, sexually-transmitted diseases, diet, viral infections, smoking, alcohol use, exposure to environmental toxins—only one factor seems to be associated with an increased risk of prostate cancer: exposure to cadmium (a heavy metal) in the workplace.

Survival Rates

When prostate cancer is detected early, there is an approximately ninety-five percent five-year survival rate. When prostate cancer is detected late (after it has metastasized), there is only a twenty-five percent five-year survival rate.

African–American Men and Prostate Cancer

In my 1997 article, "African-American Males and Prostate Cancer: Assessing Knowledge Levels in the Community," I surveyed 897 African–American men and found that less than fifty percent of them knew anything about prostate cancer. They also revealed that they would undergo digital rectal exams and other screening for prostate cancer if doctors were more assertive in initiating and explaining the importance of early detection. My study also showed a need to strengthen prevention efforts in less affluent and less educated populations. A positive result of this study was that many of the African American men I surveyed returned to their doctors and insisted that they be screened for prostate cancer.

This year, an estimated 300,000 new cases of prostate cancer will be diagnosed, and over 40,000 men will die of the disease. It is the most common cancer among men in the United States. Because African American men are routinely diagnosed with later stages of the disease, the rates of invasive prostate cancer in African–American men is reportedly thirty percent higher than in White–American men. Therefore, the survival rate for African–American men with prostate cancer is uniformly lower.

Breast Cancer

Breast cancer is the second most commonly diagnosed cancer among women in the United States. Of the approximately 182,000 women diagnosed with breast cancer this year, 40,000 will die from the disease. Although the incidence of breast cancer is a little lower for African–American women than for White–American women, breast cancer mortality in African American women is consistently higher.

There are many reasons for higher death rates from breast cancer among African–American women. The most poignant reason is that screening and prevention are often not promoted enough in African American communities. Consequently, African–American women don't seek treatment until they are in the more advanced stages of breast cancer.

What is Breast Cancer?

A malignant tumor that develops in the breast is termed a breast cancer. Breast cancers usually start in cells that line the milk ducts (ductal cancer) or milk-producing lobes (lobular cancer). A few other rare forms of breast cancer also exist. Fifteen to twenty percent of breast cancers fall into the category of noninvasive cancer, or carcinoma in situ (tiny growths that have not spread across the wall of the milk ducts or lobules). More advanced cancers are called "invasive" because they have spread beyond the ducts and lobules.

Risk Factors for and Prevention of Breast Cancer

Doctors know that there are risk factors associated with the development of breast cancer. You can change some risk factors but cannot change others. Having a risk factor does not necessarily mean that you will get breast cancer, but the more risk factors you have, the higher your chances are for developing the disease.

Risk Factors You Can Change
- Stop smoking
- Get regular exercise at least three to four hours a week (see Chapter 17)
- Stop drinking alcohol or limit consumption to no more than two drinks per week
- Restrict consumption of red meat and other sources of animal fat, including dairy fat.
- Stick to a relatively vegetarian diet
- Shed extra pounds
- If you can choose, consider having children earlier rather than later in life.

Risk Factors You Cannot Change
- **Gender**: Females are more likely than males to develop breast cancer.
- **Increasing Age**: As a woman ages, her risk of developing breast cancer increases.
- **Genetic Risk Factors:** Family history of breast cancer increases the risk.

- **Past History of Breast Cancer:** A previous diagnosis of breast cancer increases your risk of developing it again.
- **History of Benign Breast Disease:** When a biopsy has shown that atypical hyperplasia or other masses found in the breast are not cancer, your risk for malignant cancer increases.
- **Race:** Breast cancer rates are higher in White American women, but African American women die at higher rates from the disease. Fewer African American women are screened for breast cancer, and, therefore, fewer cases of early, more curable breast cancer are detected.
- **Previous Breast Irradiation:** Women who have had chest X-rays at any point in their lifetimes have a higher chance of developing breast cancer.
- **Hormonal Factors:** The following factors may increase a woman's risk of breast cancer: menstrual period starting at an early age, menopause starting at a late age, first live birth at a late age, and few pregnancies.

Risk Factors Related to Lifestyle
- **Use of Oral Contraceptives:** Women who use oral contraceptives have a slightly higher risk for breast cancer.
- **Hormone Replacement Therapy:** Hormone replacement therapy may slightly increase a woman's risk for heart attack and strokes. It also slightly increases a woman's risk for breast cancer. It may help prevent bone fractures.
- **Alcohol Abuse:** Women who drink more than 1.5 drinks a day have an elevated risk for breast cancer.
- **High-fat Diet and Obesity:** An excess amount of fat tissue can alter hormone production in women and increase the risk of breast cancer. Researchers believe changes in metabolism can increase a woman's risk as well.

Early Detection of Breast Cancer: The following guidelines aid in early detection:
- ***Breast Self-examination, Monthly after the Age of Twenty***

The most important physical symptom of breast cancer is a painless mass. Less common symptoms include persistent changes to the breast, such as thickening, swelling, skin irritation or distortion, and nipple symptoms, including spontaneous discharge, erosion, inversion, or tenderness. Among African–American women diagnosed with breast cancer, those women who have done regular breast self-examination and had annual mammograms have a five-year survival rate of 95 percent. This high survival rate is because the cancer was diagnosed early.

- *Mammography (Breast X-ray)*
  Since mammography was first introduced in the mid-1960s, it has become the most effective way of detecting breast cancer. There are two types of mammography:
  - **Screening mammography:** a routine procedure used to examine women who have no evidence of breast cancer. Two views of each breast are taken at an angle to each other.
  - **Diagnostic mammography:** used to examine a specific area of the breast when an abnormality, such as a lump, has been found. Diagnostic mammography includes special views and additional angles.

Mammography can typically spot lesions much smaller than those that can be felt by hand during breast self-examination or clinical breast examination done by a health care professional. To illustrate: an experienced examiner can feel a lump the size of a small grape; mammography can find a lump the size of a grain of rice. Overall, mammography can pick up about forty percent of cancers that are too small to detect by clinical examination.

Among African–American women diagnosed with breast cancer, those women who have done regular breast self-examination and had annual mammograms have a five-year survival rate of 95 percent.

Mammography can miss some breast changes, most often in younger pre-menopausal women with dense breast tissue. The overall "false negative" rate for screening mammography is about ten percent—in other words, one in ten lesions may not show up on a mammogram. Mammography may also have "false positive" findings, which may lead to some biopsies that in hindsight seem unnecessary. But such biopsies serve their use, by proving that a suspicious lesion is not cancerous.

The accuracy of mammography depends a lot on the skill of the radiology technologist who positions the breast and on the interpreting physician who examines the X-rays. That's why it's important to choose a facility with equipment approved by the United States Food and Drug Administration (USFDA) and with staff whose skills meet the requirements of the American College of Radiology.

Accuracy also depends on breast composition. Interpretation of mammograms of the breasts of young women, or women who are pregnant or breast-feeding, may be difficult because their breasts have more milk-producing glands and are dense. It is less difficult to interpret the mammograms of older women because their breasts are less dense and generally have a higher proportion of fat.

Women should understand that during a mammogram the breast must be compressed so it is as flat as possible. Some women will have mild discomfort during the mammogram procedure when the breast is manipulated for better imaging. Although this compression may be uncomfortable, it is seldom painful and it does not cause lingering effects.

If you have breast implants, you should be examined with special breast-positioning techniques that include pushing the implant back toward the chest wall in order to image a maximum of breast tissue. Be sure to inform the mammogram technologist if you have implants.

Types of Treatment for Breast Cancer

- *Mastectomy:* Surgical removal of the whole breast
- *Lumpectomy:* Surgical removal of the cancerous tumor and a shell of the surrounding healthy tissue. Radiation therapy follows a lumpectomy to ensure that all cancerous cells are

destroyed. This procedure is also sometimes referred to as a partial mastectomy or breast-conserving surgery.

- *Removal of Lymph Nodes:* In addition to a mastectomy or lumpectomy, doctors may opt to remove the surrounding lymph nodes since the lymphatic system is the main way cancer spreads through the body. Removal reduces the risk of metastasis.
- *Chemotherapy:* Anticancer drug treatment
- *Radiation Therapy:* Use of radiation to kill cancerous cells. Often combined with chemotherapy, this therapy can often improve your survival chances.

Emotional Responses to the Diagnosis of Breast Cancer

Talk to your doctor about any feelings you may have about your diagnosis. A woman who has just been diagnosed with breast cancer may experience any or all of the following emotions:

- *Anxiety:* A person who has generalized anxiety may feel irritable or restless, have tense muscles, shortness of breath, heart palpitations, sweating, dizziness, and be easily fatigued.
- *Depression:* Symptoms of depression include feeling down on most days, poor concentration, losing pleasure or interest in activities that you normally enjoy, change in eating and sleeping habits, fatigue and sluggishness, inappropriate guilt, feelings of worthlessness, and constant thoughts of suicide. Since cancer medication can also cause these symptoms, it is important to discuss them with your doctor and family.
- *Loss, Grief, Bereavement:* Many people with cancer experience specific phases of grief, which include shock, searching, disorganization, and organization.
- *Sexual Dysfunction:* A diagnosis of cancer and its subsequent treatment can cause both physical and psychological trauma. Nerves, blood vessels, and organs can be affected by the cancer itself, or by the treatment. Stress caused by changes in the body and self-image is a common factor in sexual dysfunction.

- *Post Traumatic Stress Disorder (PTSD):* Re-experiencing the trauma of being diagnosed with cancer can include nightmares, flashbacks, and thoughts that distract you from your normal behavior. People who have PTSD often avoid situations that remind them of the trauma, respond less to people, and show decreasing emotion.

Emotional issues related to the diagnosis of cancer or any other serious illness should always be discussed with a health care professional.

Other Types of Cancer

Cervical Cancer: An estimated 12,800 cases of invasive cervical cancer were diagnosed in 2000, and an estimated 4,600 women died of the disease. Bleeding is a common early symptom of cervical cancer.

Most doctors recommend regular cervical cancer screening with a Pap test for all women who are, or have been, sexually active. Many insurance organizations, including Medicare, recommend and cover Pap testing and pelvic examination at yearly intervals. Yearly screening is allowed for women who are at a high risk of cervical cancer or who have had an abnormal Pap smear in the preceding three years.

Risk Factors
- Age eighteen or younger at the time of first sexual intercourse
- Having numerous sexual partners
- Smoking
- Having a low socioeconomic status

Many doctors recommend discontinuing regular Pap testing after age sixty-five for women who have had consistently normal results on previous tests. Continued Pap testing for women over sixty-five is recommended for women who have had hysterectomy and for women whose cervix was removed because of cervical cancer.

Lung Cancer

Lung cancer is one of the leading causes of death in both men and women in the United States. It is a pernicious disease that has a five-year survival rate of less than fifteen percent. Smoking is the major risk factor for lung cancer. Because more young African Americans are smoking more now than they did two decades ago, more African Americans are at risk.

It is estimated that this year there will be 170,000 new cases of lung cancer and that 150,000 people will die from the disease. Lung cancer deaths account for about thirty percent of all cancer deaths in the United States. African Americans are at especially high risk—again, because of high smoking rates.

Many Americans feel that the tobacco companies have caused most cases of lung cancer, and we are finally seeing a backlash of outrage directed toward these companies. Other causes of lung cancer include passive smoke exposure, occupational and other exposure (for example, asbestos, ionizing radiation, and hydrocarbons), chronic obstructive pulmonary disease, and genetic susceptibility.

African Americans are urged to act in the following ways to decrease the risk of lung cancer:

- Don't smoke at all, or quit smoking. Talk to your doctor about smoking cessation programs.
- Try to deter young African Americans from starting to smoke.
- Get annual chest X-rays if you are at risk.

Chapter 8

Sexually Transmitted Diseases, HIV, and AIDS

S exually transmitted diseases (STDs) are diseases that you can get if you engage in unprotected sexual intercourse with someone who has an STD. In some cases, you can get a sexually transmitted disease even if you use protection. If the condom you are using breaks, or if you are using a condom not made of latex rubber, transmission of disease is possible because there is no true barrier.

HOW DO I GET STDS?

- You get STDs by having oral, vaginal, or anal sex.
- Both men and women can get STDs.
- All it takes is one sexual encounter with one infected person to become infected.
- A person can have more than one disease at the same time.
- Once a person has an STD, re-infection can occur if sexual partners, who have already contracted the disease, have not been medically treated or do not take the medication as directed by a physician.

STDs will not go away on their own. Untreated diseases may even become resistant to medications. A person can become a carrier of the disease but not have any symptoms.

STDs can cause sterility in both sexes and cause birth defects in an unborn fetus. They can also cause disease in a baby born through an infected birth canal and even cause infant death. Drugs can cure syphilis, gonorrhea, and most other STDs. However, the STDs AIDS and herpes simplex have no cure at all.

WENDY'S STORY

It is not possible to tell whether or not people have STDs simply by looking at them. A poignant case about a unique patient comes to my mind. Wendy was in her late twenties, a graduate student, and had movie star looks. She had no trouble dating or meeting men. She revealed that her sexual relations with men were frequent. I had come to like and respect Wendy for her belief in female equality, tenacity, work habits, and for her goal of settling down with a man and perhaps even raising a family.

One day she came into my office complaining of a vaginal discharge. She was shocked to find out that she had contracted a sexually transmitted disease. Wendy confided that she had always been very careful and had always practiced safe sex, except for one occasion when she had neglected to use protection, recalling that it had been with a medical intern at one of the local hospitals. Wendy said, "It could not have been him because he was a smart doctor." I patiently listened to Wendy's story and then began to explain to her a very misunderstood fact about STDs.

STDs occur in all walks of life and are not selective with regard to education, income, type of employment, or race. Wendy agreed to tell all her sexual partners that she was infected. When I treated them, I found out that the medical intern was indeed the source of the STD. As it turned out, he had not told her of his one-night stand with another man. He was bisexual but hadn't revealed this to Wendy.

Researchers from the U.S. Centers for Disease Control and Prevention (USCDC) found that a growing number of men who have sex with other men have STDs. Unfortunately, the women who have sex with these men are left holding the bag, a bag of bacterial diseases that can cause unhappiness, medical illness, and even death.

This story could very well have been a soap opera, but it is real and Wendy hopefully learned her lesson. She also took a test for human immunodeficiency virus (HIV) to be sure that she hadn't also contracted the deadly virus from the medical student; it turned out to be negative. If you suspect your partner of having sex with someone else, if you have had unprotected sex, or if you have multiple sexual partners, you should make an appointment to see your doctor.

If you have any of the following symptoms of STDs, you should seek medical care immediately:
- Burning or pain at urination
- Strange discharge or odor from the vagina
- Itching and burning or pain around the vagina or penis
- Sores on or around the vagina or penis
- Swelling, warts, blisters, or rashes on or around the genital area

HOW CAN I PROTECT MYSELF FROM STDS?

- Use a condom *every* time you have sex, unless you are in a monogamous long-term relationship where both partners have tested negative for HIV.
- Use spermicide with noxynol-9. This helps kill the germs that cause STDs. These spermicides can be purchased in most grocery and drug stores. Spermicide should be used together with a diaphragm *each* time you have intercourse.

If you suspect your partner of having sex with someone else, if you have had unprotected sex, or if you have multiple sexual partners, you should make an appointment to see your doctor.

- Women should know that use of birth control pills or an intrauterine device (IUD) will *not* protect them from STDs.
- Abstinence (not having sex at all) and monogamy (sex with only one partner) are the safest ways to protect yourself. But even for monogamous sex to be safe, both parties must be tested before having sex.

DISCUSSING STDS WITH YOUNG PEOPLE

Younger people have a harder time understanding the health consequences of contracting an STD. If you have children, discuss these issues with them before they become sexually active, so that they stay clear of the dangerous consequences of STDs. It is important to emphasize to teens that there are ways of being close without engaging in sex and sharing bodily fluids (semen, vaginal fluids, or blood).

DRUG AND ALCOHOL USE AND STDS

Most people I treat for sexually transmitted diseases contract them while doing drugs or drinking. Being drunk or high can greatly reduce your judgment, put you at risk for unprotected sex, and increase the possibility that you could be infected with an STD.

You can choose whether or not to have sex. By communicating with and getting to know your partner well, you will reduce your chances of getting an STD. One-night stands can be deadly. By choosing your sexual partners very carefully, you will ensure a healthy sex life for many years.

QUESTIONS ABOUT STDS YOUR DOCTOR MIGHT ASK

A doctor might ask the following questions if you see him or her regarding a sexually transmitted disease:

- What are your symptoms?
- How long have you had these symptoms?

- Have you tried to treat yourself?
- Have you ever had these symptoms before?
- Does urination affect the symptoms?
- Do you have a discharge? Is it thick or thin, light or heavy?
- Is there an odor?
- Are you experiencing any burning, inflammation, or itching?
- Are you presently taking any medication?
- If you are a woman, do you douche? If yes, with what?
- Are you sexually active?

COMMON SEXUALLY TRANSMITTED DISEASES
Vaginosis/Vaginitis

Vaginitis is an umbrella term for many possible vaginal conditions, including vaginosis, *Gardnerella vaginalis,* candidiasis, and trichomoniasis. These conditions occur in about twelve million women each year in the United States. Many women who have a vaginal discharge or symptoms will automatically assume that they have a yeast infection. It is important to see the doctor, rather than asking him or her to call in a prescription, because the doctor must do a pelvic examination to diagnose a yeast infection and rule out STD infection.

Vaginosis is caused from bacteria commonly found in the vagina. Overgrowth of the bacteria can cause a vaginal discharge. Many women have vaginosis during pregnancy or their periods, after progesterone therapy (Depoprovera shots), and around the time of menopause. Vaginosis is also associated with pelvic inflammatory disease and endometriosis. Vaginosis is treated with prescription medication for women who are not pregnant: Flagyl® is often prescribed, as well as intravaginal clindamycin cream (Cleocin)®, and metronidazole gel (Metrogel)®. Your doctor can prescribe the appropriate medication.

Candidiasis

Candida albicans, or "yeast" infection, commonly infects women who are obese, women who are diabetic, and women with immune deficiencies. Growth of this infection is encouraged by oral contraceptives, antibiotics, and immunosuppression. Candidiasis infection is caused by a small fungus and is not usually spread by sexual contact. Healthy women normally have a small amount of yeast in the vagina, but tight clothing, being severely overweight, warm weather, stress, antibiotics, birth control pills, pregnancy, diabetes, and steroid medication can all cause an overgrowth of yeast.

Yeast infection can cause vaginal itching; burning; a heavy, curdy, white discharge; and even pain when having sex. Candidiasis is not usually dangerous, but treatment can help the discomfort.

Women are cautioned to wear cotton underpants, because nylon underpants contain body heat and create a limited-oxygen environment in which a yeast infection can grow.

Women with yeast infection complain of vaginal and vulvar itching (vulvovaginal candidiasis), vaginal soreness, vulvar burning, painful intercourse, and pain upon urination. The vaginal discharge usually does not cause an odor. Candidiasis is easily treated with antifungal vaginal creams and/or suppositories. Recently, the oral antifungal medication, fluconazole (Diflucan®), has proven to be both popular and effective. It is taken as a single dose by mouth. However, side effects such as a headache, gastrointestinal upset, and cramps have been reported by twenty-five percent of women receiving oral fluconazole.

Yeast is a nuisance infection. To avoid problems:

- Don't douche (especially with store preparations) unless your doctor advises you to do so.
- Wipe from front to back after bowel movements. This action prevents the spread of bacteria from the anus to the vagina.
- Wear cotton underwear and loose clothing. This keeps the vaginal area dry and helps healing.
- Treat as directed by a physician and, even if the symptoms go away, take all prescription medication until treatment is completed.
- Return for a follow-up visit or as directed by your doctor.
- Use condoms to lower the chance of infections in the future.

Gardnerella Vaginalis

This bacterial infection is similar to vaginosis and can be treated with the same medicines. *Gardnerella vaginalis* is an infection caused by the interaction of multiple bacteria. Occasionally women who are not sexually active can get this infection. The combination of the bacteria does not, in itself, cause the infection, since these bacteria are present in healthy vaginas. Certain conditions, like vaginal douching, use of intravaginal spermicides, and new sexual partners can cause a change in the chemical balance in the vaginal flora fluid that triggers the infection.

Gardnerella vaginalis is characterized by a moderate to heavy grayish-white vaginal discharge with a foul, fishy odor. Although the main symptom is usually vaginal discharge, women may also complain of external vaginal itching or irritation. Men usually have no symptoms of an infection but may contribute to recurring infections in women. Tampons should not be used during treatment, as they will absorb the medication and reduce the effectiveness of treatment.

Trichomoniasis

Trichomoniasis is caused by the protozoan *trichomonas vaginalis* (a small bacterium-like organism). Trichomoniasis does not necessarily occur through sexual intercourse: fingers, the sharing of sexual toys, and use of an infected washcloth or towel can also transmit it. The organism can live in a woman's vagina and in a man's urethra. It can be transmitted by a pregnant woman to her baby during delivery, as the baby passes through the vaginal canal.

Trichomoniasis is the most common curable STD in young, sexually active women. There are an estimated five million new cases each year. It can infect a wide range of genital areas and can even involve the bladder. Some reports have indicated that the organism can also reside in the prostate.

Trichomoniasis cannot be cured with topical agents such as creams. It must be treated with antibiotics. While it is sometimes without symptoms, it can cause a vaginal discharge: foul-smelling, frothy or bubbly, sometimes yellow or green. The drug of choice is metronidazole (Flagyl®) in a single dose by mouth. Treatment is also given to the partner of someone infected with *Trichomoniasis*. A doctor can give you a prescription to treat trichomoniasis. Follow your doctor's orders regarding treatment

During treatment, do not drink alcohol. If metronidazole is taken with alcohol in any form, it can cause severe sickness or even death. When mixed with alcohol, toxins are produced and nausea and vomiting will occur.

Human Papilloma Virus (HPV) or Genital Warts

On many college campuses, human papilloma virus (HPV) is the most commonly diagnosed STD. Human papilloma virus (HPV) is not a new disease. It is the virus that causes all kinds of warts—the wart you have on your elbow, the plantar wart on the bottom of your foot, or bumps of skin ("skin tags") on your neck. Some can cause warts in other areas like hands or feet, while others tend to infect only the genital tract and can cause cancer or precancerous changes of cells, especially on the cervix. There are many different kinds of HPV, and some of these viruses only infect the genital tract.

Genital warts may look something like skin tags and may be so tiny that a doctor has to use a magnifying glass to see them. Genital warts become large only if they are left untreated. Although some types of HPV can cause cervical cancer, most HPV infections do not. Genital warts do not lead to cancer.

A Pap test will detect abnormal cervical cells, and it is particularly important for women who have abnormal cervical cells to have regular pelvic exams and Pap tests so that they can be treated early, if necessary.

Reports of genital warts go back at least 2,000 years. However, the virus that causes these warts was not discovered until the middle of the twentieth century. Today, more than sixty types of human papilloma virus are recognized.

Genital HPV is contagious and is most commonly spread through sexual contact with an infected person. Genital HPV is spread through skin-to-skin contact, not through an exchange of bodily fluid.

It is important to understand that the HPV infection also can be transmitted when warts are not present. HPV infects the top layers of skin and can remain inactive, or latent, for months or possibly years before any warts or other signs of infection appear. When genital HPV infects men, warts form on the penis and surrounding genital areas. In women, HPV generally infects the cervix.

Genital HPV can have a severe emotional impact. It can be embarrassing to obtain medical care. Two new treatments are now available that patients can self-administer: podofilox (Condylox®) and imiquimod (Aldara®).

Common Medical Treatments for HPV

- **Cryotherapy** involves freezing the wart and a small margin of surrounding skin with substances such as liquid nitrogen. This substance is applied with a cotton swab or sprayed directly onto the skin.
- **Podophyllin** is a chemical applied directly to the surface of the wart.
- **Trichloracetic acid** is a caustic agent also applied to the surface of warts.
- **Electrocautery** is the destruction of wart and surrounding tissue with an electric current that produces heat.
- **Laser therapy** uses intense light to destroy the warts.
- **Surgery** removes the warts by cutting them off.
- **Interferon** is an antiviral drug that can be injected into the warts or topically applied.

Herpes (HSV-1 and HSV-2)

There are two strains of herpes simplex virus: HSV-1 and HSV-2. Type 1 causes cold sores in or around the mouth, which are sometimes called "fever blisters." Type 2 causes blisters in the genital area.

Between 1978 and 1991, the incidence of genital herpes in the United States increased by more than thirty percent. Reports show that one in five people may be infected with HSV–2, and this number may even be higher in inner-city African–American communities.

HSV–2 is usually transmitted from person to person by intimate contact. Symptoms typically begin with pain, tenderness, or an itch in the genital area and are accompanied by fever, headache, and malaise (generally feeling ill). Blisters soon appear on the penis or on the area around the vagina.

In women, blisters may spread to the vagina and cervix, and in both sexes they may appear on the thighs and buttocks. Blisters soon erupt to form painful sores that last from one to three weeks. Other symptoms may include pain or a burning sensation during urination; a clear mucus-like discharge from the vagina or urethra (the tube that carries urine from the bladder and out of the body); a clear mucus-like discharge from the tip of the penis; and tender, swollen glands in the groin area.

The HSV–2 virus that causes genital herpes can lie dormant in nearby nerves and be reactivated later in life. The symptoms of reactivated genital herpes are similar to those of primary genital herpes but are usually less severe.

The disease can be mild to severe. Severe forms occur when the immune system is weakened, and in rare cases the brain and nervous system can be damaged. Genital herpes is particularly severe in those who are also infected with HIV and those who have compromised immune systems. The initial or primary infection is often the worst. Typically, the primary infection is characterized by extensive, multiple clusters of painful lesions (lesions can be bumps, blisters, vesicles, or rash in genital, anal, or surrounding areas).

The HSV-2 virus never goes away. After a period of acute infection that can last from two to four weeks with blisters finally crusting, the virus moves along nerve cells and lies dormant until another episode or outbreak occurs.

The following features usually occur along a predictable pathway and often make diagnosis a simple matter:

- The patient may have undergone emotional stress or trauma.
- There is a deep, dull discomfort or pain at the genital site.
- The patient may feel like he or she is coming down with the flu, with general fatigue or malaise.

- When pain changes to itching, lesions may appear. These lesions are small blister/vesicles with fluid inside. The surrounding area can become inflamed, and regional lymph nodes may swell.
- After one week, these blisters break open or dry out.
- Crusting occurs and the healing process begins. Itching can be profound during this period.
- Lymph nodes begin to lessen in size and tenderness.
- Systemic symptoms such as fever, headache, muscle aches, and pain can occur early in the cycle or through the course of the episode.

About half of the patients who sustain a first episode of genital herpes will experience another episode within six months, and in more than eighty percent, the herpes returns within one year.

Both HSV–1 and HSV–2 are contagious. They are transmitted by direct contact with an infected area. Some people infected with HSV–1 or HSV–2 have no symptoms.

The diagnosis of herpes infection is made by microscopic identification of the virus from the blister fluid. Viral culture and blood testing are also used.

This disease is usually treated with pills or creams that shorten the course of each episode or decrease the itching and discomfort. Acyclovir was the first antiviral agent approved by the USFDA for treatment of herpes simplex. Presently, there are several others that are considered to be the next generation of antiviral medications.

Chlamydia

Chlamydia trachomatis is a bacterium that causes a sexually transmitted infection. The bacterium is a major cause of sexually transmitted infection and infection transmitted from mother to infant. In parts of Africa, the same bacterium can also cause trachoma, an eye disease, which is *not* a sexually transmitted infection. Chlamydia is a very common disease, and its complications can become very serious.

The most common infection site in women is the cervix, but it can also infect the urethra. Other sites for chlamydial infection in both men and women include the tissues around the rectum and the eyes. An untreated infection can cause inflammation of the fallopian tubes or cervix, leading to infertility. The disease is particularly common among young people.

How Do You Get Chlamydia?

Chlamydia is primarily transmitted through sexual intercourse. Women with chlamydia can infect their babies during childbirth. There are usually no symptoms at birth, but symptoms begin to appear in seven to fourteen days after delivery and may result in pneumonia when the baby is two to three weeks old.

What are the Symptoms of Chlamydia?

- **In Women**
    - Stinging feeling during urination
    - Unusual vaginal discharge
    - Pain in the lower abdomen due to inflammation of the fallopian tubes
    - Pain during sex, which may be superficial (as the penis goes in) or deep (when the penis is deep inside vagina)
    - In some cases, bleeding between periods

- **In Men**
    - Stinging feeling during urination, due to inflammation of the urethra. This symptom can be quite mild, may only last for a few days, and can be easily missed.
    - Discharge from the penis and possible itchiness around the opening
    - Pain or tenderness in the testicles

In adults, chlamydia may also infect the rectum, inflaming the rectal tissues. Infection can cause a clear, sticky discharge of mucus from the rectum and pain on opening the bowels. Occasionally, diarrhea may also occur.

Chlamydial infection of the cervix often produces a pus-like discharge and makes the surface of the cervix soft and spongy. Chlamydia can be identified by microscopic examination and cell culture. During a pelvic examination, your doctor will swab the cervix and put the samples on slides for laboratory testing. The cervix sometimes bleeds during swabbing.

The symptoms of chlamydia are similar to the symptoms of gonorrhea, and sometimes the two infections can occur together. However, treatment for each disease is different, so an accurate diagnosis is important. If you have a new sexual partner or several partners at the same time and have any of the aforementioned symptoms, you should avoid any further sexual contact and make an appointment as soon as possible to see your doctor.

Chlamydial conjunctivitis can result from hand-eye contact, and the throat can even become infected after oral sex. Gonorrheal infections can occur in the same way.

Because chlamydial infection is especially prevalent among adolescents, health education and preventative strategies should be directed to them, as well as to adult and geriatric populations.

Chlamydial infections can be treated with antibiotics. Azithromycin is the usual drug of choice, but there are other alternatives that should be discussed with your doctor. It is important to treat all sexual partners to prevent the spread and recurrence of this pernicious disease. When chlamydia is treated early, there are usually no long-term consequences. Serious complications, such as sterility, can occur if the infection is left untreated.

Long-term Complications for Women

Chlamydia and gonorrhea cause approximately ninety percent of all cases of pelvic inflammatory disease (PID), an infection that spreads from the vagina and cervix to the uterus and fallopian tubes. PID increases the risk of chronic pelvic pain and ectopic pregnancy and can lead to sterility.

Limiting the number of sexual partners and using condoms during sexual intercourse greatly reduces the chance of becoming infected with chlamydia.

Gonococcal Infections

Gonococcal infections are caused by the bacterium *Neisseria gonorrhoeae*, which is found only in humans. A gonococcal infection is usually acquired through sexual contact, but it may also be passed from mother to baby during childbirth. Gonorrhea can spread through vaginal, anal, or oral sex, and can be transmitted on contaminated fingers or sex toys. Any mucous membrane can be infected, but gonorrhea is most common in the following locations:

- Eyes, especially in newborns
- Rectum and anal canal
- Throat and mouth
- Urethra in men
- Vagina, cervix, and urethra in females
- Respiratory tract

Sometimes the bacteria can spread through the bloodstream to other areas of the body. The infection may even spread to the abdomen, heart, joints, spinal cord, brain, and liver. Gonorrhea that has spread to other parts of the body may cause a rash and fever. The person may have painful, swollen joints. Other symptoms are specific to the body part that is infected. An infection in the heart, for example, may cause heart valve problems.

Most women with gonorrhea do not have any symptoms. Women who do have symptoms may notice the following:

- Abnormal menstrual bleeding
- Abnormal vaginal discharge
- Pain with intercourse
- Eye pain and discharge
- Frequent or painful urination
- Rectal discomfort
- Sore throat
- Vaginal bleeding after sexual intercourse or exercise

About half of the men with gonorrhea have no symptoms. Men who do have symptoms may notice the following:

- Discharge of pus from the penis
- Eye pain and discharge
- Frequent or painful urination
- Pus-filled discharge from the penis
- Rectal discomfort
- Sore throat

Gonococcal infections are 1.5 times more common in men than in women. They are seen most often in teens and young adults. Diagnosis of a gonococcal infection starts with a history and physical exam. For men, gonorrhea is identified through a culture of the ure-thral canal or of the discharge fluid. For women, it is identified through a pelvic exam and Pap smear.

Gonococcal infections have plagued the human race for centuries. In the African–American community, many people refer to STDs simply as gonorrhea. In fact, gonorrhea is the most widely known STD, but it is not the deadliest and can be treated easily.

Gonococcal infections can cause serious damage to a woman's fallopian tubes. The fallopian tubes, which lead to the ovaries and carry fertilized eggs to the uterus, become inflamed and narrower, preventing passage of the egg. This situation can lead to infertility or ectopic pregnancy. Blood infection (bacteremia) is another serious complication of gonococcal infections. In some cases, blood infections caused by the gonococcal organism can go to the skeletal system and cause arthritis in joints, particularly in the hands, wrists, elbows, ankles, and knees. When a young, sexually active patient comes to his or her doctor with swollen painful joints, the doctor must consider the possibility of gonococcal infection.

The cost of health care for patients with pelvic inflammatory disease caused by STDs amounts to billions of dollars each year in developing countries and in indigent, inner-city populations in the United States. STDs often infect young women of color who are economically disadvantaged, but these infections are not limited to this specific socioeconomic group. STDs affect all ethnic groups at all socioeconomic levels.

Each of us must take responsibility for the prevention and control of gonococcal and other STD infections. Since the major mode of transmission of gonococcal infection is sexual intercourse, it stands to reason that each person should choose his or her sexual partners wisely.

See your doctor for treatment of gonococcal infection. You cannot cure it by over- the-counter medication. Penicillin is no longer the drug of choice because many strains of gonorrhea have become resistant to it, but new medications have been developed.

Syphilis

"A mysterious epidemic, hitherto unknown, which had struck terror into all hearts by the rapidity of its spread, the ravages it made, and the apparent helplessness of the physicians to cure it."

This description, though written in the sixteenth century, aptly describes the HIV/AIDS epidemic today, but in fact it refers to syphilis, a new and unknown disease at the time. Syphilis is caused by the bacterium *Treponema pallidum,* a spiral-shaped organism that moves throughout the body by splitting in two about once every day. Transmission of the disease is by sexual intercourse between an infected individual and the person he or she infects. The bacterium is transferred through cuts or breaks in the skin or mucous membranes.

Each stage of syphilis has its own distinctive features. In stage one, the disease begins with a sore (chancre), which normally forms on the genital area. If untreated, this chancre will heal, but the disease will progress, possibly causing many complications.

In the secondary stage, a rash erupts. This may occur any time between six weeks and six months after infection, and the primary chancre may still be present when this rash appears. The rash indicates that the disease has entered the blood or lymph systems.

In the tertiary or late stage, the disease can infect the central nervous system: neurosyphilis, which can develop from one to thirty years after primary infection, can cause meningitis, insanity, and death. Late-stage syphilis can also be latent, meaning that there are no visible or active symptoms. In any stage of the disease, tests can be negative, making diagnosis more difficult. Syphilis can now be effectively treated with penicillin or other antibiotics (for people who are allergic to penicillin). The widespread use of antibiotics has significantly reduced the incidence of syphilis.

According to the U.S. Centers for Disease Control (USCDC), over 35,600 new cases of syphilis were reported in 1999. However, health officials suspect that more cases occur each year than actually come to their attention. In 1999, syphilis occurred primarily in people aged twenty to thirty-nine, and the reported rate in men was 1.5 times greater than the rate in women. The incidence of syphilis was highest in women aged twenty to twenty-nine years and in men aged thirty to thirty-nine. Seventy-five percent of all syphilis cases in the United States occur in African Americans, while sixteen percent occur in White Americans, eight percent in Hispanics, and one percent in other groups. *The rate of syphilis in the African American population, nearly thirty times the rate for White Americans, is one of the most glaring examples of racial disparity in health status.*

Even the geriatric African–American population is at risk. Some of my elderly patients who were infected in their youth may still have syphilis. I have seen many patients over seventy-years-old who tested positive through a blood test called RPR (reactive plasma reagin). This is the blood test used to determine whether or not a patient has syphilis. X-ray of these patients shows a metallic or opaque material in the pelvis that is arsenic, which was used to treat syphilis at the turn of the century.

Because of the stigma attached to the disease, it hard to be sure how many people die of it, but I suspect that many people have died from syphilis that was not listed as the cause of death. Three percent of the population tests positive in serological testing.

Blood Tests to Detect Antibodies for Syphilis

- **RPR: Rapid Plasma Reagin**
- **VDRL: Venereal Disease Research Laboratory**

- **FTA-ABS: *Fluorescent Treponemal Antibody Absorption***

- **MHA-TP: *Tests for antibody to* Treponema pallidum**

These tests differ in many ways and are used to identify and stage the disease. Consult your doctor for further information to determine what tests might be important for you. There are other diseases that may give false-positive results.

HIV/AIDS: Human Immunodeficiency Virus (HIV) and Acquired Immune Deficiency Syndrome (AIDS) <designer: chead>

As the twenty-first century begins, doctors who work in inner city communities in the United States are seeing the devastating impact of the HIV/*AIDS* epidemic on women of color.

For the past several years, the USCDC has worked to better understand how the HIV/AIDS epidemic impacts African Americans, and to develop intervention strategies. According to the USCDC, as of December, 1999, 733,374 AIDS cases were reported in the United States. Thirty-seven percent, or 272,881 cases, occurred in the African American population. Researchers estimate that between 240,000 and 325,000 African Americans, or one in fifty African–American men and one in 160 African–American women are infected with HIV. Currently, homosexual men and intravenous (IV) drug users account for the majority of HIV/AIDS cases, but more heterosexuals are being infected.

Under the statistics lies a frightening fact: unless something is done to slow down and stop HIV/AIDS in African–American communities, there will be little to look forward to in generations to come. HIV/AIDS threatens all of us as a community, and it is a community problem, even as it is a personal one. Anyone who practices unsafe sex risks not only his own life but the lives of countless others. This means that the most important thing we can do is stop practicing unsafe sex, and encouraging others to do the same. This is a battle that must go on not just among individuals but in our community centers and clubs and churches as well.

What is HIV/AIDS?

HIV/AIDS are diseases of the immune system. AIDS is caused by the human immunodeficiency virus (HIV). First recognized in 1983,

HIV causes both persistent and latent infections. Once the body is inoculated with the virus, the virus begins to disarm the immune system by transposing itself into the genetic makeup of cells and causing white blood cells that fight infections (lymphocytes) not to work properly. Other bodily fluids may harbor the virus, but, so far, blood, semen, and vaginal secretions are the only ones we've identified.

During the period of HIV infection, the patient has no symptoms. But, during that phase, the virus continues to replicate, infecting more and more cells until the defensive function of the immune system ceases to exist.

The three major pathways of transmission are through anal and vaginal sexual intercourse, blood transfusion, and from mother to infant during the period before birth or just after. Symptoms and Signs of Early and Late HIV:

- ***Early Infection Symptoms***
  - Weight loss
  - Fever, sweats
  - Diarrhea
  - Swollen lymph nodes
  - Ulcers in the mouth
  - Skin rashes/lesions
  - Fatigue
  - Muscle and joint pain

Signs

  - Body wasting
  - White oral plaques (oral candidiasis)
  - Fungal skin infections
  - Decreased mental cognition
  - Muscle and nerve complications: tremors, soreness, pins and needles sensation (paresthesia)

- ***Late Infection Symptoms***
  - Headache
  - Seizures

- Visual disturbances, including blindness
- Shortness of breath
- Diarrhea
- Weight loss

Signs

- Increased respiration
- Mouth sores
- Increased pressure in the brain and swelling in the optic disc
- Buildup of mucus in the chest, caused by bacteria or other organisms
- Liver and spleen enlargement
- Complication of cranial nerves that impairs the transmission of nerve impulses

The Story of Mary Jones

Mary Jones died from AIDS ten years ago. Mary was my patient, and she affected my life more than she could ever have imagined. She was a minister to the poor on the rough streets of South and West Philadelphia. With a Bible in one hand, and condoms in the other, Mary talked about God and, at the same time, advised people on the streets about the practice of safe sex. She began her crusade long before she knew she was infected with HIV.

When I first met Mary, she had little understanding of HIV/AIDS or the risk factors that contribute to this terrible disease. In fact, when she came to me with a chronic cough that simply would not go away, AIDS was the last thing on her mind. Mary did not smoke or drink, nor was she ever an intravenous drug user. But a little over a year before she had wed a man named Jeff. Together, they were on a mission to save the youths of their inner-city community.

Mary was streetwise., but she was naïve about one very important thing—Jeff's past history. Before finding God and joining together with Mary to minister to inner city youths, Jeff had had unprotected sex with several women over the years. He didn't tell Mary about his sexual encounters because he felt that that part of his

life was behind him. Mary died of AIDS less than a year after she first came to see me, and Jeff died not long after.

I have thought of Mary often over the years since her death, especially when I read the latest reports from the USCDC, which show that AIDS cases in African American women are increasing rapidly. In addition, AIDS has replaced homicide as the leading cause of death among young African–American men, many of whom are having sex with African–American women.

Because of the ostracism, shame, and homophobia that still surround homosexuality in African American communities, many African American homosexuals and lesbians are forced to live dual lives. Some men (and women) lie about their sexual histories or simply leave out the details. That's true of heterosexual people, as well as homosexuals and lesbians.

Most women with AIDS in the United States are infected through heterosexual exposure. DeVincenzi and colleagues found that male-to-female transmission occurred approximately twice as often as female-to-male transmission: twenty percent versus twelve percent, respectively. *African American women account for eighty percent of all female cases of AIDS, even though they represent less than twenty percent of all women in the United States.*

Most of my patients are very concerned about becoming infected by HIV, and they should be. More than fifty percent of all African Americans have relatives or people close to them who are either infected with HIV or who have died from it. That's why it's so urgently important that you, and all of us, become educated about HIV and AIDS. Knowledge will lessen our chances of contracting this deadly disease.

What is the Difference between HIV and AIDS?

Transmission of HIV occurs when people share bodily fluids through sexual intercourse or intravenous drug use. Before researchers knew exactly what they were dealing with, HIV was also transmitted through blood transfusions. Today, the nation's blood supply is thoroughly screened for the HIV virus.

Once you have contracted the HIV virus you cannot get rid of it. The virus lies dormant in your body, and there is no cure. Over time, HIV develops into AIDS, which is the full-blown version of the disease.

A state of emergency exists in the African American community. Take the time to seek out the facts about HIV/AIDS by talking directly with your doctor. *Heightened public awareness about the virus is the major defense against infection.* Once you have the facts, your perceptions about people infected with the virus will change. Our community needs to be able to talk publicly about this disease. That's the only way we can begin to fight back against the terrible damage it is doing.

Take the time to seek out the facts about HIV/AIDS
by talking directly with your doctor. Heightened
public awareness about the virus is the major defense
against infection.

Common Conditions Associated with HIV/AIDS

- **Skin and Lining of Mouth**
  - Lesions on the skin and the mouth are sometimes the first HIV-related symptoms for which patients seek medical care.
  - Some of these lesions are caused by candidiasis, which occurs in over ninety percent of HIV-infected patients. Common symptoms include white yeast plaques in the vagina and esophagus, redness and cracking of the surface of the mouth, and herpes around the mouth and on genital areas.
  - Herpes zoster is more common in AIDS patients, and recurrent episodes of herpes zoster have been reported in as many as twenty percent of HIV-infected people.

- **Gynecologic Conditions**
  - Vaginal candidiasis is a common condition present in forty-one percent of women with HIV infection. It is not my intent to have doctors' offices stampeded by women with yeast infections. But when a woman has frequent yeast infections, she should seek medical help.
  - Diabetics generally are susceptible to fungal infections, especially when their diabetes is complicated by HIV.
  - Human papilloma virus (HPV)—the virus that causes genital warts—is associated with HIV infection, too. Women and men with this condition should be tested for HIV.

- **Blood Conditions**
  - The most common symptom that brings HIV patients to their doctors is anemia. More than seventy percent of people with AIDS have some degree of anemia. Women who have weakness and fatigue should be screened for anemia.
  - The finding of a "low platelet" count (thrombocytopenia) is another indication for HIV testing. Platelets help the blood to clot, and low levels of platelets cause patients to bruise easily and the blood not to clot. Thrombocytopenia is present in ten percent of people who are HIV positive and in forty percent of people with AIDS. Women who have weakness and fatigue should be screened for anemia.

- *Lung Conditions*
  - *Pneumocystis carinii* pneumonia (PCP) is the most common illness contracted by people with AIDS. PCP usually starts with a dry cough and then proceeds with fatigue, fever, and shortness of breath. X-rays of the lungs show patterns of the infection. It is important to treat patients with PCP with appropriate antibiotics.
  - Tuberculosis is another lung infection common to people with AIDS.

- *Cancerous Conditions*
  - Kaposi's sarcoma is one of the first diseases to be recognized as a cancer associated with HIV and AIDS. The well-known skin lesions of the sarcoma are flat bumps, lightly pink to brown to violet. These lesions are most common on the legs, and vary in size from millimeters to centimeters.
  - Lymphomas, particularly non-Hodgkin's lymphoma, appear in AIDS patients about 200 times more often than in the general population.
  - Cervical and anal cancers are also common with AIDS patients.

Symptoms of AIDS

A person infected with HIV does not necessarily have AIDS. AIDS is the third stage of the infection.

- *Stage I (No Symptoms):* In the first stage of HIV, symptoms don't show up. People can live with HIV for years without knowing it. Blood tests will show antibodies after they form to fight the HIV virus, but if you take a blood test right after you have been infected, the virus won't show up. Antibodies appear in blood tests only after you have been infected for three months.
- *Stage II (Mild Illness):* At this stage, the virus grows within the white blood cells and destroys them. When most of the cells are destroyed, the immune system is unable to fend off infection, and the body weakens. Patients will begin to feel

tired and lose weight. They may develop a cough, diarrhea, fever, or sweating at night. A cold is more threatening to a person with HIV than to a person without the disease.

* *Stage III (Severe Symptoms):* By this time, the HIV/AIDS virus has nearly destroyed the body's immune system. The body has great difficulty fighting off bacteria. At this stage, patients can develop a rare type of cancer called Kaposi's sarcoma. AIDS doesn't kill anyone, but other infections and cancer do.

Treatment for HIV/AIDS

In 1986, AZT became the first step in AIDS prevention. AZT is a pill that has prolonged the lives of HIV-infected patients. Ninety percent of patients who take the AZT pill are still alive after one year, a fifty percent increase in the rate of survival.

Research continues to improve the survival rates of people with HIV and AIDS. Currently, there are about eighteen drugs for treating these infections, and this number is likely to rise as research continues. Drugs are used in combination, and if patients are unable to tolerate one regimen, Other drug combinations may cause fewer side effects. Fifteen percent of all patients have drug intolerance.

Side Effects from Drug Treatment for AIDS

For most patients, side effects of drug treatment go away after a few weeks. Side effects may include:

* Diarrhea
* Kidney stones
* Increased blood sugar
* Increased cholesterol
* Insomnia
* Redistribution of body fat (lumps of fat on various parts of the body)
* A typical facial appearance that is characterized by sunken cheeks

There are three classifications of drugs used to treat HIV and AIDS. These drugs work on various sites within the virus.

1) Nucleoside Reverse Transcriptase Inhibitors: Abacavir, Combivir, Didanosine, Lamivudine (3TC), Stavudine, and Zidovudine(AZT)

3) NonNucleoside Reverse Transcriptase Inhibitors: Delavirdine, Efavirenz, Nevirapine.

4) Protease Inhibitors: Indinavir, Lopinavir, Nelfinavir, and Ritonavir.

Today, the treatment preferred by most doctors is as follows:

- People who have few or no symptoms, but are at risk, are screened for the disease with a blood test to determine plasma HIV/ RNA levels and CD4 counts. When the test is positive, the following treatment is started:
- Regimen One: Combivir and Nelfinavir.
- Regimen Two, for people with advanced disease: Lamivudine, Stavudine, Indinavir, and Ritonavir. During both these regimes, additional medications are used to prevent infections and treat side effects, including Bactrim® and Azithromycin for pneumonia and some forms of lung infection. A major concern is that elevation of cholesterol is a side effect of these drugs; patients who have this side effect have to take lipid-lowering medication.

Researchers continue to look for a vaccine for HIV/AIDS. In the meantime, know the facts and prevent the disease. You'll be protecting yourself, your community, and your people.

Chapter 9

Respiratory Illness and Lung Conditions

ASTHMA

An alarming number of African Americans seek emergency care for acute respiratory complications caused by asthma. The incidence of deaths from asthma has increased in the last decade, though the specific reason is not known.

Asthma is a condition in which the airways of the lungs become either narrowed or completely blocked, impeding normal breathing. This obstruction of the lungs is reversible, either spontaneously or with medication.

How Does Air Reach Your Lungs?

Air reaches the lungs by passing through the windpipe (trachea), which divides into two large tubes (bronchi), one for each lung. Each bronchus further divides into many little tubes (bronchioles), which eventually lead to tiny air sacs (alveoli), in which oxygen from the air is transferred to the bloodstream, and carbon dioxide from the bloodstream is transferred to the air. Asthma involves only the airways (bronchi and bronchioles), and not the air sacs.

Although everyone's airways have the potential for constricting in response to allergens or irritants, the asthmatic's airways are over-sensitive, or hyper-reactive. In response to stimuli, the airways may become obstructed by any of the following:

- Constriction of the muscles surrounding the airway
- Inflammation and swelling of the airway
- Increased mucus production that clogs the airway

Once the airways have become obstructed, it takes more effort to force air through them, so that breathing becomes labored. This forcing of air through constricted airways can make a whistling or rattling sound, called wheezing. Irritation of the airways by excessive mucus may also provoke coughing. The air sacs (alveoli), although not directly damaged, become deprived of oxygen and shrink, so that less oxygen is delivered into the blood.

How is Asthma Diagnosed?

Asthma is diagnosed by physical examination, personal history, and lung function tests. During a physical examination, your doctor looks for typical symptoms of asthma, such as wheezing or coughing. The personal history provides additional clues, such as allergies or a history of asthma in the family. Lung function tests may be as simple as measuring peak flow with a peak flow meter (a plastic cylinder with a mouthpiece at one end, a place for the air to escape at the other end, and a calibrated meter along the side). When you blow into the peak flow meter, a marker is pushed along the scale and comes to rest at a point that indicates your air flow. Lung function can also be measured by a simple spirometer (a hose you blow into with a gauge attached to measure air flow), or by a battery of spirometry tests in a pulmonary function lab.

The Most Common Triggers for Asthma

- Viral respiratory infections, such as influenza (the flu) or bronchitis

- Bacterial infections, including sinus infections
- Irritants, such as pollution, cigarette smoke, perfumes, dust, or chemicals
- Sudden changes in either temperature or humidity, especially exposure to cold air
- Allergens
- Emotional upset and stress
- Exercise

Treatment for Asthma

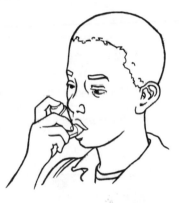

Mild asthma is usually treated with short-acting, inhaled bronchodilators to relieve occasional symptoms as they occur. Moderate or severe asthma is treated with both bronchodilators and anti-inflammatories to alleviate both the constriction (closing down) and inflammation of the airways. Bronchodilators are drugs that open up (dilate) the constricted airways, while anti-inflammatories are drugs aimed at reducing inflammation of the airways.

Taking anti-inflammatory drugs (usually inhaled corticosteroids) daily for moderate to severe asthma is a relatively new approach to treating asthma. The idea behind it is that if the underlying inflammation of the airways is reduced, the bronchi may become less hyper-reactive, making future attacks less likely. Such anti-inflammatory therapy, however, must be taken regularly in order to be effective. For asthma that is strongly triggered by allergies, allergen avoidance can often greatly reduce the need for medication.

Educating yourself about asthma is very important. Learning how to measure peak flows, use inhalers, and avoid allergens and other substances that trigger attacks may well save your life or the life of someone you know who has been diagnosed with asthma.

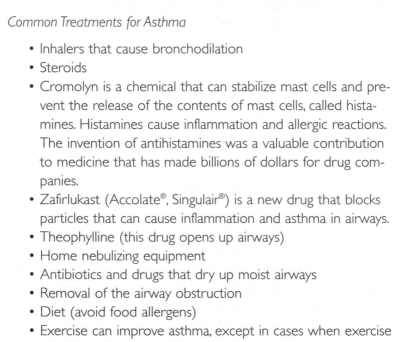

Common Treatments for Asthma

- Inhalers that cause bronchodilation
- Steroids
- Cromolyn is a chemical that can stabilize mast cells and prevent the release of the contents of mast cells, called histamines. Histamines cause inflammation and allergic reactions. The invention of antihistamines was a valuable contribution to medicine that has made billions of dollars for drug companies.
- Zafirlukast (Accolate®, Singulair®) is a new drug that blocks particles that can cause inflammation and asthma in airways.
- Theophylline (this drug opens up airways)
- Home nebulizing equipment
- Antibiotics and drugs that dry up moist airways
- Removal of the airway obstruction
- Diet (avoid food allergens)
- Exercise can improve asthma, except in cases when exercise may in fact cause asthma

CHRONIC OBSTRUCTIVE PULMONARY DISEASE (COPD)

While many diseases affect African American men, the major causes of death are chronic obstructive pulmonary disease (COPD), pneumonia, diabetes, heart disease, and kidney disease. The impact of these diseases is costly, as are the frequent hospitalizations they may require.

What is COPD?

COPD is a general term used for diseases that obstruct the airways—in particular, chronic bronchitis and emphysema, one rarely occurring without a degree of the other. The American Medical Association defines COPD as "a disorder characterized by reduced maximal expiratory flow and slow, forced emptying of the lungs, features that do not change markedly over several months." This limitation in airflow is only minimally reversible with bronchodilators.

The Story of Mr. Thompson

Mr. Thompson came into my office with a cough and fever, symptoms that he had almost on a monthly basis. Once a virile shipyard worker, he was thin, sickly, and looks much older than his sixty-five years. Mr. Thompson had resisted all of my suggestions to stop smoking by saying that it was the one thing left that he enjoyed. Since his first visit three years ago, his condition had steadily worsened. Mr. Thompson had chronic bronchitis, and was well on his way to developing emphysema. Many men and women who do not take care of their health end up with chronic obstructive pulmonary disease (COPD) and share Mr. Thompson's story.

What are the Main Symptoms?

Mr. Thompson's chronic cough and shortness of breath were the outward signs of his disease. When he coughed, sputum was expelled from his lungs. People with chronic bronchitis, like Mr. Thompson, have increased amounts of mucus in their lungs. The excess mucus buildup in his body also made Mr. Thompson puffy. Tests revealed poor oxygen levels in his blood (less than ninety percent), causing a dull, ruddy complexion; premature wrinkling of his skin; and a blue hue in his skin and nails. The medical community sometimes refers to people with these symptoms as "blue bloaters."

People with emphysema have expanded chests and difficulty breathing after even minor exertion. They are often called "pink puffers" because they lack oxygen and breathe rapidly. Destroyed lung tissue is a characteristic of emphysema.

If you have symptoms, see your doctor! A doctor will offer support and treatment for COPD. In Mr. Thompson's case, I finally convinced him to start a program that included both short-term reachable goals and a long-range plan.

What is Your Risk for Developing COPD?

Fourteen million Americans suffer from COPD. Over 90,000 people die each year from COPD, and, in the last few decades, the diagnosis of and death rate from COPD for African American men has increased significantly. Statistics show that more men than women suffer from the disease. Bronchitis is the most common precursor.

What Causes COPD?

Cigarette smoking is the major cause of COPD. The more cigarettes and the longer a person has smoked, the greater the chance of getting the disease. Mr. Thompson had smoked a pack of cigarettes a day for over forty years, but since he retired five years ago, his cigarette smoking had increased to three packs a day. He blamed the increase on being bored and depressed, even saying, '"Why should I quit at my age?"'

It is important to note that a person does not have to smoke to develop COPD. Other causes are allergens from air pollution, occupational hazards such as working in a job where the air is polluted with chemical fumes or large amounts of dust, and childhood respiratory illnesses. People who are exposed to cigarette smoke for long periods of time are also at an increased risk for developing COPD. The death rate from COPD is generally higher for people working in blue-collar jobs.

How is COPD Diagnosed?

Your doctor will review your medical history, and may ask you a series of questions, such as:

- Are you a smoker, or have you ever smoked?
- Do you have symptoms such as shortness of breath, persistent coughing, or mucus production?
- Are you exposed to chemical fumes or dust on a regular basis?

General Body Types Associated with COPD

Overweight:
- Chronic bronchitis
- Water retention in feet and legs (peripheral edema)
- Poor skin tone resulting from reduced distribution of oxygen to the body tissues

Underweight:
- Emphysema
- Tendency toward weight loss
- Poor appetite
- Apparent muscle wasting: chest, arms, and legs look bony

- Are you often fatigued, or do you have problems sleeping?
- Does anyone in your family have a history of lung problems?

In addition, your doctor may order the following tests to evaluate, diagnose, and manage COPD:

- Pulmonary function
- Office spirometry
- Chest X-ray
- Arterial blood gas (this test takes a sample of blood from an artery.
- CAT scan of the chest
- Pulse oximetry (this test measures oxygen levels in the body)

In order to make a proper diagnosis, your doctor relies on the comparison of several different tests.

What to Expect During Testing

- ***Office Spirometry:*** Spirometry measures lung function. I instructed Mr. Thompson to breathe into a tube that was attached to a meter machine. As he exhaled into the device, a reading on the meter told me how strong his lungs were. The measurement was useful in determining the exact diagnosis and the management of Mr. Thompson's COPD.

- **Chest X-rays:** Every African American man forty years of age or older should have a routine chest X-ray. A baseline X-ray helps the doctor determine the degree of change in future X-rays. It also shows if you have pneumonia, cancer, tuberculosis, or lung destruction from COPD. Bronchitis will show increased mucus and prominent vessels in the lungs. Emphysema reveals a flattened diaphragm.

- **Electrocardiogram (EKG or ECG):** Sometimes patients with COPD will also have heart disease. Since Mr. Thompson had high blood pressure, there were some changes on his electrocardiogram that indicated that he had heart disease.

- **Arterial Blood Gas Analysis:** This test determines the level of oxygen present in the blood. If the oxygen level is low, portable oxygen can be prescribed.

After some or all of these tests have been done, the following treatment options are available. Talk to your doctor on which one is best for you. If you are a smoker, the doctor will almost certainly recommend that you stop. The doctor may prescribe the following medications, separately or in combination:

- Bronchodilators
- Steroids to reduce inflammation
- Inhaled anticholinergics
- Other drugs mentioned in the asthma section—i.e., leukotriene anatagonist, theophylline, home oxygen, and antibiotics to treat infections that commonly affect people with COPD

Check Your Knowledge of COPD (True or False?)

1. Chronic obstructive pulmonary disease (COPD) is caused only by smoking.
2. COPD can be life-threatening and is a leading cause of death.
3. COPD affects men and women with equal frequency.
4. More COPD patients suffer from emphysema than from chronic bronchitis.
5. The effects of COPD are usually only present after a person exercises.
6. A chest X-ray is the only sure way of diagnosing COPD.
7. Good eating habits are important to an individual diagnosed with COPD.
8. A good habit for a patient with COPD is to eat three big meals a day.
9. People with COPD should avoid exertion of any kind.
10. Exercise programs for people with COPD should be limited to aerobics.

Answers

QUESTION 1: FALSE.
CORRECT ANSWER: Although smoking is the major cause of COPD, other contributing factors are air pollutants, occupational exposure to dust and fumes, infection, heredity, allergies, and aging.

QUESTION 2: TRUE.
CORRECT ANSWER: COPD is currently the fifth leading cause of death in the United States. More than ninety-five percent of all deaths from COPD occur in people over the age of fifty-five.

QUESTION 3: FALSE.
CORRECT ANSWER: Far more men than women get COPD. Differences in smoking habits probably account for this fact, but, with more and more women smoking, this difference will disappear as the population grows older.

QUESTION 4: FALSE.
CORRECT ANSWER: Emphysema afflicts an estimated two million Americans. Chronic bronchitis, though less well known, afflicts more than 12.6 million people in the United States.

QUESTION 5: FALSE.
CORRECT ANSWER: People with COPD can experience difficulty breathing at night, while at rest, or with specific activities like eating, talking, or walking. Patients may talk in short sentences or purse their lips to exhale. An exercise program, good eating habits, and maintaining normal weight are essential to lessening the effects of COPD.

QUESTION 6: FALSE.
CORRECT ANSWER: A chest X-ray is not very sensitive or specific in diagnosing COPD. A pulmonary function test is critical in the diagnosis of COPD. Any other laboratory test will only confirm the diagnosis or uncover complications like pneumonia or lung tumors.

QUESTION 7: TRUE.
CORRECT ANSWER: For people with COPD, eating is as important as breathing. Because a person with COPD has to work harder to breathe, the muscles used in breathing can burn up to ten times more calories than the muscles of a healthy person. Eating foods from each of the basic food groups is essential for good nutritional support.

QUESTION 8: FALSE.
CORRECT ANSWER: It might be better to eat six small meals per day. The smaller quantity of food will not fill a person's stomach and will make breathing easier. Avoid foods with little nutritional value. Limit salt intake because excess sodium can cause fluid retention, which interferes with breathing.

QUESTION 9: FALSE.
CORRECT ANSWER: Exercise, on most any level, improves the oxygen utilization, work capacity, and state of mind of a person with COPD. If an individual with COPD can use energy more efficiently for breathing, then more energy will remain for daily activities. Exercise coupled with good dietary habits can improve the quality of life for people with COPD. Physician direction of an exercise program is essential.

QUESTION 10: FALSE.
CORRECT ANSWER: With physician approval, a COPD patient can swim, weight train, or perform exercises like walking or low-impact aerobics. If the patient is allowed to participate in different kinds of activities, varying routines help reduce boredom and contribute to enjoyment of the activity. Any exercise is better than none. Even if a patient wears a supplemental oxygen setup, some exercise is possible.

How Can You Prevent COPD?

The best way to prevent COPD is never to smoke, or, if you are a smoker, to stop. For three years, I tried to persuade Mr. Thompson to stop, but never succeeded. It is a difficult habit to break. Making every attempt to work in a healthy environment with clean air dramatically reduces your risk for developing COPD.

Setting Goals for Lifestyle Changes

Contemplation

First, Mr. Thompson was to contemplate why he needed to stop smoking. We talked about the damage that had been done, and I told him that his quality of life could change if he reinvented himself. The question he needed to ask himself was, "Am I willing to stop smoking?"

Preparation

Preparing for a mental and social change is perhaps the most difficult part. Mr. Thompson's smoking was a social habit when he played cards with his friends. He also smoked to blow off steam when he was agitated or angry. Making a time frame for when he would smoke his last cigarette was our first goal. He started the mental process by telling his friends, loved ones, and buddies that he would be quitting by that date. He also decided to throw away all but one ashtray in his home.

Getting started

Just do it! Mr. Thompson's goal was to reduce his smoking by three cigarettes every day. When the date he chose came, he would only have three cigarettes to smoke. When those three were gone, he'd quit smoking.

Toward the end of the process, I put Mr. Thompson on smoking cessation patches to assist him in his withdrawal from nicotine. He had a supportive network of family and friends, and even a few of his buddies joined in the process with him. Perhaps the biggest motivating factors, in addition to suffering from the disease itself, are a supportive doctor and network of family and friends.

Maintenance

Your doctor, family, and friends will help to maintain the "smoke-free" you. Throughout the process, regular visits to your physician will ensure that you stick with the plan of action.

Treatment

Smoking Cessation

Smoking cessation is absolutely necessary and should be the first line of therapy. I had Mr. Thompson set a date and let his family know about it. I encouraged him not to let anyone smoke in his home. He had a grown son who lived with him and who smoked, and his son agreed to smoke on the back porch. I also gave him some medicine to calm his nerves. It was understandable that this experience was anxiety-provoking for Mr. Thompson.

I also discussed the use of a nicotine patch for Mr. Thompson. Although reluctant, he agreed to use it if he had problems quitting on the chosen day. He understood that smoking made his COPD worse, exacerbated his high blood pressure and heart disease, and put him at risk for stroke and atherosclerosis. The truth of the matter is that nicotine replacement therapies, when used with behavioral therapy, make a good, balanced smoking cessation program. Some other nicotine replacements are nicotine inhalation systems, nicotine nasal spray, Nicoderm®, and Nicorette® gum. Studies have shown that these kinds of nicotine replacement are safe.

Pharmacological Therapy

The aim of pharmacology is to reverse narrowing of the airways, increase lung function, decrease inflammation, and control infection. The following drugs are commonly used:

- **Atrovent®:** This drug is an anticholinergic (acetylcholine-blocking) medication that is given as an inhaler, in order to minimize airway narrowing. In Mr. Thompson's case, it was important that he learned how to properly use a metered-dose inhaler (MDI) that was filled with Atrovent®. He was taught to inhale the mist into his lungs instead of holding it in his mouth.

- **Albuterol:** This drug is also given as an MDI (it can also be in pill form). Albuterol is a beta- adrenergic drug that expands the small airways (called a bronchodilator). You can use Atrovent® and albuterol together.

- **Theophylline:** This drug is usually administered in pill form and also expands the airways. Although theophylline was used frequently in the past, it is no longer the first drug of choice. Nevertheless, if a patient is taking theophylline when he or she sees a new doctor, chances are that the doctor will continue the drug. Theolair® and Theodur® are some of most common brand names for these preparations.

- **Steroids:** These drugs (*not* the kind of steroid that increases muscle mass) are used to decrease inflammation in the lungs. Steroids can be given in pill form (predisone) and in an MDI (Azmacort® or Vanceril®).

- **Zyflow® and Singulair®:** These new medicines can prevent worsening of inflammation and bronchoconstriction. You should ask your doctor about them.

- **Antibiotics:** Mr. Thompson was coughing up green mucus. He had an infection, and needed antibiotics. Antibiotics are indicated for patients with COPD because they are at high- risk for lung infections and contagious pneumonia (called community-acquired pneumonia).

Asthma is considered to be a form of chronic obstructive pulmonary disease (COPD). The same medications are used for asthma, bronchitis, and emphysema, because much of the pathophysiology is similar.

NonDrug Therapy

- **Surgery:** Removing some of the damaged lungs can help a person to breathe better. But surgery is usually used as a last resort.

I hinted to Mr. Thompson that surgery was an option if he was unable to quit smoking or take the prescribed medication. Needless to say, he was even more motivated to quit.
Vaccinations: All patients with COPD should receive the pneumococcal vaccination that is given in a one-time dose (vaccinations will be discussed in the section on pneumonia). All COPD patients should also be given the influenza vaccination (flu shot). Vaccinations help the body build up immunity to pneumonia and the flu, which is especially important for people who suffer from COPD *Long-term Oxygen Therapy:* Many of the people you see walking around with portable oxygen tanks have COPD. In fact, long-term oxygen therapy is one of the few therapies that have been shown to actually improve the survival rates of people with COPD.

How Can You Help Yourself?

Accepting the fact that you have COPD can be a difficult challenge, but remember that, by accepting it, you also empower yourself to take control of your situation. Learn as much about COPD as you can by establishing a close relationship with your doctor and reading about good health. You can take the following steps:

1. Have your family go through the education process with you.
2. Stop smoking and don't cheat; get support from your family and your doctor.
3. Make sure you understand how to take your medicine. This knowledge can prevent problems in the future.
4. If you are overweight, try to lose weight. If you lose that abdominal girth, you can breathe better.
5. Take care of yourself: avoid infection by getting the vaccinations that will protect you. Eat well, get plenty of rest, and dress appropriately when out in the cold.
6. Work on your psychology. If you are angry or depressed, talk to your family and doctor about your feelings. African–American men sometimes have trouble opening up.

One important thing that Mr. Thompson did for himself was to participate in a pulmonary rehabilitation and exercise program. The aim of this program was to decrease air flow obstruction by exercising. Exercise decreases air flow obstruction and raises blood oxygen levels, thereby helping you breathe better. A pulmonary rehabilitation and exercise program benefits participants physiologically and psychologically, by lowering blood pressure and decreasing depression. Mr. Thompson found that, by exercise training and learning proper breathing techniques, he experienced fewer episodes of shortness of breath. Pulmonary rehabilitation also helps lower the cost of health care by decreasing the rate of hospitalization.

What is the Outlook for People with COPD?

Only one-quarter of people with COPD are able to stop smoking. People who cannot stop smoking have a poor prognosis. COPD is the fourth leading cause of death in the United States.

Because COPD is a combination of various functional and physiologic abnormalities, no one treatment plan will fit every person. To have the same success as Mr. Thompson, a person must be motivated and work in collaboration a doctor. Because Mr. Thompson stuck to the treatment plan, he was able to live a quality life. I thank him for his contribution in this chapter.

Who Else Can Help?

Your higher power! By becoming more spiritual, you can feel better. Work on balancing your personality. Spirituality can lessen rage, anger, fear, and depression. Recruit the cooperation and encouragement of your family and friends. Ask the National Heart, Lung, and Blood Institute (http://www.nhlbi.nih.gov/) or the American Lung Association (http://www.lungusa.org/) for information about support groups in your area. Your doctor and local hospital will have information about local support groups.

COMMUNITY-ACQUIRED PNEUMONIA

Community-acquired pneumonia (CAP) is caused by a bacteria or viral infection of the lungs. Bacterial organisms cause the lungs to become inflamed, and mucus accumulates, preventing the flow of oxygen. If enough oxygen can't get to vital organs like your brain and heart, you may die. Community-acquired pneumonia (CAP) is the most common pneumonia I encounter in my practice. It is called "community-acquired" because people contract the lung infection from other people, especially in crowded living conditions. Most CAP doesn't require hospitalization, and patients are simply treated with antibiotics and sent home to rest and recover.

African–American men and some African–American women tend to put off medical treatment for illness. They don't seek out a physician for their symptoms until inflammation and mucus in the lungs makes them unable to breathe. African–American men sometimes walk around coughing with fever and chills (hence the phrase "walking pneumonia"). For older Americans, CAP is the sixth most frequent cause of death.

The Story of Elmer Smith

The case of Mr. Elmer Smith makes me think about the terrible impact of community-acquired pneumonia on the Black community. Mr. Smith was a man who rarely went to see a doctor. He was a good man, a deacon at his church and a city activist for human rights. At seventy years of age, Elmer had been married to his childhood sweetheart for fifty-five years and had many great, great grandchildren. He was a pillar of society and an indelible influence on everyone who crossed his path.

One winter day, Elmer came to see me with a dry cough, shortness of breath, chest pain, and mild confusion. His medical history included adult onset diabetes mellitus, mild kidney disease, and congestive heart failure. He had not sought treatment for these disorders in years.

On physical examination, his temperature was over 100 degrees (normal is 98.6). His pulse was 130 beats per minute (normal is 60–90); respiration, 22 per minute (normal is 18); and blood pressure of 90/50 (normal is 120/70). When I listened to his chest, I heard crackles in the base of his lungs. This abnormal sound indicates fluid and abnormal lung function. I was very concerned.

As I examined Elmer, his weary eyes seemed to follow my every move, as if he knew that I was going to hospitalize him—and he turned out to be right. My suspicions were confirmed after an oxygen function test and subsequent X-rays: Elmer had a severe case of community-acquired pneumonia.

Two days after being hospitalized, he was transferred to the intensive care unit because of progressive respiratory failure. After eight days, Elmer passed away. If he had come to see me at the onset of his symptoms, he probably would have survived.

What causes CAP?

The most common cause of CAP is the bacterium called *Streptococcus pneumoniae*. This form of bacterium predominates in about seventy-one percent of patients in whom bacteria can be found when doing a sputum culture. *Streptococcus pneumoniae,* followed by viruses, are common causes for pneumonia. Other bacterial causes are *Haemophilus influenzae,* commonly found in smokers, and, less commonly, *Staphylococcus aureus, Legionella,* and *Mycobacterium* tuberculosis.

Diagnosis: Determining the Type of Pneumonia You Have

In order to determine the type of pneumonia you have, the doctor will ask the following questions:

- Do you smoke? *Haemophilus influenzae* bacteria cause lung infection in people who smoke.
- Are you at risk for HIV? *Pneumocystis carinii, Mycobacterium* tuberculosis, or fungal infections are common in people with HIV infection.
- Do you drink or use drugs? People who use alcohol or intravenous drugs, and people with diminished consciousness, impaired gag reflex, or recent vomiting can be susceptible to aspiration pneumonia.

- Have you had a recent viral infection or flu-like symptoms?
- Are you a nursing home resident?
- Have you stayed in a hotel or hospital, or flown on an air-plane within two weeks of the onset of symptoms?
- Have you recently been exposed to farm animals or pregnant cats?
- Have you recently traveled or resided in the Southwest? Infection from the bacterium *Coccidioides immitis* is com-mon to this area of the United States.
- Have you recently traveled or resided in the Ohio-Mississippi Valley? The bacterium *Histoplasma capsulatum* is common to this area of the United States.

Common Symptoms of Pneumonia

In younger people, the most common symptoms are cough, fever, chills, and chest pain. The elderly, besides having the same classical symptoms found in young people, may also feel confused and agi-tated. Older people may not experience chills, fever, shortness of breath, and chest pain.

When I saw Elmer, he had all of the signs, but that isn't always the case. The early stages of CAP can be subtle. Sometimes, older people with CAP simply "feel different," and actual symptoms don't appear until it is too late. If you are over the age of sixty-five, it is important to have regular checkups, so that your doctor can diagnose pneumonia in its early stages.

What is Your Risk?

The older you become, the more likely you are to catch pneumonia and die from it. As a person ages, the immune system doesn't clear bacteria and other toxins from the body as efficiently as it did when the person was younger. Older people are less mobile, often poorly nourished, and have other diseases—diabetes, cancer, liver disease, and kidney disorders—that put them at risk for pneumonia.

People with heart disease, who are given morphine for the pain of a heart attack, are at risk for aspiration pneumonia. Morphine decreases the cough/gag reflex, making it difficult to clear mucus from the airways and increasing the possibility that bacteria will remain and proliferate in the lungs. (This kind of pneumonia is a danger to people whose health is badly weakened, and who may be bed-ridden because of breathing troubles.)

Alcoholics and people confined to jails and nursing homes are also at risk for pneumonia.

Prevention

There is no substitute for an active, healthy lifestyle. Regular exercise and good nutrition can help prevent pneumonia, along with a host of other diseases. See your doctor for regular checkups and whenever you sense changes in your body or mind, and have the recommended vaccinations against disease. These precautions may save your life.

> There is no substitute for an active, healthy lifestyle. Regular exercise and good nutrition can help prevent pneumonia, along with a host of other diseases.

The U.S. Centers for Disease Control and Prevention (USCDC) recommend that all people over the age of sixty-five receive an influenza vaccination every year and a vaccination for pneumonia at least once in their lifetimes. Patients who are particularly susceptible to respiratory illness, because of disease or a compromised immune system, should receive a second vaccination for pneumonia, if the first was given after five years of age.

Unfortunately, elderly African Americans are far less likely to get flu shots than elderly White Americans, and the gap seems to be widening. James Singleton of the USCDC's National Immunization Program thinks this gap is not related to limited access to medical care. Instead, he found the causes in these common attitudes among African Americans:

- General apathy about their own health
- Suspicion of doctors
- Macho personality
- Belief in the myth that you will get sick from the injection
- Limited understanding about health issues

Remember: good health is the responsibility of the individual and the community. Doctors obviously aren't of use to patients who don't come in. Community centers of various sorts, from churches to libraries, or wherever people gather in your community, can provide programs through which people learn how to take better care of themselves by getting flu shots and in other ways.

Nurses in the community can help get such programs going. For further information about organizing such programs, see *Congregational Health,* by Kristen L. Mauk, Ph.D., RN; Cynthia A. Russell, DNS, RN; and Jack Birge, MD: Roscoe, IL: Hilton Publishing (2003).

Vaccinations for pneumococcal infections can be given at the same time as flu shots, except to patients who have acute cardiopulmonary illness.

Most local community health centers offer free vaccination programs.

Treatment

Pneumonia is treated with antibiotics, sometimes during a hospital stay, depending on the condition of the patient and the severity of the disease. Patients need to rest and drink lots of fluids, which help clear the lungs of phlegm. Treatment has been complicated in recent years because thirty percent of the bacteria that cause it are now resistant to penicillin.

That's a good reason not to ask for antibiotics when all you have is a cough and a runny nose. Overuse of antibiotics (frequent and careless use of antibiotics by the general public and the sometimes too-ready willingness of doctors to prescribe them) has caused these resistant strains of bacteria.

Chapter 10

Kidney Disease and Renal Failure

Kidney disease is strongly associated with diabetes and high blood pressure, and African Americans have these disorders more often than other ethnic groups. Yet kidney disease is preventable and treatable. All that you need to protect yourself and your loved ones is a little basic knowledge.

ABOUT YOUR KIDNEYS

The kidneys are two bean-shaped organs, each about the size of your fist. They are located in the lower middle of your back, just below your rib cage, on either side of your spine. Although the kidneys are small organs by weight, they receive nearly twenty percent of the blood pumped by the heart. The large blood supply to your kidneys enables them to:

- Regulate the composition of your blood
- Keep the volume of water in your body constant
- Remove wastes from your body (urea, ammonia, drugs, toxic substances)
- Help regulate your blood pressure

- Stimulate the production of red blood cells
- Maintain your body's calcium levels

RENAL FAILURE

There are two types of renal failure:

Acute renal failure (sometimes referred to as "renal insufficiency") results when your body can't get rid of waste products. These wastes normally pass out in the urine, which is produced and processed by the kidneys for excretion. But if the kidneys start failing and can't produce enough urine to eliminate toxic waste products that accumulate in the blood and body, the result is that wastes that ordinarily eliminate in the urine will remain in the blood. If renal failure is not treated properly, pulmonary edema, electrolyte imbalance, heart rhythm abnormalities, and even death can occur.

Chronic renal failure is the progressive and generally irreversible decline of kidney function. Most people who are on dialysis have chronic kidney failure. Although chronic kidney failure has many causes, the major causes are diabetes, high blood pressure, and heart disease. Obesity is often an underlying cause of these diseases. These diseases are frequently found in African–American men, and many African American men also have kidney disease.

Some over-the-counter and prescribed medications can cause renal failure. For example, nonsteroidal anti-inflammatory drugs (NSAIDs) like Motrin®, Advil®, and Celebrex® have been implicated in kidney disease. NSAIDs can cause injury to the kidneys by blocking the production of prostaglandins, fatty acids that are needed for proper kidney function. Information on the impact of NSAIDs on African Americans is limited. The high incidence of renal failure in the African American population calls for more research on this subject.

Common Symptoms of Renal Failure

The buildup of waste products in the blood from protein and toxins can result in heart problems, anemia, excessive bleeding, nausea and vomiting, muscle weakness, central nervous system disorders, and other metabolic malfunctions. This build up of wastes is progressive, and if it is not treated early can cause kidney failure.

Common symptoms of renal failure:

- Inability to urinate
- Buildup of fluid in the arms and legs
- Shortness of breath
- Mental confusion
- In some people, sudden onset of high blood sugar

What are Your Risks?

Approximately 200,000 Americans are treated each year for renal failure. Many of them are on dialysis and/or waiting for kidney transplantation. We can't say for certain what percentage of those people are African American because the research is still spotty. But one report states that almost forty percent of cases of end-stage renal disease occur in African Americans, even though African Americans make up only thirteen percent of the total U.S. population. This means that African American men are four times more likely than White American men to have renal failure. Kidney disease also seems to run in families.

> African–American men are four times more likely than White American men to have renal failure. Kidney disease also seems to run in families.

Prevention

Most causes of renal failure can be prevented. All that's required is that you have a close relationship with your doctor. Your doctor can guide you to the kind of healthy lifestyle that isn't likely to lead to renal failure. That means good nutrition and exercise, which help reduce body fat and keep blood pressure low. Obesity and high blood pressure are major risks for kidney disease. Not smoking seems to decrease the incidence of kidney disease, and your doctor can help you give it up if you're a smoker.

Your doctor can also perform simple blood and urine tests to find out if you are at risk. The earlier renal failure is detected, the more effective the treatment.

Treatment

Dialysis

In 1861, chemists began applying techniques of dialysis, extracting urea from urine. Almost one hundred years later, the dialysis machine was developed as a treatment for irreversible renal failure. In 1960, in Seattle, Washington, the first patient with long-term renal failure underwent dialysis. Since then, hundreds of thousands have had their lives extended by this procedure. Currently, there are over 200,000 patients on dialysis in the U.S.

A doctor who implements dialysis is called a "nephrologist." He uses a dialysis machine, which is essentially a filtering device that removes waste from the body in the same way the kidneys do.

There are two types of dialysis:

- **Hemodialysis:** This type is usually used in the hospital for individuals with severe renal disease.

- **Peritoneal dialysis:** This type is simpler and can be used at home. The patient administers his or her own dialysis.

Although dialysis saves lives, patients who undergo many years of dialysis can develop serious side effects, including psychological illnesses like depression and anxiety; even heart attack has been known to occur as a result of long-term dialysis.

Dialysis may require from twelve to twenty-eight hours a week. Your doctor will strongly recommend the type of dialysis that works best for your particular physical condition.

While dialysis can be a burden, for many people it means being able to live a full life, to work, and to travel. Doing so just requires a little planning ahead.

Kidney Transplantation

Early research in the 1900's paved the way for kidney transplantation. With advances in blood matching and the development of better immunosuppressants, life expectancy and quality of living have improved.

In most cases, kidney transplantation occurs after the patient has undergone many years of dialysis. After kidney transplantation, blood pressure returns to normal in patients who have had uncontrolled hypertension for many years. Patients are usually excluded from participating in kidney transplantation programs if they have cancer, severe atherosclerosis, liver disease, or lung disease, because these illnesses may destroy the new organ.

Screening for Kidney Transplantation

Most programs use the following criteria to screen the donors and recipients:

- Patients are evaluated for their ability to understand the risks, benefits, and treatment regimes involved in organ transplantation, because such understanding is critical for the success of transplants.
- Both the mental and physical health of patients is assessed.
- Organ, tissue, and blood compatibility are tested.
- Each patient's motivation for participation is evaluated.
- An assessment is made of the recipient's willingness to cooperate with treatment guidelines, followup, and behavior modification after receiving the new organ.

Chapter 11

Sickle Cell Disease and Trait

Sickle Cell Disease (SCD) is an inherited, or genetic, disorder of the blood common among African Americans. The disease specifically affects the protein inside the red blood cells, causing the roundness of the cells to collapse and become sickle-shaped. Sickle-shaped red blood cells interrupt blood flow in small blood vessels, leading to tissue damage and extreme pain. It is possible have the sickle cell trait but exhibit no the symptoms of the disease. Still, if you have the trait, you can pass it on to your children.

SYMPTOMS OF SICKLE CELL DISEASE

Patients with sickle cell disease often have the following symptoms:

- Generalized pain in long bones and joints
- Abdominal pain
- Nausea and vomiting
- Poor appetite
- Swelling in hands, feet, and joints
- Fever and fatigue

DIAGNOSIS OF SICKLE CELL DISEASE

The most common test for sickle cell disease is called a "hemoglobin electrophoresis." The Sickledex test can also detect the disease. Sickle cells can be seen clearly under a microscope.

When doctors suspect sickle cell disease, they look for anemia, increased heart rate, fever, and shortness of breath, as well as a swollen abdomen, jaundice, enlarged spleen, liver, and heart.

Many patients with sickle cell disease are very young and in pain. Some patients require the continual administration of narcotics. Patients may also have damage to internal organs, especially spleen infarction. People with sickle cell disease are susceptible to infection caused by salmonella bacteria, which can penetrate bone and cause osteomyelitis. SCD can also cause heart disease.

Characteristics of a Normal Blood Cell	Characteristics of a Sickled Blood Cell
Disc-shaped	Sickle-shaped
Soft (like a bag of jelly)	Hard (like a piece of wood)
Easily flows through small blood vessels	Often gets stuck in small blood vessels (causing extreme pain)
Lives for 120 days	Lives for 20 days or less

TREATMENT

A person who has an episode of sickle cell anemia must be given oxygen so that more cells do not sickle. Infections are treated with the appropriate antibiotics, and massive amounts of fluids are administered.

The sickle cell patient is usually dehydrated because of the nausea and vomiting associated with the pain. Pain management is important, and some people will require blood transfusions.

Education for patients and their families, providing insight into the disease, has proven to lessen crises. By knowing what to expect, and what to do when it happens, a crisis becomes a manageable problem.

Patients and their families should also be counseled on travel, exercise, and healthy lifestyle. It is imperative that the patient's doctor be readily available for close follow-up. It is also imperative that a person with sickle cell drink lots of water.

INCIDENCE OF SICKLE CELL DISEASE[1]

Sickle cell disease is present in one out of four hundred African Americans in the United States. It is the most common genetic disease in this country. That's why all newborn babies should be tested at birth for sickle cell disease, so that prevention efforts can begin right away.

Sickle cell disease is not just found in African Americans. The disease is also found in Africans, Turks, Greeks, Saudi Arabians, Egyptians, Iranians, Italians, Latin Americans, and Asian Indians.

HOW DO I KNOW IF I AM A CANDIDATE FOR SICKLE CELL DISEASE?

Sickle cell disease is an inherited disease. Here's how it works.

- If both of your parents are trait carriers, and both parents passed a sickle cell hemoglobin gene on to you, then up to forty-nine percent of your red blood cells may have sickle cell hemoglobin. (The rest of the hemoglobin in your red blood cells will be normal.) If your parents passed the gene for sickle cell disease to you, it can have many different implications for your children.
- If you carry the sickle cell trait (SA), and your partner has normal hemoglobin (AA), you have a fifty percent chance of

1. This section is from James W. Reed, MD, et al, *The Black Man's Guide to Good Health* (Roscoe, IL.: Hilton Publishing: 2001), pp. 158–59.

conceiving a child with normal hemoglobin (AA), and a fifty percent chance of having a child who carries the sickle cell trait (SA). There is no chance that any of your children will actually have the disease.

- If you have sickle cell disease (SS) and your partner has normal hemoglobin (AA), all the children you conceive will carry the sickle cell trait (SA); none of them will be born with normal hemoglobin (AA). But the good news is, none of your children will actually have sickle cell disease (SS).
- If both you and your partner carry the sickle cell trait (SA), you have a twenty-five percent chance of having a child with normal hemoglobin (AA); a fifty percent chance of conceiving a child who carries the sickle cell trait (SA); and a twenty-five percent chance of having a child with sickle cell disease (SS).
- If you carry the trait for sickle cells (SA) and your partner has the disease (SS), you have a fifty percent chance of having a child who carries the trait (SA), and a fifty percent chance of conceiving a child with sickle cell disease (SS).
- If both you and your partner have sickle cell disease (SS), all your children will have the disease as well (SS).
- If neither you nor your partner carries the trait or has the disease (AA), there is no chance that any of your children will have sickle cell disease.
- Certain hemoglobin traits can combine with sickle hemoglobin to cause cell diseases such as Hemoglobin C, D, and Beta thalassemia.

Years ago, if both partners carried the trait for sickle cell disease or had the disease itself, doctors commonly discouraged the couple from having children. Today, doctors will generally make parents-to-be aware of the health problems their child may encounter, but the choice of whether or not the couple chooses to have a child is ultimately left up to them. (For further information on sickle cell disease and sickle cell trait, see Allan Platt, Jr., and Alan Sacerdote: *Hope and Destiny: A Patient's and Parent's Guide to Sickle Cell Disease and Sickle Cell Trait.* Roscoe, IL: Hilton Publishing, 2002. See also http//www.emory.edu./PEDS/Sickle)

Chapter 12

Hepatitis C

Hepatitis C virus (HCV) is a viral infection that affects the liver. Because of the small size of the virus, the immune system does not respond to it, and the virus can reproduce itself, undetected, in liver cells. In other words, unless you see your family doctor regularly for checkups and tests, you may not know you're infected until it is too late for effective treatment.

Hepatitis C is a serious public health problem in the United States that affects four million people. Unfortunately, this disease has been increasing in the African–American community: twenty percent of people living in inner cities are infected! Studies show that 3.2 percent of African Americans have HCV, compared to 1.8 percent of White Americans. Each year, close to 10,000 people die of the disease.

WHAT CAUSES HEPATITIS C?

The most common way people are infected with HCV is by coming in direct contact with the virus. Groups at-risk for HCV include:

- Hemophiliacs who received blood transfusions before 1990
- Patients with kidney failure who undergo dialysis

- People who come into contact with the blood of an infected person
- IV drug users
- Drug abusers who use instruments for intranasal application of cocaine and are infected through the nose
- Alcoholics
- People who have multiple sexual partners
- People who travel to Africa and Asia

SIGNS AND SYMPTOMS

> Early detection is the key to identifying the infection so that treatment can be started immediately.

Early detection is the key to identifying the infection so that treatment can be started immediately. Unfortunately, most people don't know they have HCV until their condition has become chronic. Even people with acute infection may not show many symptoms.

Only twenty percent of people with hepatitis C have yellowing skin (jaundice) and fatigue, and a small percentage will have stomach pain and no appetite. In chronic disease, the doctor may see muscle aches and joint pain, skin eruptions, kidney problems, and sometimes gallbladder disease. Some women will also experience thyroid disorders.

Some patients may have cirrhosis and liver failure. In the event of liver failure, a liver transplant is necessary or the patient will die. Five percent of people with chronic hepatitis C will develop liver cancer.

DIAGNOSIS

HCV is diagnosed by the following tests:

- A blood test for liver function
- A viral ribonucleic acid (RNA) blood test to determine the amount of the virus in your body

- A biopsy to find out how much the virus has damaged the liver (To do the biopsy, doctors insert a very small needle into the liver, remove a piece of the organ, and examine the specimen under a microscope.)

TREATMENT

Some people's immune systems are able to keep the infection at bay, while others require treatment. Treatment usually consists of a twelve-month course of three to five million units of the drug alpha interferon given three times weekly. Alpha interferon works as an antiviral agent and can cause nausea and vomiting, for which your doctor will prescribe remedies. Fifty percent of patients response positively to interferon. Another medication, ribavirin, is sometimes used with interferon and has been shown to strengthen its effect.

IF YOU ARE DIAGNOSED WITH HEPATITIS C

- Don't drink alcohol.
- Don't infect others, especially loved ones. Practice safe sex by using condoms.
- A healthy diet and regular exercise have been shown to help patients, both emotionally and physically.

Unfortunately, no effective vaccine is currently available for HCV. Hepatitis A and B vaccines, however, are recommended for patients with HCV.

- People with chronic hepatitis C are usually monitored for the development of liver cancer for ten to fifteen years.

HCV is not a death sentence, as many people tend to believe, but a close working relationship with your doctor is critical.

Part III
Health Issues Specific to Children, Women, and Men

Chapter 13

Children's Health Issues

IMMUNIZATIONS

Immunizations combat disease and keep children healthy. In the past half century, immunizations have dramatically decreased outbreaks of whooping cough (pertussis), measles, diphtheria, and polio. Be sure your child gets immunization shots as scheduled. You can't afford to neglect them.

Immunizations help to prevent the two kinds of infections that could make your child ill. One group of infections is caused by a virus— a microorganism smaller than a bacterium and incapable of growth or reproduction apart from living cells. Viruses enter cells, interact with the genetic machinery of the cell, and then continue their life cycle.

The other group of infections is caused by bacteria. A bacterium is a single cell microorganism that contains its own DNA. Unlike viruses, bacteria do not need a living host and can live on their own. Antibiotics are used for the treatment of bacteria but not for viruses. Because the common cold is a virus infection, doctors do not treat it with antibiotics.

Vaccines aimed at holding common viruses and bacteria in check are combined with one another so that children do not have to be given that dreaded "shot" from the doctor too often. Here is a chart to help you with these schedules:

*United States Recommended Childhood Immunization
Schedule for 2001*

Hepatitis B
First dose: between birth and two months
Second dose: between one and four months
Third dose: between six and eighteen months
Eleven to twelve years: vaccine to be given if previously recommended doses
were missed or given earlier than the recommended minimum age

**DTaP- Diphtheria and tetanus toxoids and acellular
pertussis vaccine**
First dose: two months
Second dose: four months
Third dose: six months
Fourth dose: between fifteen and eighteen months
Fifth dose: between four and six years
Sixth dose: (Td—tetanus) between eleven and sixteen years

Hib- H. influenza type B
First dose: two months
Second dose: four months
Third dose: six months
Fourth dose: between twelve and fifteen months

OPV- Polio
First dose: two months
Second dose: four months
Third dose: between six and eighteen months
Fourth dose: between four and six years

MMR- Measles, Mumps, Rubella
First dose: twelve months
Second dose: either between four and six years OR eleven and twelve years

Pneumococcal Conjugate
First dose: two months
Second dose: four months
Third dose: six months
(catch-up if indicated—twelve to eighteen months)

Varicella (Chicken Pox)
First dose: eighteen to twenty-four months
Eleven to twelve years: vaccine to be given if previously recommended doses
were missed or given earlier than the recommended minimum age

Hepatitis B Vaccine

In recent years, the hepatitis B vaccine has become available for infants, children, and adults. The vaccine can prevent hepatitis, a disease in which the liver becomes inflamed and functionally impaired. This form of liver disease can cause cancer and sometimes even death. The prevalence of hepatitis in the African–American community is high.

People in the following categories should also get the vaccine:

- Institutionalized children (regardless of age) and adults
- High-risk professionals, including health care providers
- Patients with sexually transmitted diseases
- All IV drug users, including crack users, and alcoholics
- Inner-city African Americans

Hepatitis B is a viral infection. There are a wide range of symptoms, and the disease progresses differently in different people. The patient may have no complaints at all, then have a rapid, progressive sickness, and may even die. Hepatitis can also cause cancer of the liver.

Even though there are different forms of hepatitis (A, B, and C), at this time immunizations are available only for hepatitis B. When a person is infected with hepatitis B, the virus is present in virtually all body fluids and secretions. Hepatitis B is commonly transmitted through IV needles, blood transfusions, and unprotected sex. It can also be transmitted from mother to infant during the birthing process.

Diphtheria, Tetanus and Pertussis

Diphtheria, tetanus, and whooping cough (pertussis) are bacterial infections that primarily infect children. They can cause severe sickness and even death. Diphtheria can cause life-threatening upper respiratory infections when a pseudo-membrane thickly coats the nose, throat, or airway. This disease can also cause interruption of the normal functioning of the nervous system and skin abnormalities.

Tetanus bacteria invade the body through a cut or wound, causing serious, painful spasms of all the muscles that can lead to locking of the jaw and an inability to swallow. Pertussis, like diphtheria, spreads when bacteria pass from an infected person to the noses or throats of other people, and can cause whooping cough, pneumonia, and jerking and staring spells (seizures).

Haemophilus Influenzae Type B (Flu)

H. influenzae B is a bacterial infection that primarily infects the respiratory tract, skin, or mucous membranes. These bacteria can also become blood-borne and lead to meningitis, blood infection, epiglottiditis (infection of the throat), endocarditis (inflammation of the outer wall of the heart), arthritis, and cellulitis (skin infection). *H. influenzae* type B is spread from person to person and is the most common cause of meningitis of children.

Polio

Polio is a serious disease caused by a virus that is passed from person to person, usually by mouth, which can cause paralysis and death. There are two kinds of polio vaccines. Oral polio vaccine (OPV) is the one most often given to children and is given by mouth as oral drops. Inactivated polio vaccine (IPV) is given as a shot, usually in the leg or arm.

Measles, Mumps, and Rubella

Measles is a viral disease that causes a highly contagious infection characterized by a fever, cough, pink eye (conjunctivitis), and skin rash. It can be fatal when a secondary bacterial infection and pneumonia develop.

Mumps is a systemic viral infection of children that infects the salivary glands. It can also cause infection of the testicles, meningitis, pancreatitis, and inflammation of other internal organs.

Rubella, also called German measles, is a viral infection that causes a rash and involves the lymph nodes. This disease can cause infection of the brain (encephalitis). When pregnant mothers are infected, the baby that is born can be infected, too. Postnatal death of the infant is common.

Chicken Pox

Varicella is a virus that causes chicken pox and shingles. In the last decade, a live vaccine for chickenpox has been developed. Its use is recommended for all children, starting at age one year. The vaccine can prevent rash and systemic disease.

Children infected with varicella have skin lesions and high fevers. Most patients don't feel well and, in rare cases, may develop nervous system involvement. Sometimes, in extreme cases, pneumonia develops. Treatment of the disease is the same as for a common cold. The rash and itching can be treated with topical lotions and oral Benadryl®.

COMMON CHILDREN'S INFECTIONS AND THEIR TREATMENTS
Sore Throat

Common Sore Throat

Mothers and fathers frequently summon me for advice when their children have sore throats. The parents' voices are usually urgent and, more often than not, they request antibiotics. Mothers tend to assume that sore throats are caused by strep infection and that antibiotics are necessary. In fact, most sore throats, like most coughs and colds, are not caused by strep bacteria but by viruses, and antibiotics are ineffective for treating them.

If your child is sick with a sore throat caused by a virus, the illness will run its course and there is no need for antibiotics, unless there is a secondary bacterial infection. Your doctor will be able to determine what kind of infection your child has.

Keep in mind that unnecessary use of antibiotics can be dangerous in itself. If people take antibiotics every time they get sick, some bacteria can become resistant and continue to grow and multiply.

Not all complaints need to be treated with medicine. A home humidifier or simple decongestant may be all that is needed for your child, or you, to get relief from an ailment.

Strep Throat

Strep throat is caused by bacteria. Complaints range from generally not feeling well to severe fever, abdominal pain with vomiting, and blood infection. If the infection is left untreated, pus can form in the throat. Strep infection can also cause rheumatic fever and a kidney infection, and may even require hospitalization.

If your child develops a sore throat, always consult your doctor so that strep may be ruled out. Strep throat must be diagnosed by a laboratory test.

Strep infections primarily affect children five-to-fifteen-years-old and usually occur in the winter and early spring seasons. The disease is contagious, and sometimes several people in the same family have to be treated.

Parents Should Look for:
- Sore throat
- Pain when swallowing
- Fever
- Gastrointestinal complaints
- Abdominal pain
- A very red tongue

- A fine, diffused red rash. (Please note that in African–American children, the rash may not appear red, but the same color as the child's skin. If you rub your hand across the surface of the rash, it will feel rough or as if there were sand on the skin. The rash may also indicate scarlet fever.)

Many doctors may choose to take a throat culture, by swabbing the throat with a cotton stick, and wait for the results. As a precaution, a doctor may prescribe antibiotics while waiting for the test results but will ask the patient to discontinue using antibiotics if the test results prove to be negative. Normally, it takes twenty-four hours (one day) to get test results.

Strep throat is usually treated with penicillin or erythromycin. Newer antibiotics can work just as well, but penicillin should be tried first, with the more modern drugs reserved for severe or resistant infections, or if the patient has intolerance for penicillin. Treatment for strep infection should continue for a period of seven to ten days. After your child is treated with antibiotics, it is not uncommon for his or her skin to peel.

An important reason to treat this disease promptly is to prevent rheumatic fever. Rheumatic fever can be a sequel to strep infection and can affect the heart and heart valves, in some cases making heart surgery or even a heart transplant necessary in adulthood.

As always, it is important to follow your doctor's recommendations very specifically so that your child's health is not compromised.

Swollen Glands

Lymph nodes are small round tissues that are part of the immune system. Their function is to screen diseases from the body so that infection does not occur. Lymph nodes help keep the immune system strong and healthy. Lymph node cells eat up viruses, bacteria, parasites, and cancerous cells. They usually do their job well, but not always. An overabundance of microorganisms can overcome the lymph cells and threaten the body.

During their battle against microorganisms, lymph nodes swell. Lymph nodes that enlarge from viral and bacterial infection are usually tender to the touch. Enlarged lymph nodes caused by cancer are not tender to the touch. Cancer cells that invade the lymph nodes become larger and begin to change the total architecture of the node itself.

Lymph nodes are located throughout the body. They lie adjacent to organs and form a chain. The major sites for lymph nodes are at the neck, armpits, and groin. For example, small lymph nodes from the breasts drain into the armpit nodes and lymph nodes for the external genitalia drain into the pelvic (groin) nodes.

The location of a swollen lymph node can point to the possible cause:

- *Neck (Cervical Nodes)*
  - Infections of the head and neck
  - Mononucleosis, other viral infections
  - Tuberculosis
  - Head and neck cancers and lymphomas

- *Neckline/Shoulders (Nodes Just Below the Clavicle)*
  - Lung diseases
  - Gastrointestinal diseases
  - Lymphomas
  - Infections and cancers of the chest and pelvis (such as breasts and testicles)

- *Groin (Pelvic Nodes)*
  - Infection and cancer of the gastrointestinal and urinary tract
  - Extremities (legs)
  - Genitals (vagina, testes, penis, and rectum)

Diagnosis of enlarged lymph nodes can also depend on:
- Blood tests and radiological assessment
- Surgical removal and laboratory analysis
- Cultures and examination of the cells under a microscope

CHILD ABUSE

I often read in the newspaper that yet another African–American child has died as the victim of physical abuse by a parent or guardian—the very person whose role is to protect and give love. Child abuse has been increasing at an alarming rate. The offenders are often young and single, burdened by limited finances, and poorly educated. Offenders are often drug or alcohol abusers. Many of them were themselves abused as children. They are usually people who lack the means to cope with the everyday stress of life.

As a doctor, I am required to approach every patient in a non-judgmental way. I would like to share the following case because it challenged my efforts to stay open-minded.

The Story of Ms. S.

Ms. S. was a twenty-five-year-old African–American woman with four children. She was a single parent who had a live-in boyfriend and was a recovering drug addict who had been clean and sober for a little over a year. She had come to see me because her youngest son had a respiratory infection. Several weeks earlier, Mrs. S's mother had told me that Ms. S. was doing drugs again.

When Ms. S. brought her son to my office she seemed anxious and hostile. She told me that I must hurry the exam so that she could get to another appointment. I asked politely, but somewhat sarcastically, if she had a job interview. (She'd told me a dozen times before she was in a rush for this reason.) She ignored my question. By this time I'd noted that her appearance was disheveled and her eyes sleepy and dull.

Her child sat quietly on the examining table. As I inspected him, I noticed small, well-defined scars scattered along both arms. Some of the scratches were old, and others were more recent.

As I examined them, Ms. S. interrupted me. Pointing to the child's neck, she shouted, "His throat hurts! Look there!" Her finger extended toward her child's neck, and I noticed that her nails were well-manicured, long, and colorful. They looked like daggers. I saw the swollen lymph node on the child's neck. I also noticed that when his mother lifted her arm and extended her hand toward the child, he recoiled away from her as if he were frightened of being struck.

I continued with my exam. "Could you take off his shirt?" I asked. When I moved behind the child to listen to his lungs, I was caught off-guard by large bruised areas on his back. There were two well-defined welts just under the shoulder blades that resembled fist prints and looked new. The child flinched with pain as I touched them. When I turned to look at his mother, she cast her eyes downward to the floor and refused to make eye contact with me.

Ms. S. was an emotionally stressed parent with a drug problem. Later I learned from family members that she also battered her child. This unfortunate case might have been hopeless, but I intervened on behalf of her child, who was temporarily cared for by an aunt until Ms. S. was effectively treated.

With the help of family members, I persuaded Ms. S. to talk to a social worker and to begin a drug detox program. After treatment and monitoring, Ms. S. is reunited with her children. She has been without drugs for six months.

Ever since this case occurred over a year ago, I have been on guard when an aggressive and unfriendly young mother or father brings her or his child into my office. I take the time to closely examine the child and note the interaction between mother and/or father and child.

Steps for Coping and Seeking Help

Many African Americans face social and economic stress that makes everyday living very difficult. The following steps can help parents cope with young children. You will find that helping yourself can be a way to help your child.

Admit You Need Help and Seek It

Realizing that you cannot cope and are powerless is the first step toward recovery. If you are not able to ask for help from family members and friends, seek aid from your doctor. See him or her as a friend. Your doctor has at his or her disposal a vast referral system for all kinds of social problems that people may encounter. Fear and helplessness create anger and abuse. The doctor can help you change fear into creative power.

Make Yourself Available

The old phrase "don't take your work home" applies to parents, too. Make time for your children. Interact with them and play with them. Clear your head and get into the heads of your children. Not only do adults teach their children, but also children can teach their parents how to play and have fun. You may find that spending time with your children will become a pleasant habit.

Know When You Have Had Enough

When you spend all of your waking moments with your children, the quality of your relationship with them may begin to suffer, especially if you are in a high-stress environment. The rambunctious child can often make you feel like you are going to blow your stack, especially if you are already stressed. Organize your daily schedule so that you don't attempt to do everything in one day. If you feel like you are

about to explode, stop and take time to clear your head and calm your mood.

Ask Family and Friends for Help

Call a family member or a friend to come and watch your child while you go for a walk. Remember, there is always time to take a short break, and it will help you avoid getting overly angry with your child.

Be an Actor on the Stage of Life

We perform everyday as actors on the stage of life. Why not utilize these skills with our children? We all have days when we are not in a particularly good mood. One way to circumvent the stress and feelings of gloom you may feel on those days is to pretend that you are the director of a movie. Simply devise a "script" for your day.

On such days on my way to the office, I turn on music and go through the steps of my day as if they were scenes in a comedy—perhaps a comedy of errors, but an amusing one nonetheless. I make a firm decision to approach my day with humor instead of negativity. When I enter my office, I have a cheerful laugh, and continue in a good humor throughout the day.

Your approach towards life should be based on the positive and not the negative. You'll find that once you give yourself a positive scenario, even the people around you tend to become cheerful.

This method applies not only to your life outside of your home but also to your family. Your attitude has a direct effect on your children and how they behave, and even affects their view of the world around them.

Try assuming the role of "nutty professor" or "queen for a day" and, as your young son or daughter becomes Sir Lancelot or Princess Ann, you will all have smiles and a story to remember of your "adventure."

Don't Threaten Your Child

Sure, at one time or another everyone does it. However, words can hurt terribly. Husbands and wives should never threaten to hurt each other or leave each other when they are angry. Harmful words leave resentment and a fear of abandonment in the hearts of those who hear them. You don't take control by threatening your child or each other. Quite the contrary, you destroy any emotional safety they feel and replace it with anxiety and preoccupation with their security.

Mean What You Say

If you say something to your child involving discipline, follow through with the promise. If you do not follow through, your child will distrust the things you say or even view you as a liar. This may cause the child to manipulate the parent.

For example, a mother might say, "If you don't eat your vegetables, you do not get dessert." The child does not eat the vegetables, but later gets a piece of pie anyway. The child may come to believe that bad behavior is, in fact, rewarded. This sends a mixed message to the child that can later foster manipulative and generally bad behavior both at home and away from home.

Don't Instill Guilt

Parents should not feel guilty for enforcing reasonable "rules of conduct" for their children. Likewise, parents should never make a child feel guilt. Parents make their children feel guilty by sending them hidden messages and playing mind games with them. Children are too young to understand these messages and the games can backfire.

By being open, up front, and dealing with situations head-on, you can lay a firm foundation for your children's futures. Children learn by what they see and what they hear. They will emulate behavior and incorporate it into their own lives. Make sure that the model you give your child is a positive one, not one driven by negativity and guilt.

Parents Must Become Teachers

African–American children need to become more informed. It surprises me how little knowledge the average African–American person has and how many African–American parents don't read to their children. Parents must also encourage their children to achieve academically.

Parents also teach their children about life. You cannot expect your child not to steal if you steal yourself. When you boldly announce that you have illegal cable television or handicapped stickers when you don't have a handicap, you are sending the message to your child that it is okay to steal.

Set Limits, But Be Reasonable

It is important to understand that children will be children. Remember that limits require discussion and fairness from both sides. Be open about your reasoning with your child, and make sure that he or she is comfortable with it. Open communication builds a strong and ongoing parent/child relationship that will grow fuller as the child moves into adulthood.

Regroup and Start Over

It is okay to say you're sorry to your child. When something goes wrong, set a time to discuss matters. Review these steps and start over. Everyone backslides because of stress.

In order to have healthy and happy children, you must communicate with them on an impartial and fair level. Keep in mind that parents have their own faults and often try especially to control their children's lives in areas that have been problems to the parents themselves.

Consult your doctor if there seems to be no way to resolve an issue or if you need a mediator. The doctor may help you find a new approach to problem resolution that works better than the old ways.

TEENAGE PREGNANCY

Recently, the parents of a twelve-year old girl asked me to help find out why their daughter was gaining so much weight. The girl had always been sunny and friendly, but now she'd become glum and isolated. She spent a lot of time in her room not wanting to be bothered. Her school grades had begun to drop. She had not taken physical education classes for years because of her mother's note to the principal asking that she be excluded because of her asthma. The note was never signed by a doctor and did not come to my attention until this visit.

Although the child had become obese, her appetite had not changed; in fact, her frequent bouts of nausea and periods of vomiting prevented her from eating much at all. "She must have thyroid disease, like me," her mother explained nervously as I began my examination of her daughter. But when the routine blood test results came in, I was surprised and saddened to find that the girl did not have thyroid disease. She was pregnant.

Teenage pregnancy is a preventable calamity, but as the incidence continues to increase (for White–American and African–American teenagers alike), it appears that we aren't doing enough to prevent it. It drastically undermines the futures of our young people, who, growing up with the added burden of raising a child, are often denied more productive choices and opportunities.

The Statistics

Studies show that children who are fatherless, poor, and have limited education are more likely to become pregnant. This makes for a vicious circle. Poverty promotes teenage pregnancy and teenage pregnancy causes poverty. Two thirds of unwed mothers raise their children in poverty. In 1993, nine million children were on welfare and, unless the cycle is broken, these children will have children who will grow up and repeat their mothers' lifestyles and economic status. What is needed to break the cycle is a collective educational effort by federal, state, and local governments and health care providers.

African–American teenagers have twice the pregnancy rate of White American teenagers. Forty percent of African–American girls become pregnant by the age of eighteen. An international teenage pregnancy study done in 1985 concluded that teen pregnancy rates are lower in countries where there is greater availability of contraceptive services and sex education. To our shame, the United States has a higher rate of teen pregnancy than some of the developing countries.

Society often pays the cost of caring for these babies. Teenage mothers often receive inadequate prenatal care because they seek care late in their pregnancies and, often, fail to follow their doctor's instructions. The result is that their babies are born with medical complications.

Even when the babies are born healthy, families are often disrupted. In my practice, I find grandmothers raising their grandchildren, because the teenage mothers have poor parenting skills.

The Consequences for African Americans

- Young mothers, fathers, and their children are at greater risk for socioeconomic disadvantage throughout their lives.
- Teenage parents are less likely to achieve academically.
- The younger the mother, the greater the likelihood that she and her baby will experience health complications.
- Each year, the U.S. government spends twenty-five billion dollars on behalf of families in which a teen gave birth, including direct aid, Medicaid, and food stamps.
- Children of teenage mothers are at greater risk for behavioral problems than children of older mothers.
- Daughters of teenage mothers are more likely to become teenage parents themselves.

Solutions

Achieving a solution to the problem of teenage pregnancy in the African–American community is difficult. Historically, it was common for African–American women to have children while they were young. In the period following Reconstruction, families were intact—fathers and mothers lived together and were able to meet the needs of their children. Times are different now, and single parent families with limited social and economic opportunities are more common. Still, real solutions are possible.

Public Responsibility

The appropriate agencies must work together with the African–American community to address the problem of teenage pregnancy. Strategies must be developed to change public perceptions about teen pregnancy. Health organizations and educational systems have to teach children about prevention and about the cost of early pregnancies. Parents must be held accountable for the education of their children, help them avoid social perils, and show them how to work toward real opportunities that will create better lives. If children do become pregnant, government, health organizations, and families must come to the aid of these young mothers, so that they and their babies receive adequate health care and financial support.

Preventative Education

Young women have to understand how much harm they do themselves by becoming pregnant. A national campaign must be launched to get the word out. We must teach young men that it is not okay for a man to father a child he does not support. Young women at risk of becoming mothers too soon must be given incentives for making other choices.

Chapter 14

Women's Health Issues

African–American women must ask themselves: "I give a lot of myself to others, but do I also take time for myself? Do I give proper attention to my own physical and emotional well being?" Current health statistics suggest that you do not. In the not so distant past, women were healthier and were outliving men. Today, African–American women are dying from diabetes, heart disease, and cancer at an alarmingly high rate. More than fifty percent of African–American women are obese, stuck in social situations they feel powerless to escape, and depressed. And when it comes to basic health maintenance, most African–American women do not exercise at all.

The bad news about the health of African–American women is no secret. It appears regularly in the newspapers. Yet too many of our women accept the fact passively, as if it were simply their fate.

It is my hope that you will be moved by this book to take control of your own health, change your lifestyle, join a gym or exercise program, eat a healthier diet, and, most importantly, take more positive time for yourself. You cannot take care of other people if you do not take care of yourself.

The following sections provide open and frank discussions on the obstacles you face every day. Hopefully, you will be able to identify the dilemmas in your own life and gain insight from other women's experiences, so that you can make your own plan to become a healthier person. Knowledge can make you free. Take the time to read and understand what this chapter offers, and you will find that where once you had felt helpless, now you feel energized and in control of your own destiny. It is just a matter of moving step by step, as you might move through a new recipe.

YOUR RECIPE FOR A NEW LIFE

We begin with the basic ingredients that will make you healthier: mental, physical, emotional, and spiritual stability. These ingredients go hand in hand. When you are physically fit, you also become healthier in mind and spirit. At the same time, spiritual and emotional calm can be the right background for renewed physical health.

In order to be healthy, you have to see yourself in a positive light. That means having a purpose in your life, identifying and coping with the sources of mental stress, and learning to express your feelings. When you can do these things, you can begin to enjoy the self-esteem that's essential to good physical, emotional, and spiritual health.

Maintaining a positive image of yourself doesn't depend on high social standing or a fat salary. My mother never completed high school because she had to work, but she was a wise and confident woman. She read newspapers, watched educational documentaries on television, and was well informed about current events. The wisdom she drew from what she read and experienced allowed her to teach her children to become more educated than she was. She would say to me, "It doesn't matter if you're poor; you can still succeed if you're educated."

To achieve higher self-esteem, you have to move beyond what you perceive your limits to be. Learning to exercise regularly is a remarkably efficient way of doing just that. If you move your body first, your mind will tag right along. Exercise lets you set small goals and achieve them. Each achievement means greater self-confidence. And, as your body becomes active and energetic, you'll find that your mind too wakes up to new energy.

One of the things that have held African–American women back from developing their full capacities is the traditional notion that being a good wife and mother was a woman's sole "purpose." Today, when women make up a larger percentage of the nation's workforce than ever before, that traditional notion is often complicated by the double burden of keeping a family and keeping a job. Too many of our women feel themselves to be kinds of sacrificial victims who, by denying themselves everything, can serve to hold the family together.

I think it's time to change that notion. Women have to begin to see themselves as multidimensional people who set goals for themselves and are driven by a sense of purpose. That means discovering a self that is independent of your partner and your children. By doing so, you'll find you become more useful to others even as you are serving yourself. When you are happy, you are better able to make others happy as well.

There are all sorts of ways to activate a new life. Try keeping a daily journal of your activities and thoughts. Describe your feelings about other people. Be honest with yourself. By keeping this journal of self-discovery, you may find out that there are things you want to do that you hadn't fully realized before. You may discover love, and, yes, anger, where you didn't see it before. By discovering and acknowledging what you really feel, you'll find yourself better able to recognize what you want and don't want, and set about sorting out your life with a new active energy.

And it's not all about other people. Maybe you'll discover that you want to begin a new hobby, or even a new job or career. Maybe you'll finally take out that membership at the Y you've often thought about. Maybe you'll turn to schooling or new social contacts. The list goes on. Start that garden you've dreamed of, become an advocate for children, a church worker, an artist, a musician. Find out what aspects of your self have been waiting to be born. Follow the tendency in all of us to learn and evolve.

I see that hunger all the time when children come into my office after they leave the examination room. Sure, they go to the jar of jellybeans. But they also notice the chalkboard that I used for teaching medical students and young doctors. The kids write on it, rehearsing their schoolwork or number systems they've just learned. Sometimes they ask me to teach them something, using the boards. They're curious and open, and eager to learn and grow. Their openness is something we need to keep when we grow up.

Yes, many African–American women are single parents trying to make ends meet and are more apt to sacrifice their own needs or desires to provide for their families. But even if you are in this situation, you can find some time for yourself, for the sake of your mental health. That's far better than feeling yourself to be a slave, doing nothing that you want to do, and becoming depressed. When that happens, you're not much use to others or to yourself. (For more about how to rid yourself of stress and enjoy the experience of an active and fulfilling life, see Marilyn Martin: *Saving Our Last Nerve: The Black Woman's Path to Mental Health.* Roscoe, IL: Hilton Publishing, 2002.)

QUESTIONS FROM
AFRICAN AMERICAN WOMEN

Taking your own physical wellness in hand, as the writer Maya Angelou put it, is an important way to begin a recipe for a new life that is healthy and vital. The first step is to understand and actively take part in a program of preventative medicine that your doctor can work out with you. Let's start learning by looking at some health questions my patients often ask me. By understanding how and why your doctor carries out some basic tests, procedures, and treatment plans, you'll learn to see them as part of your own effort to keep yourself vital and strong.

PELVIC EXAM

What is a Pelvic Examination and What is a Pap Smear?

The pelvic examination is a "checkup" of your vagina (inside and outside), the opening of the uterus (cervix), and the womb (uterus). Your doctor will look inside the vagina with a "speculum" (an instrument that lets the clinician see inside the vagina), and, once a year, will also do a Pap smear and tests for gonorrhea and a bacterial disease called chlamydia.

During the pelvic exam, drops of discharge from the vagina may be checked under a microscope for yeast, *Trichomonas*, bacterial vaginosis, and irritation or infection of the cervix. To check for genital warts (HPV), herpes, or syphilis sores, the doctor carefully examines the inside and outside of the vagina.

In the second part of a pelvic examination, the doctor puts two fingers inside the vagina and checks the uterus, fallopian tubes, and ovaries for normal development, infection (such as pelvic inflammatory disease), tubal pregnancy, or ovarian cysts. The pelvic examination is normally not painful.

Pap Smear

A Pap smear is not the same thing as a pelvic exam and is done once a year. In special circumstances, as when a woman has had previous abnormal results from a Pap smear or has a history of genital warts, she may have to get a repeat Pap test every three to six months, until the cells return to normal.

To do a Pap smear, the doctor gently scrapes the loose cells at the opening of the cervix. The cells are put on a glass slide and examined under a microscope for any changes or abnormalities. The Pap smear is an important tool that doctors use to detect precancerous and cancerous conditions of the cervix and microorganisms and inflammatory conditions that cause STDs. Every woman, whether sexually active or not, should have a Pap smear.

Sometimes, the abundance of inflammatory cells from STDs make it difficult to determine whether or not cancerous cells are present. Some STDs may cause cancers of the cervix.

The Pap smear can produce any of several results:

- It can be read as "normal" (satisfactory, without signs of cancer).
- It can be read as "atypical" (mildly abnormal cell changes).
- It can be read as "inflammation" (irritation of the cells,

maybe from a vaginal infection or STD, such as Trichomonas).
- It can be read as "abnormal changes in the cells" (suggesting HPV infection or, sometimes, precancerous changes in the cells.)
- It can be read as "unsatisfactory" (not a good specimen, has to be repeated).

In most cases, your doctor will not contact you if your Pap smear result is normal. However, if there is anything abnormal about your Pap smear, you will receive a phone call or letter from your doctor.

Treatment of Abnormalities Revealed by Pap Smear

Getting such a call or letter is a disturbing and frightening experience. Most women agree that they tended to think the worst and fear for their lives. Let the doctor know your fears and concerns.

Treatment of abnormalities revealed by the test includes:

- Colposcopy
- Conization
- Cryocauterization
- Laser therapy

Talk over the advantages and disadvantages of these treatments with your doctor. Each procedure has a cure rate of over ninety percent. The more you know about the procedures in advance, the less anxiety you're likely to experience.

The doctor who performs the above mentioned procedures will probably ask the following questions:

- When was your last period?
- What type of birth control do you use?
- Do you have any history of previous abnormal Pap smears? What was the treatment?
- Do you have any history of pelvic pain or infection?
- If applicable, what is your history of past colposcopic exams?

- **Colposcopy**
  When a patient has an abnormal Pap smear, she is referred for a colposcopy. Colposcopy is a procedure that allows your doctor to look more closely at your cervix through a colposcope (essentially a magnifying glass), and, if necessary, take a sample of tissue from the cervix (this procedure is called a biopsy).

  By applying a special solution to the surface of the cervix with a cotton swab, the doctor is able to see precancerous and cancerous cells clearly. If such cells are present, the cervix is numbed and a sample is taken from both the cervix and uterus. The total procedure can take from fifteen to ninety minutes and is painless. Most doctors instruct women not to douche, use tampons, or have sexual intercourse for about a week afterwards.

  In the laboratory, cells taken from the cervix are examined to determine the severity of disease. When the results are determined, the appropriate treatment is begun. In unusual circumstances, the colposcopy does not allow an adequate view of the cervix and another procedure, called conization, is necessary in order to obtain a tissue biopsy.

- **Conization**
  During a conization procedure, your doctor will remove the entire area of abnormal tissue, so that a thorough laboratory analysis can be performed to rule out of the presence of invasive cancer.

  Conization is done under anesthesia on an outpatient basis. There are risks from this procedure that are associated with the administration of anesthesia. Talk to your doctor about these risks.

- **Cryocauterization**
  If cells on your cervix turn out to be premalignant—that is, showing signs that they could turn into cancer cells—your doctor may recommend cryocauterization. Cryocauterization is a safe and simple surgical procedure in which the cervix is cooled with liquid nitrogen. Touching the frozen, abnormal cells with a probe causes them to slough off. After cryocauterization, a watery vaginal discharge can last for several weeks.

- **Laser Therapy**
  Laser light produces electricity that runs through a gas. Laser therapy is used to vaporize abnormal cells. The laser light beam is pointed toward the area of abnormal cervical tissue. The heat from the laser causes the abnormal tissue to die, and it sloughs off. This procedure may be painful, but it causes less cervical scarring than other procedures.

- **Risks**
  Before you undergo any of the above procedures, you will be asked to sign a consent form that outlines the procedure's possible risks. Be sure that you understand the risks prior to giving your consent, and if you are at all unsure, *ask your doctor questions*. The risk is minimal, but, nevertheless, bleeding and pain may occur, and it is possible that the procedure will not eliminate all of the affected cells. If you have heavy vaginal bleeding, abdominal pain, or maloderous discharge, return to your doctor's office immediately.

Dysfunctional Uterine Bleeding

It seems as though I have my period every two weeks. Is this frequency normal? My moods change terribly during this time. What is going on?

Irregular or excessive menstrual bleeding is a complaint that plagues a small number of women. Most cases of dysfunctional uterine bleeding (DUB) are associated with menstruation that occurs even if no ovulation has taken place. Abnormal bleeding is common among women who have just started menstruating and, then again, in the several years preceding menopause.

When you don't ovulate, the estrogen and progesterone levels in the uterus are disturbed, and irregular and abnormal bleeding results. Endometriosis and fibroids are the most common causes of excessive bleeding. Stress and illness can also trigger DUB. Other causes can be thyroid disease, infections, and cancers.

If you bleed for longer than a week and/or bleed frequently

(more than every three weeks or so), and/or bleed between periods, and/or bleed excessive amounts, you should see your doctor.

Dysfunctional uterine bleeding causes moodiness, pain, embarrassment, anxiety, and fatigue. Women who bleed excessively may even develop anemia. Medical and surgical costs to treat this condition can be considerable. If you have DUB, I would recommend short-term disability insurance to cover the days you have to take off from work. Dysfunctional uterine bleeding can usually be medically treated.

Diagnosis

Treatment for DUB begins only after blood tests and X-rays rule out other serious diseases. You can help your doctor determine the heaviness of your bleeding by describing the number of menstrual pads or tampons you use. Endometriosis and fibroids are the most common causes of excessive bleeding.

Treatment Options

The goal of treatment is to stop the bleeding and avoid long-term complications. Because of the disturbed levels of estrogen and progesterone, doctors usually prescribe nonsteroidal anti-inflammatory drugs (NSAIDs), such as Motrin®, Naprosyn®, and Advil® as the first drugs of choice. (However, if you have a history of kidney or peptic ulcer disease, you should not take these drugs.) NSAIDs inhibit prostaglandin production. These drugs are readily available, cheap, and have few side effects, especially when used short-term. In most cases, they decrease uterine bleeding significantly.

Another form of treatment for women (who do not plan to become pregnant) is hormone therapy. Estrogen, progesterone, and oral contraceptives of various strengths or in combination can be used to control dysfunctional uterine bleeding. Oral contraceptives are easy to use, and women do not experience serious side effects.

Hormone therapy should be used only with caution, after careful discussion with your doctor. Recent studies at the Mayo Clinic suggest that the risks may include a greater likelihood of heart disease, stroke, blood clots, as well as dementia and loss of thinking power.

Complaints about hormone therapy may also include weight gain, hair loss or thinning, nausea, and bloating (water retention). However, there are usually few if any side effects. Although the duration of medical therapy depends on the individual patient, most studies show a change in uterine blood flow within three months.

Surgery as a Last Resort

Surgery is the treatment of last resort. Surgery usually involves the removal of the uterus (hysterectomy) and is recommended only when repeated medical therapy has failed. Laser therapy has been used as an alternative to hysterectomy and does not cause infertility.

A hysterectomy can be psychologically taxing, and it is important that you share your concerns, fears, and emotions with your doctor. Women who undergo a hysterectomy often feel low self-esteem.

Fibroids, noncancerous tumors that cause excessive uterine bleeding, may have to be surgically removed if they grow large and cause pelvic pain. Fibroids are common and, in most women, are without symptoms.

Dilation and curettage (D and C) is another surgical procedure that can be used as a temporary measure. D and C involves scraping of the inner lining of the uterus to remove excess tissue that can cause excessive bleeding. This procedure does not cause infertility.

Endometriosis

I have been diagnosed with endometriosis.
I'm unclear about what is going on in my body.
What does it mean to have endometriosis?

Endometriosis is a common cause of dysfunctional uterine bleeding. Tissue from the lining of the inner wall grows outside of the uterus in the pelvis or in another location inside the abdominal cavity. During the menstrual period, these displaced cells also bleed.

Endometriosis causes pelvic pain, excessive bleeding, infertility, appendicitis, chronic back pain, and urinary obstruction. Pain usually occurs around the time of the menstrual cycle, and this helps your doctor make the diagnosis. Pelvic pain caused by endometriosis may sometimes occur in postmenopausal women.

Diagnosis

During pelvic examination, women with endometriosis may complain of severe pain that worsens on manual manipulation of the cervix and ovaries. The diagnosis is confirmed by laparoscopy, a procedure in which a scope with a small camera is placed into the body to visualize endometrial tissue outside the uterus. This surgical procedure is done when the patient is under anesthesia. This disease tends to run in families.

Treatment Options

The treatment for endometriosis is the same as for dysfunctional uterine bleeding. Laser therapy is often used to treat endometriosis.

Osteoporosis

I am fifty-years-old and my doctor says I'm at risk for osteoporosis. What is osteoporosis, and can it be prevented?

While the aging process is inevitable, by exercising, eating a proper diet, and living a healthy lifestyle, you can achieve a happier, older age and a relatively disease-free life. As African–American women age gracefully, diseases such as heart disease, cancer, and osteoporosis need not stake their claim and thwart the potential joy that older women deserve.

Osteoporosis is a bone-weakening disease. Bones that were once strong become weak, brittle, and prone to fracture through loss of bone mass. Bone loss may lead to small breaks in the spine. As more small breaks occur, people get shorter and tend to look "bent over." Some people are unaware of these changes and may only notice that their clothes don't fit quite the same way.

This disorder results from the normal aging process or from other diseases, like hyperparathyroidism. The process of losing bone mass also appears to be related to a decline in estrogen (a hormone that increases the strength and mass of bone) and in vitamin D production and absorption. Vitamin D is needed to help the blood absorb calcium. Patients who take steroids to treat inflammatory diseases, such as arthritis and asthma, are at risk for osteoporosis.

How Common is Osteoporosis and Who is at Risk?

More than twenty-eight million Americans have osteoporosis or are heading toward it, and eighty percent of these people are women. In the United States, ten million people already have osteoporosis, and eighteen million more have been diagnosed with low bone mass, a precursor to the disabling disease. An alarming one in two women over the age of fifty will experience an osteoporosis-related fracture during her lifetime. Only ten percent of African-American women over the age of fifty have osteoporosis and an additional thirty percent have low bone density, putting them at risk for developing the disease. The assumed reason that fewer African–American women are affected is that, in general, they have greater bone density.

Although osteoporosis is more common in the older population, it can strike at any age. And it is likely to grow worse before it grows better. During the next twenty years, as women live longer, tend to be more obese, don't get hormone replacement therapy, and live more sedentary lifestyles, the incidence of osteoporosis is expected to increase by fifty percent.

- **Risk Factors for Osteoporosis**
  - Increased age
  - Female gender (although men can have osteoporosis also)
  - White or Asian American ethnicity (although the number of African American women who have osteoporosis is steadily increasing)
  - Family history of osteoporosis
  - Early menopause
  - Low calcium intake
  - Being tall and thin

- **Preventable Risk Factors**
  - Sedentary lifestyle

- Cigarette smoking
- Alcohol abuse

More About Your Bones

Bone is a living, growing tissue, constantly being renewed. During childhood and early adulthood, new bone is added to the skeleton faster than old bone is removed. After age thirty-five, more bone is removed than is replaced. Women begin to lose bone tissue more rapidly after menopause when circulating estrogen levels in the body are low. Bones become weaker if bone tissue is not replaced as rapidly as it is lost.

Normally, the inside of bone looks something like a sponge. With osteoporosis, the holes in the sponge become larger and more numerous; the bones become weaker and are more likely to break. Women can lose up to twenty percent of bone mass in the five to seven years following menopause, making them more susceptible to osteoporosis.

Diagnosis

The diagnosis of osteoporosis is determined by a person's medical history, lab tests, and, most importantly, by an advanced X-ray technique called DEXA, a bone density measurement test called a Bone Densitometry Test (BMD). There are several methods for measuring bone mass density (BMD). The technique that has yielded the most benefit is a specialized X-ray called "Dual Energy X-ray Absorptiometry" or Dexa.

The common X-ray is used to diagnose vertebral fractures in people with back pain and to detect possible secondary conditions related to osteoporosis, like rib fractures. Certain blood tests are helpful in determining if vitamin D levels are low or if parathyroid disease exists.

Treatment

All women who are postmenopausal and who have low BMD and several of the risk factors listed above should be on medication to prevent future painful and debilitating fractures. Common medications include calcium, vitamin D, bisphosphonates, and, though increasingly rarely, HRT.. There is also a lot you can do to protect your bones without medication. By exercising, getting balanced nutrition, and avoiding smoking and excess alcohol, you can take control of your risk and reduce the progression of osteoporosis.

• **_Supplements and Medication_**

   Calcium Supplements: A sufficient intake is important. I inform all my female patients, both young and old, to take calcium. Studies have shown that the foundation of healthy bone is laid during the twenties and thirties, a foundation that can later (at menopause) prevent or offset the occurrence of osteoporosis. Ask your doctor for the proper dosage of calcium.

   Hormone Replacement Therapy (HRT): Hormone replacement therapy has been used to prevent osteoporosis and to lower cholesterol levels. Some studies show it to be effective in treating those conditions. Estrogen is the primary hormone given to patients with osteoporosis. Progestin (Provera®) is also used, along with a calcium supplement, to achieve the best benefit. Estrogen enhances the total process of bone production and absorption, and thus helps prevent loss in bone density. That's important, because elderly women who have suffered bone loss are often frail and unsteady on their feet, and therefore at risk for falling and for bone fractures

Be Aware! Until recently, it was thought that prolonged estrogen use reduced the risk of heart disease among postmenopausal women. Now, several recent studies suggest that the benefits of hormone replacement are outweighed by the serious risks. A study at the Mayo Clinic by Sharonne H. Hayes, M.D., suggests that the risks may include a greater likelihood of heart disease, stroke, blood clots, as well as dementia and loss of thinking power. The benefits, according to this study, are fewer bone fractures and less likelihood of cancer of the lower colon. Talk to your doctor or your health care provider about the advantages and disadvantages in your particular case.

Newer Drugs

- *Bisphosphonates*: Newer drugs, like Fosamax®, are now used to increase bone mass. They may inhibit bone breakdown. These drugs are poorly absorbed through the intestines and therefore should be taken on an empty stomach with only water. Heartburn and indigestion appear to be the common side effects. I advise my patients to take Fosamax® with their calcium supplements.

- *Calcitonin*: Calcitonin, a hormone made in the thyroid gland, can inhibit bone breakdown and thus improve bone mass. Calcitonin also acts like estrogen in preventing fractures. Calcitonin was previously given by injection just under the skin. But with improved medical technology, it is now available as a nasal spray. The only side effects from the spray are minor nasal irritation or sneezing.

Love and Sex After Menopause

My grandmother has started dating a younger man, and it's driving the family crazy. Isn't my grandmother too old to be in love and have sex?

Physical changes in your body that accompany menopause, life experiences, and general health can affect your ability to enjoy sex. But there are ways to deal with these changes, so that you can continue to feel sexy, romantic, and adventurous.

What is Menopause?

Some women consider menopause to be a major turning point in their lives, and some women mourn the loss of fertility and the feeling of getting older that goes with that loss. But many women feel freer physically, emotionally, sexually, and spiritually, and enthusiastic about being able to be more sexually spontaneous, not having to worry about premenstrual syndrome (PMS) or pregnancy.

You will probably live one-third of your life after menopause, and this can be the most rewarding time of your life. Women who are of menopausal age tend to be more financially secure, have more leisure time, and have a better self-image than younger women, all of which can lead to richly romantic and intimate times with a partner.

In the 19th century, doctors spoke of menopause as "a function of God's wisdom and kindness." The implication was that menopause spared women from bearing children in their later years, and spared the child the early death of a parent.

In strictly medical terms, menopause occurs when a woman's ovaries stop releasing eggs, her menstrual period stops, and, therefore, she can no longer reproduce. In some women, the change happens abruptly, but, in most cases, the change is gradual, and it may happen over a period of years. The average age for women to experience menopause is fifty-one.

The period prior to menopause itself is called"perimenopause." During perimenopause, many hormonal, bodily, and emotional changes occur. A woman's estrogen production slows down, and she can experience the same hormonal changes that occurred during puberty, though usually in a more intense way.

The period after menopause is called "post-menopause." Women are also considered by health professionals to be postmenopausal after surgical removal of the ovaries or when chemotherapy treatments damage the ovaries.

"Stress menopause" is another type of menopause, according to the North American Menopause Society. This type can occur most often to women in their thirties or older who do not have a period over long stretches of time because of stress, illness, bulimia, excessive exercise, anemia, grief, and chemotherapy.

Symptoms of Menopause

Of course, one of the most obvious signs of menopause is when a woman's period becomes irregular or stops altogether. Some other signs of menopause include:

- Achy joints
- Hot flashes
- Night sweats
- Early wakening
- Insomnia
- Change in sexual desire
- Extreme sweating
- Frequent urination
- Difficulty concentrating
- Vaginal dryness
- Mood changes
- Headaches

These symptoms can be so unpredictable that a woman may think she's "going crazy" because she is unable to control them. The good news is that, according to Planned Parenthood of America, postmenopausal women have a greater overall sense of well-being and are the least likely group of all women to be depressed.

Hormone Replacement Therapy (HRT)

Doctors often recommend HRT to combat hot flashes and insomnia associated with menopause or to increase the bone density of post-menopausal women. HRT has also been shown to reduce vaginal dryness and atrophy and to alleviate the mood swings associated with menopause. HRT appears to encourage skin thickness and elasticity so that there are fewer wrinkles.

If you regularly see a doctor or health care provider, you will eventually need to make decisions about whether to use HRT, and, if you do, for how long. Roughly thirty-eight percent of American women were on HRT, as of a few years ago. One suggests that women in the lower socioeconomic group are less likely to get HRT treatment than women of other groups. You should always weigh the risks against the benefits while you are making your decision. (See the Osteoporosis section above for more on advantages and risks of HRT.)

Concerns about HRT center on the risks of endometrial cancer and breast cancer, especially after long-term use (more than ten years). Many women decide against using HRT because they choose to avoid the risks of these cancers. Often, they prefer to take other steps such as exercise and a well-balanced diet along with calcium supplementation to reduce their risk of osteoporosis and heart disease.

Sex and Menopause

Vaginal dryness, referred to by health professionals as "vaginal atrophy," is a common complaint of sexually active, postmenopausal women. Dryness in the vagina can cause intercourse to be painful. It can be treated with estrogen creams and over-the-counter lubricants. HRT can also prevent vaginal atrophy.

It is important for you to understand that if you have vaginal dryness, you may not actually have vaginal atrophy. The truth is, older women simply may need more stimulation from their partners, along with the aid of lubricants. Talk to your doctor about treatment options for vaginal dryness and an accurate diagnosis of vaginal atrophy.

A Time for New Challenges

During and after menopause, women can take on new activities, exercise, and hobbies they didn't have time for when they were young. At this stage of life, women also need to focus on proper nutrition, even if they haven't done so before. Estrogen-like hormones can be obtained from soy products, yams, carrots, corn, apples, and oats. More protein in the diet can help keep your body strong and flexible. Women who feel better physically have increased sexual drive.

Women have small amounts of testosterone, a hormone typically associated with men, that can increase sex drive. Testosterone levels decrease during menopause. Doctors sometimes prescribe very small amounts of testosterone to help increase a woman's level of desire. If you are interested, ask your doctor.

In summary, an older woman's poor health can impede a healthy sex life. Heart disease, diabetes, high blood pressure, and depression can all affect the ability to have and enjoy sex and romance. So talk with your doctor about sex. He or she can help you experience a healthy, enjoyable sexual life in your later years.

What are Urinary Tract Infection and Urinary Incontinence?

A few years ago, when I was sixty-five, my husband and I stopped going out socially because I started to have embarrassing moments. Coughing, sneezing, and laughing all cause me to wet myself. My doctor told me that I had a chronic urinary tract infection and a condition called "incontinence." Why is it happening and is there any help for me?

Both urinary tract infection and urinary incontinence are common conditions affecting older women and can appear together or alone. A urinary tract infection does not cause urinary incontinence even though bacteria can be an underlying cause.

Twenty percent of women between the ages of sixty-five and seventy have bacteria in their urine. Bacteria buildup in the urine increases with age and can occur without symptoms. But if the patient has diseases like diabetes or heart disease, or if bacteria in the urine build up beyond the normal increase, symptoms can occur. If another disease is present, symptoms can feel flu-like, with fever, painful urination, and blood in the urine (hematuria).

Urinary tract infection can involve both the lower urinary (bladder) and the upper urinary tract (kidneys). If urinary infections are left untreated, the bacteria can even invade tissue and cause serious septic conditions in the body. For example, if bacteria invade the kidneys, it is not uncommon to become very sick with a fever, experience an increased heart rate, shortness of breath, nausea, and vomiting. Changes in mental status can also occur. The worst scenario is a build-up of bacteria in the blood so heavy that it causes organ systems to fail and, ultimately, death.

There are two major bacteria common to urinary tract infection: *Escherichia coli* and *Staphylococcus saprophyticus*. Doctors perform urine cultures to determine which antibiotics to use. Ordinarily, doctors use a dipstick test (a stick with an indicator on it and placed into the urine) to look for nitrites, blood, and high white blood cell counts. In some cases, people attempt to treat their own symptoms with old antibiotics that have been previously prescribed, but that's dangerous. Such treatment can lead to a false negative result from the urine test. All old medications should be thrown away.

Aging and Anatomical Changes

As women age, changes in the anatomy can also cause urinary tract infections. Family physicians will often refer patients to urologists for a proper diagnosis of anatomical problems.

Urologists often test for anatomical problems in the bladder by inserting a scope into the urethra, the tube through which urine passes. The doctor can then determine if there have been any structural changes to the bladder as a result of aging.

Another test, performed by a radiologist, involves taking an X-ray of the urinary system, which will reveal any stones, tumors, or abnormal anatomy.

Older women who have had children and who have low levels of estrogen can have weakened ligaments that fail to keep the bladder and uterus in normal position. The uterus can lie on the bladder, preventing it from emptying completely. Because of stagnant urine in the bladder, bacteria can increase.

Treatment for Urinary Tract Infection

Short–course antibiotic treatment (three to five days) seems to work well for younger women. For older women who have chronic problems, the ordinary course of treatment is ten to fourteen days.

Antibiotics like nitrofurantoin (Macrodantin® and Macrobid®) work well for young women but can be dangerous for older women because side effects may include liver disease. The following drugs have been successful for treating older women with urinary tract infection: trimethoprim sulfamethoxazole DS, Bactrim DS®, norfloxacin (Noroxin®), and ciprofloxacin (Cipro®). Prophylactic treatment, when antibiotics are given continuously, should be used only as a last resort. Frequent bladder emptying, estrogen therapy, and maintaining good hygiene are all recommended treatments for urinary tract infections.

Urinary Incontinence (UI)

Urinary incontinence is a common condition that can affect women and men of all ages. UI is one of the most common reasons that elderly patients are admitted to nursing homes. This condition may occur even in schoolgirls (one to three percent). Among elderly men and women, UI rates run as high as forty to fifty percent in some studies. Some people with UI fail to talk to their doctors about it out of embarrassment. Many doctors don't ask their patients questions, either.

The leading theory about the cause of UI is that, as children, we learn to hold off urination until the appropriate opportunity by learning to place tension in the muscles that control the bladder and colon and assist in maintaining proper position. After years of this form of tension, muscular dynamics in your body can change and can put you at risk for UI.

It is important to talk to your doctor if you experience urinary incontinence. He or she will ask you questions about your history and what medicines you've been taking, and will do a test to determine if you have an infection or some anatomical problem.

Age-Related Changes

Several age-related changes in the body and mind can cause UI:

- Changes in brain chemistry, particularly with the neurotransmitters that pertain to mood and body balance (for example, the brain controls the body's need to quench thirst and to void)
- Changes in the nervous system that controls impulses to the bladder
- Changes in the way the bladder responds to fluid. Bladder hyperactivity increases as we age.
- Changes in the way the bladder contracts to expel urine
- Urinary tract infections, as well as weakening of muscles and

ligaments that contributes to the sinking down of organs like the bladder and uterus. Such infections increase with age.
• The walls of the bladder and uterus become thinner as levels of estrogen decrease.

Types of UI

• **Stress:** When pressure is applied to the bladder, as from coughing, sneezing, or laughing vigorously
• **Urge:** When the patient has a strong desire to void and, then, a sudden loss of urine. This condition occurs when the bladder becomes hyperactive.
• **Overflow:** When the bladder becomes too full, urine will leak out
• **Functional:** Inability to reach the bathroom in time

Treatment for UI

Each type of urinary incontinence is treated differently. In the past, surgery was a leading treatment. Today, drugs, which have fewer side effects, are the treatment of choice, along with behavioral modification. Exercise and biofeedback have good results, too. Included in this process is relearning how to contract the muscles of the pelvic floor. This may sound complicated, but it really is not. You can learn to isolate those muscles by using accessory abdominal, gluteal, and thigh muscles. If it is hard to envision, simply watch children shake or cross their legs when they have to go to the bathroom.

Patients have had excellent results with exercises that strengthen the pelvic floor. These are called "Kegel exercises," and information about them can be found at http://www.kegel-exercises.com/. Other less common forms of treatment include electrical stimulation, mechanical intravaginal devices, and bladder neck support prostheses.

• ***Drugs Used to Treat UI***
    1) *Stress:* Phenylpropanoline hydrochloride, pseudoephedrine and Premarin®
    3) *Urge:* Detrol®, Ditropan®, Tofranil®, and Bentyl ®

4) *Overflow:* Urecholine®

5) *Functional:* No drugs for this form of UI

Remember: there is no reason to feel ashamed. You are not alone. There is help for women who suffer from UI. Tell your doctor, and the two of you can discuss UI openly.

Yes, women's bodies change as they age, and some of those changes aren't what we'd order if they were on the menu. But though you can't always avoid medical problems, by going in for regular checkups and when you have physical complaints, you can catch the problem early. By understanding what your doctor is doing and why, you can become an active partner in your own recovery and in the maintenance of your good health.

Chapter 15

Men's
Health Issues

Of the many obstacles that prevent African–American men from keeping healthy is our buying into the myth of the macho man. African–American men have long been socialized to believe that we are stronger, tougher, and more virile than all other groups of men. This expectation has its roots in the abuse and pain African–American men endured during slavery. Regardless of how far we have come, the struggle to live up to the image of the long-enduring male has created poor health habits among large numbers of African–American men.

A result of false pride is that African–American men have more health problems than men from other ethnic groups. For example, to put it bluntly, some men feel that to let a doctor put a finger in the rectum is not manly. Not only are they embarrassed and afraid, but the chance of any doctor finding something wrong threatens a virile and impenetrable self-image. Pride is laced with fear, anger, and rage at any threat to an African–American man's sense of self. The sad result is that far too many cases of prostate cancer are diagnosed only after it is too late to treat them most effectively.

Social, economic, and cultural pressures can combine to erode our resilience and reduce our physical immunity to illness and disease. The stress of being responsible for our families is so often taken for granted as simply part of the job. Without exercise, a healthy diet, time for reflection, and regular visits to the doctor, our bodies will fail us, and our souls will fade as well.

Your family practitioner can help you in culturally sensitive ways. By becoming partners with your physician, you can begin to take control of your health and ultimately improve the quality of your life.

On the following pages, I will take up some of the tough issues that my patients have raised to me through their questions.

QUESTIONS FREQUENTLY ASKED BY AFRICAN AMERICAN MEN

My uncle is having problems in his marriage, and I feel that if something isn't done soon, he and my favorite aunt will get divorced. My uncle has always been very strong and independent. He spent two tours in Vietnam. He's fifty now, and though he still looks to be in his thirties, for the last few years he has been dealing with severe high blood pressure and diabetes. He hardly ever goes to see his doctor, and his wife gets mad and worried because, even when he does go, he doesn't do what his doctor tells him.

My aunt says his personality has changed, and he seems distant and depressed. Just the other day I heard her telling my mother how he hasn't touched her in a long time and how she figured he was cheating on her. She said she was going to get a divorce if things didn't change. I know my uncle is a "macho" guy, but he loves his wife, and I don't think cheating is the problem. He told me that he wasn't too much of a man anymore, but he wouldn't say anything more. I think he has problems with impotence and is too proud to tell anyone. Is this possible?

ERECTILE DYSFUNCTION (ED)

Although the term impotence is often used to refer to sexual problems, doctors now use the phrase "erectile dysfunction" instead. Both terms mean an inability to achieve or maintain sufficient penile rigidity for sexual intercourse.

Causes of Erectile Dysfunction

- Nervous system disease (Parkinson's disease, Alzheimer's disease, multiple sclerosis)
- Hormonal imbalance (testosterone deficiency, estrogen increase, diabetes)
- Circulatory disease (arteriosclerosis, cardiovascular disease, high blood pressure)
- Psychological problems (most cases are not psychological, although feelings of rage, anxiety, and depression can hinder sexual performance)
- Pelvic surgery
- Enlarged prostate gland
- Cancer surgery
- Sickle cell disease
- Smoking too heavily
- Alcohol or drug abuse

Who Has Erectile Dysfunction?

ED affects approximately fifty percent of the male population in the U.S. between the ages of forty and seventy, and is probably underreported because of its sensitive nature. Currently, there is little data about the number of African–American men affected with some form of erectile dysfunction. I suspect that the number is high because of the high incidence among African–American men of diabetes and hypertension and because many African–American men smoke cigarettes, drink alcohol, or take drugs. Habits that are bad for your body in general are also bad for your sexual performance. Rage, anxiety, and depression can also hinder sexual performance.

Viagra and Other Treatment Options

The day after the release of Viagra® into the market, I arrived early at my office and found three African–American men waiting for me. They were eager to see me, which was unusual, because none of these men had been conscientious about keeping doctor's appointments. In fact, I had tried for years to get their wives to bring them in for physical exams and routine laboratory tests. Not surprisingly, they all wanted Viagra®. I subsequently found that two of them had ED because of the diseases they had and the medicines they were taking. The other man simply wanted to improve his sexual performance.

I learned a great deal that morning. Rather than see a doctor, these men had gone to extreme efforts to hide their inability to perform sexually. They hid it from their loved ones so as not to appear less manly. Their behavior caused stress in their relationships. The good news is that the marketing of Viagra® paved the way for many African–American men to finally come forward, and come forward they did.

Viagra® has been shown to increase vascular problems, such as blockages of blood flow to the penis caused by thickened vessels as a result of high blood pressure, high cholesterol, and heart disease. Patients who take nitrates for heart disease should not take Viagra®. Viagra® may also worsen other cardiovascular problems such as heart attack, stroke, or life-threatening arrhythmias. Because Viagra® dilates vessels, it may worsen low blood pressure (hypotension). Vacuum devices, injections, and penile implants are other ways to treat ED.

Asking for Help

Talking about ED with your doctor is one of the best ways to combat its effects. Erections require a harmonious integration of the nervous, circulatory, and lymphatic systems. Often, it is best understood as a medical problem. For example, according to one study, men with untreated diabetes are three times more likely to experience ED than patients with treated diabetes. Asking for help from a doctor does not make you any less of a man.

Here are some ways to help yourself and to get help from others:

- Get an annual medical checkup.
- If you have diabetes, heart problems, and/or high blood pressure, follow the doctor's instructions closely.

- If you are having difficulty achieving or sustaining an erection, talk to your doctor.
- Don't define your self-image by whether or not you have ED.
- Don't isolate yourself. Tell your companion or a close trusted friend what you're going through.
- Stop smoking and drinking, and get plenty of rest to alleviate the stress in your life.
- Work to develop a healthier lifestyle.

Negative behavior that can result from ED—such as anger, ignoring mates, or blaming loved ones—jeopardizes relationships and thwarts communication between otherwise loving people. In most cases ED is a treatable physical condition that can be effectively managed by a qualified, knowledgeable physician.

Part IV

Emotional and Spiritual Health Issues for African Americans

Chapter 16
Emotional Illness and Emotional Health

Many African Americans, both young and old, and in all socioeconomic levels, will experience anxiety, depression, sleep disturbance, and/or physical ailments linked to anxiety. But experiencing such disturbances doesn't mean we need to be ruled by them. That's why early treatment can be so valuable. It can be the way of nipping a potentially big problem in the bud.

The bad news is that African Americans, along with Latinos, are less likely than Whites to receive mental health care. Something must be wrong here. Given our history of discrimination, violence, and poverty, we know there's plenty of pain, even for those of us who have made it.

WHO SUFFERS FROM MENTAL ILLNESS?

The percentage of African Americans who suffer from psychological disorders is unknown, but, from what I see in my own patients, I assume it to be quite high. I am alert to mental illness in my practice and gather as much information as I can about complaints and history. Then, for patients who do have symptoms that may need treatment, I can assign the patient to the appropriate category of mental

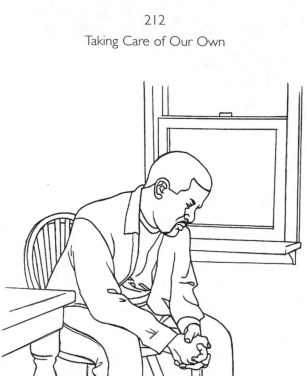

illness (as the law requires) and recommend a suitable treatment plan. If I feel that the treatment needed is more than I can provide, I will refer the patient to a mental health practitioner.

As we know, you can lead a horse to water, but you can't make him drink. I often see patients who are seriously neurotic but who avoid my recommendation to seek counseling. I see husbands and wives sitting and waiting for their marriages to fail, when they could have avoided reaching that point if they'd been willing to go to marriage therapy.

Whites enter therapy for woes much less severe than the problems African Americans tend to bear without turning toward help. African Americans have to be willing to seek therapy when they need it. Mental illness can be treated once it is diagnosed. With the help of treatment, which can be given for short or long periods of time, depending on the severity of the problem, many people recover to live happy and productive lives.

MENTAL ILLNESS COMMON TO AFRICAN AMERICANS

The following categories of mental illness occur most commonly in African Americans:

- Anxiety
- Depression
- Anger and rage
- Addiction
- Bipolar Personality
- disorder

Anxiety

What is Anxiety?

Anxiety is characterized as having a painful uneasiness or abnormal apprehension about an event or upcoming situation. That means that anxious people worry to the extreme about things that don't need worrying about. They eat up their lives finding things to worry about. Such generalized anxiety is quite common among African Americans.

The trick to controlling anxiety and the stress that goes with it is sorting out the things you *can* change from the things you can't, and then working on the ones you can. In this way, sources of anxiety can become an inspiration for brave, inventive, and purposeful approaches to your life.

What Causes Anxiety?

Usually, a particular emotional stress sets anxiety going. In such cases, you may react in one of two ways. For some people, anxiety may be over-excitement and fluttery nervousness. For others, it may be depression, which often feels like an inability to do almost anything at all or to take pleasure in anything.

Anxiety has a lot to do with body chemistry, and some people are more prone to it than others. But even if you're one of those people who tend to have high levels of anxiety, you can learn to manage it, sometimes by avoiding the sources but, more often, by facing them and finding solutions.

Your mind can help take care of your body once you learn ways of coping, and you will find that you are less anxious. Energy that you used to put into worrying now can flow into your enjoyment of the day and into your ability to do things—big things—like managing work, family, and relationships.

What Are the Symptoms of Anxiety?

The major symptoms of generalized anxiety are the following:

- Excessive worry and anxiousness over real or projected problems
- Lack of energy or always feeling fatigued
- Chest pain and/or heart palpitations
- Difficulty breathing
- Gastrointestinal problems like indigestion
- Inability to sleep
- Agitation
- Tremors
- Excessive sweating
- Poor ability to concentrate
- Hyperventilation (Rapid breathing)

How Anxiety Affects the Body

People can make themselves sick by beating themselves up mentally all the time. This process is called "somatization," and it occurs when anxiety makes itself felt in the body in the form of physical symptoms.

This process can have its beginnings in childhood. For example, a child can become anxious because of overly protective parents, or because of an emotionally traumatic experience.

Children can also develop acute anxiety after a severe illness. The actual illness fades and no longer exists, but as time passes, these children, who have now grown into adults, have recurring complaints with no underlying organic cause. For example, people who are anxious or depressed often have multiple tender spots on their body. The tenderness is often exaggerated. Some people yell out if the doctor just touches their skin.

Diagnosis and Treatment of Generalized Anxiety

Anxiety requires close attention by a doctor. Your doctor will take a thorough family and medical history to rule out any physical cause for the anxiety. He or she will try to determine the intensity of your anxiety and its effects on your life and health. Depending on the doctor's findings, he or she may recommend medication and psychological counseling. Don't be afraid to take advantage of what such treatments have to offer. Getting to know yourself better can be a great adventure. So can renewed interaction with other people.

Neurosis and anxiety tend to isolate us from other people. We get lost in our own troubles and may find ourselves without anyone to talk to. That's why counseling and support groups work so well in the treatment of generalized anxiety. Often, by talking openly about what creates your anxiety in the first place, you can reduce the anxiety. Just by being clearer about the sources of your problem, you come closer to dealing with it.

Besides giving you a chance to talk and listen to other people's stories, support groups provide tools for coping. They can also offer effective methods for working with the specific living situations that are the source of your anxiety. You'll like the feeling you get at group meetings—the feeling that now, maybe for the first time in a while, you're taking charge of your life, making the necessary changes, and feeling the excitement that comes when you take a big step forward.

In addition, there are medications to treat generalized anxiety, but they are not the first course of action, due to their addictive potential. Doctors are more likely to prescribe antidepressants specifically aimed at controlling anxiety. Talk to your doctor if you experience anxiety. Once you have discussed specific issues, the doctor can recommend an appropriate course of treatment.

Major Depression

What is Depression?

When you're depressed you feel heavy with sadness. You don't feel like doing anything, and you have a hard time thinking about or concentrating on anything. On top of this, you may feel constantly fatigued or, sometimes, constantly restless. You might lose your appetite, and you might go through sudden mood swings.

Researchers are finding more and more depression in the African–American community. If you're like most of us, you've probably seen, or experienced, enough depression to know something about how it works. Depression can come and go for no obvious reason, and isn't necessarily dependent on your immediate outward circumstance. Some people go through bouts of depression and learn to deal with it. Other people go through their lives depressed without knowing it. They come to accept their misery as a lifelong companion.

What Causes Depression?

Some causes of depression are the same as those for anxiety. The immediate cause may be a particular circumstance, or it may be something in your body chemistry that makes you feel bad much of the time, or periodically. The latter cause of depression can be hereditary. Illness, like a stroke or chronic cancer, can also cause depression.

What are the Symptoms of Depression?

Certain kinds of feelings are associated with depression. Not all depressed people feel them, but if you've ever gone through a depressive episode, or known someone who was depressed, you will recognize some of them.

- **Resignation**
  Feelings of "Why bother?" or "What's the point in anything?"

- **Unhappiness**
  We are all unhappy sometimes, but in a depressed person the level of unhappiness is deeper than a nondepressed person could

imagine. Gloom, doom, and misery are at the forefront, and it's impossible to take pleasure in anything.

- *Anxiety and Paranoia*
  These two emotions are common in depressed people because of a chemical imbalance in the brain. Feelings of anxiety and panic attacks can occur quite frequently, particularly in stressful situations where the physical senses are overwhelmed. Paranoia is the irrational feeling that someone is taking an unnatural interest in your life. You assume that when people are talking together, they are talking about you. At its extremes, you may believe that everyone you know is secretly plotting against you or listening outside your door.

- *Going Through the Motions / Dreamlike State*
  One of the most common complaints from depressed people is that they're just going through the motions. Although they are doing all the things that they used to do before, nothing gives them any pleasure. They feel like robots going through life, or actors rehearsing a play. Other people, and even their ordinary lives, seem distant and unreal. Some people liken the experience to living in a dream.

- *Detachment*
  Detachment is the feeling that you are watching your own life take place, that you are sitting behind your own eyes and observing your actions as if they were someone else's. At its worst, the sufferer feels as though he or she is trapped inside his or her own head, unable to reach out and connect with real life. Some people experience this as the soul becoming disconnected from the body.

- *Time Distortion*
  One of the stranger effects of depression is that the sufferer's perception of time can be distorted. Events that happened years ago can seem as though they happened yesterday, while the far distant future feels like it is right around the corner. Experiences long-since forgotten can be recalled in sharp detail. In some

cases, the sufferer can pick a time of his or her life, go to it, and see it as vividly as though it were the present day. Although this may sound like an interesting experience, it is in fact very confusing, because the sufferer's perception of "Who am I?" blurs with "Who was I?" and "Who will I be?" An identity crisis is the last thing a depressed person needs.

- *Fear of the Future*
  Depressed people see nothing but gloom and misery in the future, and because of the effects of time compression, they believe that they can see to their own death and even beyond to the end of all mankind. This leads back to the feelings of resignation.

- *Guilt*
  You'll often hear depressed people say, "It's all my fault," usually accompanied by tears. However irrational the reasoning may seem to someone in good mental health, anything from a friend's misfortune to population starvation on the other side of the world can feel like the fault of the depressed person. The weight of the world's woes is truly on the shoulders of the depressed.

- *Magnification*
  One of the scariest feelings of all is the impression of "magnitude." This is a hard one to explain, but it's the sensation that every single thing you do has a profound effect on the world around you and your own life, to the extent that you start to analyze every action before doing it. Even the smallest task can become an immense challenge because of the profound effect the sufferer feels that task will have. By comparison, the day-to-day life that the sufferer experienced before the depression can seem shallow and irrelevant.

This distancing from one's ordinary, everyday life can be a barrier to escaping from depression. The sufferer may feel that the depression is far more profound and important than the old, nondepressed life and may feel guilty about getting on with things and enjoying them again. The term "uplift anxiety" has been used to describe this feeling of guilt.

Treatment for Depression

Researchers have learned a lot about depression during the past two decades. Doctors today can determine if a depression is caused by stress and emotional issues or by problems in your body chemistry. For example, because thyroid disease slows down the body's metabolism, it can often lead to depression.

Several medicines, including Prozac® and Paxil®, have been successful in treating major depression. But pills aren't enough in themselves. Eating a healthy diet and getting good exercise are also part of a good treatment plan. Psychotherapy and support groups can also be essential in helping bring the depressed person back to an emotionally healthy life.

Qualified therapists can lead you to healthier behavior patterns that will help you control your depression. A sensitive family doctor can often make good recommendations, too.

Physical Illness Linked with Depression

In most cases, depression leads to physical symptoms because, when we are under stress, our bodies secrete hormones like cortisol and adrenaline. Once these chemicals are released into our blood stream, they can cause damage to blood vessels that lead to plaques and heart disease. In addition, diabetes, cancer, high blood pressure, and obesity have been found to occur more in people who are depressed and "stressed out."

Suicide is also closely linked to depression. There are slow suicides as well as fast ones. By "slow suicides" I refer to people who use drugs and alcohol on a daily basis and who partake in high-risk behavior that puts their lives, or other people's, in jeopardy.

Taking Control of Your Depression

Here are some strategies you can try after talking them over with your family physician or counselor:

- Try to be more consistent in what you say and do.
- Learn to see and say more clearly what's bothering you.
- Always be open to feedback.
- Keep jealous feelings in check.
- Always consider compromise.
- Don't mind-read or expect others to read your mind.
- Reduce or eliminate sarcasm when speaking to others.
- Exercise your mind by reading more.
- Write your feelings in a journal.
- Don't live in the past or get caught up too far in the future.
- Connect yourself with a spiritual community, and get involved in spiritual practice.

Your doctor will be glad to discuss these strategies with you. He or she knows that your depression is a threat to your general health and that, by taking charge of it, you are heading in the right direction.

After you talk to your doctor, open up to your family. Your doctor may even help plan a family conference for you. Once you've begun to thrash matters out and are ready to face them, as a step toward healing, here are other steps you may wish to take:

- Find a support group or seek individual counseling.
- Start an exercise program under your doctor's supervision. Exercise is a useful tool for preventing and easing the symptoms of depression.
- Talk to your doctor about what medicines you can take to feel better. Selective Serotonin Reuptake Inhibitors (SSRIs) work very well and have few side effects.

Some drugs may cut down on your sex drive, but others, like Paxil® and Zoloft®, can be taken without loss of libido.

- Be realistic in your goals. Have your doctor help you create a daily activity chart. When you're depressed, it's hard to mobilize energy or be motivated to do new things. Getting organized can help get the motivational process started.

- Find something enjoyable to do with your free time and do it with your family or friends. If you don't have extra time, then create it.
- Make an effort not to be negative. Try not to find fault with people and events.

By practicing the tools I have outlined, by seeing your doctor on a regular basis, and by eating properly and getting regular exercise, you can be happier and healthier. Depression is not something to be ashamed of. Once you own up to it, you can join a community of others who have experienced it and learned how to deal with it.

You aren't the best doctor in this case. The only way to determine whether or not you are depressed is to seek professional assistance from your physician. He or she can make the diagnosis and prescribe proper treatment for depression.

Anger and Rage

Anger can be a healthy emotional response to situations that threaten us. Such situations could be as simple as a car alarm going off or as complicated as our reaction to some catastrophe in the neighborhood or the world. We all get angry sometimes, and in itself anger isn't a symptom of mental illness. But when it gets hidden and grows, it can be a strong destructive power. Some people act it out passively, showing their anger to others by their refusal to be happy, or even social. Others act it out in frequent bouts of aggressive rage. In either of these cases, constant or frequent anger ("chronic anger") can be a serious symptom.

People who suffer from chronic anger are more likely to experience psychological stress or even physical pain. Chronic anger, as a kind of mental illness, can be emotionally, and even physically, destructive and dangerous to yourself and other people. It's also true that people who have been angry for a long time may no longer notice that they're angry. That's true of *all* people, but for African Americans, who have had to wrestle with the history and presence of racism, it can be a particular problem, especially for young Black men.

You might ask, "What is the difference between feeling angry and feeling rage?" Anger is usually conscious, and it's usually a reaction to something tangible and immediate. Rage, on the other hand, is subconscious, something a person carries around most of the time, regardless of the situation.

The Rage Pie Gauge

If you chronically feel like three or more slices of the pie, you could be described as someone who feels rage. So that your anger does not hurt your life or the lives of others, you should seek professional intervention.

Rage can prevent you from taking control of your health. When faced with the possibility of illness, some people react in the following ways:

- Becoming alienated from others
- Behaving in a self-destructive way (such as drinking too much or abusing drugs)
- Inflicting pain on others
- Becoming even more physically challenged (as in obesity, heart disease, and diabetes) through bad diet and lack of exercise
- Falling into patterns of self-criticism and self-loathing

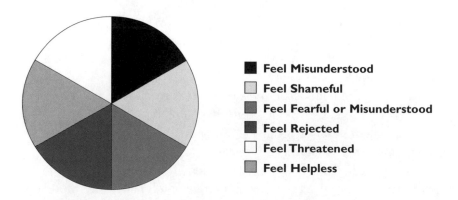

Taking Control of Rage

The following exercises will help you to keep rage in check and improve your health:

- Set aside time to think about your reactions to situations that feel negative and set short-term goals for taking control of your health. Meditation, which can help you become more spiritual, is the best defense against rage.
- Take responsibility for how you feel. Learn how your feelings affect your physical, emotional, and spiritual health.
- Connect with two people who love you. Talk about your fears and your goals for better health. Ask for support.
- Keep a journal so that you know how, where, when, and why your rage occurs.
- Forgive and begin to love yourself. Loving yourself can mean doing nice things for yourself. But it also means learning to see yourself as you are, warts and all, learning to change the things you can and want to change, and learning to live with what can't be changed.

Anger and Illness

Like other forms of emotional illness, chronic anger can cause health problems and complicate health problems you already have. Some studies have shown that anger causes a release of certain hormones (for example, epinephrine) that can worsen heart disease. Anger may also increase heart rate and elevate hypertension.

Addiction and Alcoholism

Until recent years, alcoholism and drug addiction were thought to be character defects or emotional disorders. Specialists who study substance dependency now recognize that addiction and alcoholism are predictable diseases that can be treated effectively. Alcoholism has its stages, and each stage calls for a specific treatment. There is some evidence that a predisposition to alcoholism can be carried in the genes.

The Impact of Addiction in the African–American Community

Ethnicity and culture may play a major role in determining why one person is more likely than another to become addicted to alcohol or drugs. African Americans have higher rates of alcoholism and drug addiction when compared with the general U. S. population. As to gender, more men than women have these diseases, but, in my practice, I see more and more women who use drugs and alcohol excessively. Many of these women are victims of sexual violence and physical abuse.

Genetics may also contribute to alcoholism and drug abuse. Sons and daughters of addicted parents are more likely to be alcoholics and drug addicts than if they have non-user parents, even when these children are separated early and raised by adoptive parents.

There's some good news. Some studies show that African–American high school students use alcohol and drugs less often than high school students from other population groups. But alcohol and drug use remains a leading health and social problem for African Americans. African–American entertainers and athletes commonly set bad examples by abusing alcohol and drugs. Alcohol manufacturers in their advertisements especially target African–American communities.

Are You at Risk for Addiction?

Some of the risk factors for alcohol and drug abuse or addiction are:

- **Weak Parental Attachment:** When parents pay little attention to their children and children learn to pay little attention to their parents, children tend to be rebellious against rules and not committed to school. They also tend to become alcohol and/or drug users.

- **Antisocial Behavior:** Aggressive or hyperactive children are more likely to use alcohol and drugs, and possibly become addicted, especially if they are isolated or alienated from parents, friends, and family.

- **Other-directed Tendency:** Children who want to be part of the crowd and who believe that fate guides their lives are more likely to be influenced by peers to use alcohol and drugs.

- ***Sensation-seeking Personality:*** People, especially young adolescents, who consistently take risks (like driving fast) are more likely to become addicted to alcohol and/or drugs.

Identifying Addiction

There is usually one event that calls attention to a person with an alcohol or drug problem: perhaps being fired from a job, being arrested, getting a DUI (driving under the influence) violation, having an automobile accident involving alcohol, or sustaining a head injury as the result of a bad fall.

Often, family and friends notice the signs later than they might. Maybe, they just didn't notice. Or maybe they just wanted to cut the person who was abusing as much slack as possible. Here's what they might have seen if they'd been looking:

- A friend might notice that, when he or she goes out for a drink with the person who has the problem, that person just doesn't want the drinking to stop.
- Friends and family might notice that the person seems to be always getting into some kind of trouble.
- Friends and family might notice that the person is often unable to carry on normal social functioning.
- A spouse might notice that his or her mate's habits are changing and that the mate's moods shift suddenly and unpredictably.

Often, by the time others notice there's a problem, the other person's disease has become a full addiction. At that point, the consequences to the person's health and ability to function can be tragic.

Symptoms of Addiction

Most addicts simply deny their problems and never seek a doctor. But the following symptoms are common:

- Abdominal pain
- Diarrhea

- Palpitations (usually from cocaine)
- Sexual dysfunction
- Depression
- Blackouts
- Seizures
- GI bleeding
- Injuries from falls or accidents

Other changes in the body can occur as the result of addiction. Men may develop large breasts, and for all addicts, common symptoms include large livers, abdominal tenderness, red blotchy skin lesions, swollen neck glands, high blood pressure, and problems with balance (for example, dizziness). Tremors and alcohol breath are common as well.

There are no laboratory tests that screen for addiction, but blood and urine tests can detect the presence of alcohol and drugs. Other blood tests may show abnormal liver blood counts (anemia), high lipids, an abnormally functioning pancreas, and sodium and potassium (electrolyte) abnormalities.

Intervention and Treatment

Frequently, in order for an addict to own his or her problem and get treatment, someone has to step in to convince that person to acknowledge and accept that he or she needs professional treatment. This kind of stepping in, usually planned in advance, is called "intervention."

Once the addict has owned the problem, several courses of treatment are possible:

- Pharmacotherapeutics (such as Methadone, Clonodine, Disulfiram, Antabuse®)
- Group counseling
- One-on-one substance abuse counseling
- Life skills counseling
- General health education

- Peer support groups (for example, Narcotics Anonymous (NA) and Alcoholics Anonymous (AA)
- Social and athletic activities
- Alternative housing
- Relapse prevention (monitoring by sponsors, counselors, doctors)

Al-Anon is an organization that helps family members and loved ones recover from the effects of living with someone with a drinking problem.

African Americans can benefit greatly from treatment programs. However, since there are only a limited number of addiction programs that are operated by African Americans and are culturally sensitive, be sure to choose a program that:

- Identifies the learning styles of African Americans in recovery
- Identifies the specific issues that African Americans bring with them to the recovery process
- Understands the history of drug and alcohol use and abuse by African Americans

A culturally sensitive program, created in Seattle, Washington in the early 1980s by Dr. William James and Reverend Stephen Johnson, involves these eleven steps:

Seattle's Afro-centric Program
1. Gain control over my life.
3. Tell my story to the world.
4. Stop lying.
5. Be honest with myself.
6. Accept who I am.
7. Feel my real feelings.
8. Feel my pain.
9. Forgive myself and forgive others.
10. Practice rebirth: a new life

11. Live my spirituality.
12. Support and love my brothers and sisters.

I strongly recommend such programs as avenues of help. Your doctor can educate you about culturally sensitive organizations and will usually have literature from Alcoholics Anonymous and Narcotics Anonymous available in the office. Your doctor probably also knows about reliable rehabilitation and treatment centers for quick referrals. Your doctor can also help you after detoxification by talking with you about your progress or about any problems that come up.

Bipolar Disorder

Bipolar disorder, also known as "manic depression," is a mental illness involving episodes of serious mania and depression. These days, most of us know someone whose moods swing from overly high and irritable to sad and hopeless, and then back again, with periods of normal mood in between.

Bipolar disorder typically begins in adolescence or early adulthood and continues throughout life. It is often not recognized as an illness, and people who have it may suffer needlessly for years or even decades.

They don't have to. Effective treatments are available that can often prevent the devastating complications of bipolar disorder—marital breakups, job loss, alcohol and drug abuse, suicide—and greatly ease the suffering it causes.

Marked changes in a person's emotions can confuse doctors, family members, and spouses. Spot observations and diagnosis are difficult. By observing someone over time, however, mood changes become easy to identify, and sometimes even follow a predictable pattern.

In some cases, manic episodes can resemble schizophrenic psychosis. The person may be out of touch with reality, and out of control. In some cases, manic episodes are triggered by addiction.

People with bipolar disorder are usually young, between twenty and thirty years of age, but the disorder can also occur in middle age as well. The cause of bipolar disorder is unknown.

Symptoms of Bipolar Disorder

Bipolar disorder involves cycles of mania and depression. Signs and symptoms of mania include periods of:

- Increased energy, activity, restlessness, racing thoughts, and rapid talking
- Excessive "high" or euphoric feelings
- Extreme irritability and distractibility
- Decreased need for sleep
- Unrealistic beliefs in one's abilities and powers
- Uncharacteristically poor judgment
- A sustained period of behavior that is different from usual
- Increased sexual drive
- Abuse of drugs, particularly cocaine, alcohol, and sleeping medications
- Provocative, intrusive, or aggressive behavior
- Denial that anything is wrong

Treatment

Prior to any specific therapy, an adequate medical workup is necessary to rule out any underlying medical dysfunction. Manic or psychotic features can be treated with medication, just as with schizophrenia. Lithium therapy is usually the drug of choice. Patient education, therapy, and support groups can also be helpful. Prognosis depends on the frequency of episodes of highs and lows. Currently, only fifteen percent of patients improve, usually with the help of Lithium compounds (Lithobid®), or other medications.

A person with bipolar disorder should be under the care of a psychiatrist skilled in the diagnosis and treatment of this disease. Help can be found at:

- University-or medical school-affiliated programs
- Hospital departments of psychiatry
- Private psychiatric offices and clinics
- Offices of family physicians, internists, and pediatricians

People with bipolar disorder need strong encouragement from family and friends to seek treatment. The family doctor can make the referral. If the patient will not seek help, loved ones must take him or her for proper mental health evaluation and treatment. That can be done without making the patient feel threatened if it is done with kindness. Do what you can to explain to the patient what kind of treatment he or she can expect. Try to convince the patient, without bullying, to recognize that he or she must take steps to restore his or her own mental health. Armed with that knowledge and with love, the family can often convince the person of the need to see a psychologist who can evaluate the condition and recommend treatment if needed.

A person in the midst of a severe episode may have to be committed to a hospital for his or her own protection and much needed treatment. Anyone who is considering suicide needs immediate attention, preferably from a mental health professional or a physician. School counselors and members of the clergy can also help detect suicidal tendencies and make a referral for more definitive assessment or treatment. With appropriate help and treatment, it is possible for a person to overcome suicidal tendencies.

It is important for people to understand that bipolar disorder will not go away, and that continued compliance with treatment is necessary to keep the disease under control. The patient needs ongoing encouragement and support after treatment because it may take a while to discover what forms of therapy work best.

Chapter 17

Spirituality and Good Health

S pirituality, as I'm using the term, is a force that helps integrate the personality so that the inner self emerges and begins to take charge. Some people cultivate spirituality by going to church, others by meditation and self-reflection.

Spiritual searching of the inner self does not mean that the searcher lacks real faith, and having faith doesn't mean we have all the answers. Read the *Book of Job* or the *Psalms* to be reminded that faith means asking hard questions—that is, searching for a more intense understanding of divinity.

By soothing internal conflicts, spiritual practice makes you more calm, sensitive, and compassionate. Such practice can refer to "direct" relationship with God or a higher power, or it can be a form of self-reflection, free of external attachments, that draws your consciousness inward toward some deeper core of yourself. In either case, a key benefit of practice is the feeling of well-being that comes out of acknowledging and surrendering to a power greater than yourself.

Such spiritual practice is like prayer, but without desiring or effort. Unlike a prayer that asks for good health, safety, or success or that confesses something verbally, self-reflective spirituality requires you to do nothing but concentrate on your own inner peacefulness and calm. The state you experience is a quiet personal communion that leads to a deeper understanding of yourself. And, while you're gaining that understanding, you will also gain a deeper sense of "your higher power"—that is, the force or principle or spirit that you hold yourself in account to. You'll find that regular spiritual practice will allow you to you look at the world, the people around you, and yourself, with a new love and compassion.

REFOCUSING FOR BETTER SPIRITUAL HEALTH

Changes in routine take an investment, including time, and if you're like most of us, you probably feel that you already don't have enough time to keep up with all your obligations. Maybe you're married with children and working. Maybe you've got a new job that's causing some stress and requiring a lot of your attention. We all know there are a hundred ways of being too busy.

Think of it this way: by taking time to find your spirituality you'll cope better with the stress of giving to other people, and you'll have more to give, both to them and to yourself. Sometimes, just by giving so much, we become drained, unmotivated, and fatigued. In that kind of state, we may feel that we're buried under our responsibilities, and suffocating. Sometimes, in that state, we say, "Well, I'm powerless, I'll just leave it to God."

I'm not saying that we shouldn't put our trust in God, only that, as the familiar saying tells us, God helps those who help themselves. We help ourselves by spiritual practice that gives us some moments of peace and quiet, free of our ordinary responsibilities and worries. Here we will find a pool we can return to daily, where we can bathe and be renewed by feeling the calm that lets us bear our earthly tribulations and that can restore us to energy and joy.

Most people who meditate daily find they are better able to focus on what's good in their lives and in the people around them. By becoming more comfortable with themselves and treating themselves with kindness, they also become more ready to treat others with that same kindness we call compassion.

Many of the patients who come in to see me pray, believe strongly in God, and have strong spiritual roots. Religion and spirituality were *all* that African slaves had to hold on to, and experiencing life in that way gave them the strength to survive. But often in the process, spirituality came to mean leaving *all* the care and management of their bodies to God, without taking on any of the responsibility themselves. But though faith can move mountains, you also have to bring your shovel. As we are reminded in *First Corinthians*: "The body is your temple. Love and nourish it as you would your love for me." You can help do that by giving daily attention to your spirit and, in this way, getting to know your higher self.

THE STAGES OF SELF-REFLECTION

Here are steps to take on the way to finding your higher self:

- *Awareness:* When you feel irritated, bored, angry, fearful, or excited, pay strict attention to your prejudices and motives. Try to see the reasons you feel as you do, without judging those reasons as good or bad.
- *Reflection:* Reflect on what is happening to your life and whether your priorities are clear to you. Do you feel that you're being pushed, or dragged, around by circumstances and not in control of your life? Think about what's working and what isn't working. Where personal relations are the problem, work on setting boundaries so that the other person doesn't control your life.
- *Self-Transformation:* Undertake a program to change circumstances or behaviors that aren't in keeping with your deepest values. For example, if you feel trapped in a bad relationship, or a bad job, be ready now to make the necessary changes. If you know that some bad habits are destroying your health, decide now to remove those habits from your life.
- *Daily Deepening:* This is the formal meditation component of self-reflection. Give yourself at least twenty minutes each day to calm yourself down and become more deeply aware of what you need and want. In this way, you will begin to be comfortable with your innermost consciousness.

HOW TO MEDITATE

Find a place for privacy. Sit comfortably on a chair or on the floor with a soft cushion to support you. Keep your back straight. You may close your eyes or keep them half open, with a "soft focus" on a spot a few feet in front of you.

Start your meditation by relaxing your entire body. Be aware of any tension in your head, neck, shoulders, arms, body, legs, and feet. Breathe evenly, and, as you breathe out, concentrate on the feeling you get when you become more relaxed.

Be aware of any emotional tension, and let it go. You may picture a white light flowing through your entire body that harmonizes your feelings. Sometimes, a good way to let tension go is by concentrating your thought on it. After a while, the tension will soften and go away.

Be aware of your thoughts, and let them settle down naturally. (This part may take many sessions before you can master it. You are trying to discipline a mind that may have been undisciplined for many years.)

Use an image, a sound, or a point in your head as an anchor for your attention. You may count your breaths: one when you inhale, two when you exhale, three when you inhale, and so forth (counting helps you become focused and helps you come back to your meditation if you are distracted by your thoughts)

As your thoughts stabilize, let your mind wander to an infinite, relaxed, and timeless place, and let your ego fade. Stay in silence. Meditation is the gateway to self- realization, which is the gateway to exploration of the divine.

As you come out of meditation, slowly become aware of your mind, your emotional state, and your physical body. End with thoughts of benevolence and peace toward the people in your home, workplace, community, nation, and world. Reaffirm your willingness to help alleviate the suffering of humankind and become a selfless instrument for unity and goodwill.

Be patient. Try meditation for at least three weeks, do not jump around within the steps, and be sure to adhere to the sequence during the relaxation period. Through meditation and self-reflection, you will find strength and focus to meet life's challenges effectively, to develop your potential much more fully, and to discover a happier and more meaningful life.

Part V
Prevention:
Nutrition and Exercise

Chapter 18

Nutrition

Good nutrition is the cornerstone to building and sustaining a healthy and disease-free life. Once you know what your body needs and what hurts it, you'll find it easy to nourish yourself and your family with food that helps keep all of you healthy and strong. It's just a matter of learning the simple ABCs.

> Good nutrition is the cornerstone to building and sustaining a healthy and disease-free life.

The ABCs of Nutrition

Carbohydrates

Carbohydrates are the primary source of energy for our bodies. The body breaks down starches (for example, corn, wheat, and potatoes) and sugars into glucose, which the body needs for metabolism, brain and nerve function, blood sugar regulation, and energy production.

Carbohydrates may be classified as simple or complex. The more complex they are, the better they are for you.

- ***Simple Carbohydrates:*** Sugars are the simplest of carbohydrates. Glucose, sucrose, lactose, and fructose are examples of simple carbohydrates. Glucose is usually rapidly absorbed and utilized by the body, but sucrose, fructose, and lactose are more slowly utilized, because they have a slightly different structure.
- ***Complex carbohydrates:*** The complex carbohydrates—starch, cellulose, and glycogen—are rapidly absorbed and metabolized. Examples of high starch products are corn, wheat, and potatoes.

Often patients mistakenly feel that all carbohydrates are fattening, which is not true. Vegetables, fruits, legumes, and whole grains like brown rice are carbohydrates that provide energy with little or no fat.

Simple sugars, such as candy, should be avoided. Fruit, however, is a simple sugar that is good to eat, so long as it is not eaten in excess.

In a healthy diet, carbohydrates should make up forty percent of each meal.

Fiber

The structural components of plants are called fiber. Fiber resists rapid digestion in the intestinal tract. Fiber helps to protect you from some types of cancer. That's why it makes sense to eat plenty of vegetables, especially raw ones.

Protein

The major function of protein (which the body turns into amino acids) is building and maintaining muscles, tendons, ligaments, the circulatory system, brain, organs, the immune system, and skin. Because cells are continually sloughed off, protein must be replaced continually. If it is not, tissues will break down. The consumption of protein helps the body produce enzymes, hormones, and antibodies, and helps balance fluids within the body.

Meats, fish, chicken, and turkey are good sources of protein. Choose lean meats such as flank steak, chicken, turkey, and fish. They are better for your health. Protein can also come from milk, eggs, legumes, grains, and vegetables.

People who do not consume enough protein will have muscle wasting, obesity, bad skin, bad hair, fatty livers, and edema. The best way to get protein is in servings of 50–60 grams a day, taken over four meals. Eating an adequate amount of protein and exercising regularly, particularly with weight training, reduces body fat.

Fats

Fat is the primary form of stored energy in the body. It provides more than twice as much energy as the same amount of stored carbohydrate. If it were not for fat, we would have to eat constantly to meet our energy needs. Fat also helps maintain cell and tissue structure, insulates from the cold, cushions internal organs, and protects these organs from trauma. Fats are even necessary for the absorption of vitamins A, D, E, and K.

> Too much fat in the diet, in the form of triglycerides and cholesterol, causes obesity, heart disease, cancer, and diabetes.

While we need fat in order to stay alive, most of us get much more than we need. Too much fat in the diet, in the form of triglycerides and cholesterol, causes obesity, heart disease, cancer, and diabetes.

Fats can be saturated or unsaturated. People should avoid saturated fats, such as animal fats. Unsaturated fats, like those found in fish oils and canola and olive oils, are healthy.

In a healthy diet, fat should make up thirty percent or less of each meal. For maintenance of a healthy body weight, fat composition should be less than twenty-three percent.

Vitamins

Vitamins, essential for life, are found in food. They do not provide the body with energy, but rather help it digest, absorb, and metabolize nutrients. There are thirteen vitamins, each playing its own special role in making a body healthy:

Vitamin A

- Vitamin A aids vision and helps prevent night blindness, maintains the health of tissues (especially the skin), strengthens the immune system, and promotes bone growth.
- Children who have don't get enough vitamin A do not grow properly. At the same time, too much vitamin A can cause birth defects, blood disorders, gastrointestinal problems, and skin dryness.

B Vitamins

- B vitamins help the body use energy. They also help the body to multiply cells and to deliver energy to all living cells. When the body doesn't get enough B vitamins, it lacks energy. The B vitamins are thiamine, riboflavin, niacin, pantothenic acid, and biotin.

Vitamin C

- Vitamin C is an antioxidant. This means that it helps the body to get rid of waste products that could be poisonous. Vitamin C is often used to treat colds, but why it works is still unknown. Vitamin C also assists the B vitamins by helping the body utilize energy from the major nutrients. Vitamin C deficiency can cause bleeding gums and scurvy, a disease that causes bone abnormalities in children. Lack of vitamin C also causes poor wound healing.

Vitamin D

- Vitamin D is unique because the body, with the help of sunlight, can make it. Because the liver and kidneys help produce vitamin D, people with bad kidneys and livers will also tend to have vitamin D deficiency. Deficiencies of vitamin D can cause rickets, a bone disease that primarily afflicts children, and osteomalacia, a similar disease that softens the bones of adults, particularly women. Too much vitamin D may lead to high calcium levels in the blood and stone formation in organs and tissues.

Vitamin E

- Vitamin E is the body's chief antioxidant. By preventing lipids from oxidizing and forming plaques on blood vessel walls, it helps you avoid blood vessel problems that can lead to heart disease. Vitamin E is essential to the lives of cells. Deficiency of vitamin E can cause red blood cells to break up lead to damage to the nervous system. Vitamin E may also play a role in preventing fibrocystitic breast disease. High doses of vitamin E (over 899 mg) can cause problems with blood clotting.

Vitamin K

- Vitamin K helps blood clotting; deficiencies can cause bleeding. Patients who take the blood thinners warfarin or coumadin and who have bleeding problems often have to be given vitamin K intravenously so that their blood will clot.

Minerals

Minerals are elements necessary to the bones, teeth, and the body fluids. Minerals like calcium are necessary to sustain body structure, while chromium can aid in glucose metabolism and can be of benefit to diabetics. Minerals can be found in fruits and vegetables and as supplements in multivitamin tablets.

Water

Most people do not drink enough water. If you're physically active, try to drink at least a gallon a day, most of it during the normal workday. Everyone should drink at least eight glasses (8–ounces) of water a day. Water is the main ingredient of almost every tissue in the body. It is also necessary to the crucial activities of the body, like digestion, excretion, and absorption.

The body's metabolism itself generates some water, which assists in the transportation of vital materials to cells. Water also helps remove waste products from the cells and carry them out of the body.

Chapter 19

Physical Fitness

Your family doctor will want to know how much physical activity you do each day and may make recommendations to improve your exercise routine. Regular physical activity can help the human body maintain, repair, and improve itself to an amazing degree. Even older people with illnesses or disabilities can take part in moderate exercise programs. People who exercise regularly are less likely to suffer fractures or other accidents. It stands to reason, for example, that if your body is in good condition, you're less likely to fall.

Exercise must become one of those things that you do without question, like bathing and brushing your teeth. When you're first starting, the trick is patience. Don't try too much too soon, and don't quit before you have a chance to experience the rewards of improved fitness. You can't gain in a few days or weeks what you have lost by years of sedentary living, but you can become fit if you persevere.

THE BENEFITS OF EXERCISING

- Strengthens your heart and lungs
- Lowers your blood pressure

- Helps protect against the start of adult-onset diabetes
- Can strengthen your bones, slowing down the process of osteoporosis
- Helps you move about more easily by keeping joints, tendons, and ligaments more flexible
- Helps you lose weight (when combined with good eating habits) or maintain ideal weight, by burning excess calories and by helping to control your appetite
- Improves your appearance and self-confidence
- Gives you energy to keep socially active, which is good for your mental health
- Helps you sleep better
- Promotes a sense of well-being
- Improves digestion

KINDS OF EXERCISE

The most beneficial form of exercise is "aerobic"—exercise that makes the heart and lungs work hard and steadily to supply oxygen to the muscles. Over time, aerobic exercise increases the efficiency of the cardiovascular system. That means it not only helps you to feel better, but it also helps you to live longer.

Common aerobic exercises are brisk walking, swimming, jogging, bicycling, cross-country skiing, folk dancing, modified aerobic dancing, calisthenics, and yoga.

People who have kept in good condition may be able to participate in a wider range of exercise activities. Just tailor your program to fit your own level of ability and special needs. For example, jogging is not for everyone and may be dangerous for those who have unsuspected heart disease or joint problems.

EXERCISE PROGRAMS

An exercise program works best when you've designed it around activities you like. Depending on your temperament, you can decide whether you want to join a group, exercise with a friend, or exercise

alone. If you exercise alone, tell someone of your schedule and plans in case you need assistance.

Some people love working out in gyms or with groups elsewhere. Others prefer to take walks outdoors or ride bicycles. Some exercise in the morning, others in the afternoon or even in the evening. Whatever kind of program you choose, make your exercise program part of your daily routine.

Most communities have centers where people can join exercise classes and other recreational programs. Find out about fitness programs at a local church or synagogue, civic center, community college, park or recreation association, senior citizens' center, or check the yellow pages in your telephone directory under *Exercise*.

> Most communities have centers where people can join exercise classes and other recreational programs.

If you are convinced that regular exercise is not for you, try to stay active in other ways. Activities such as bowling, nature walks, arts and crafts, card and table games, gardening, and community projects will not offer all the benefits of regular, moderate exercise, but they will help you remain active, possibly adding years to your life.

PULLING IT ALL TOGETHER

Physical fitness can pull everything together in a strong and surprising way. Besides making you stronger and making you feel good, with more energy, exercise is one of the best relievers of stress. That's why it's so important to "just do it." This is a magic that really works.

Here are suggestions that will make your personal program a success:

- Make time for yourself, like making an appointment
- Keep a daily journal
- Connect with other men or women who have the same goals
- Talk to a friend or life partner about your plan

MOTIVATING YOURSELF TO EXERCISE

At first, exercise seems a lot like work. Be easy on yourself. Maybe you've spent a lot of time letting yourself get into bad physical shape. Be willing to spend a little time getting back into good shape. If you begin slowly, you will notice increased energy and strength in a short time, say, three weeks or a month—that is, as long as you keep at it regularly, at least three times a week, and, ideally, more. Even during those days that you don't schedule your program, you'll find yourself wanting to do something to keep yourself physically active. Your body will be hungry for that good feeling it gets from *working*.

Of course, it takes energy to change, and most of us, when we're first thinking about changes in our lifestyles, have a lot of resistance. We think it's going to be too much work, or that we won't be up to it, and it will feel like just another defeat. A negative attitude creates negative energy, and it is a fact that if you really think you can't, you won't. Your mental and spiritual self can't grow with an "I can't" body and will.

Getting into a routine is a little like trying on clothes—you put on this and that and you look at yourself in the mirror, to see if this is something you're going to enjoy wearing. With a routine, in the beginning, you're a beginner. Being a beginner means trying it out. If you're lifting weights, start with really light ones, and get some instruction. If you've decided to walk, start off walking to the corner and back, where you ordinarily drive. After a week of that you might want to go around the block a few times. Later, who knows where you might want to go.

Go to a local YMCA or community center or anywhere else nearby that can help you get started. If you want to get into some form of group exercise, such places provide programs.

I've seen it work hundreds of times: physical fitness is the foundation for a sense of well-being. A fit, healthy body houses a healthy mind and spirit that will create energy, hope, and direction. Accomplishing your goals will be easier when you exercise. The beautiful thing about exercise is that, at any level, you can set small, achievable goals, so that each time you reach one you will feel a sense of real accomplishment. Such experiences give you a better sense of self and purpose.

COMMON EXCUSES NOT TO EXERCISE

I've heard all the excuses, and you have, too. Maybe there have been times when you've used one of them as a reason for not exercising:

- My hair will get messed up.
- By the time I get out of work I'm beat, and I'd have to get up three hours early to do it in the morning.
- I am embarrassed to go to a gym looking like this, so out of shape.
- It's too expensive.
- I don't want to grow muscles like those women in the magazines who look like men.
- My man likes big women.
- I have to work all of the time and provide for my family.
- My family keeps me too busy.
- I am too tired to exercise.

Get past the excuse phase. Do something positive for yourself, something that, for millions of people, has led to better health and greater happiness.

JUST DOING IT

Your doctor will tell you if you should restrict your exercise routine because of the condition of your health. Even if this is the case, your doctor can probably help you work out an exercise program that's right for you. It's just a case of finding what's right for you, whatever your condition. Cost doesn't have to be an obstacle. Most insurance companies reimburse you for gym memberships. Even if you don't have such insurance, you can find exercise programs that don't cost anything.

Some women are afraid that if they exercise they will look like the female weightlifters you see in magazines. Don't worry. These women spend much more time at it than you will need to in order to stay healthy and fit. For most of us, regular exercise in a gym simply means a kind of toning. You can work out without losing softness in the right places.

If you feel that you haven't time to go to a gym, or prefer to exercise without people around you, work out at home. The thing is, recognize reasons like those I listed for what they are: excuses. What you want from yourself is not excuses but action—action that means a healthier, more energized, and longer life to do all the things you want to do for yourself and for those you love.

Once you get to a gym, if that's where you decide to exercise, you'll find all kinds of bodies—fat ones and skinny ones, athletic ones and others, maybe like yours, that aren't so athletic. Remember that what's respected above all in a gym is steadiness and effort. People don't care about how you look but about the growing determination and energy that you give to and take from your routine.

Exercise may tire you at first, but before long, you'll find that it gives far more than it takes. You will enjoy your new energy so much that you'll be more and more eager to do what it takes to get it. Being energized keeps you motivated and excited.

A lot of people make exercise more fun by exercising with a friend or family member. Some people recruit neighbors, and pretty soon they're exercising with a team. A team effort is a good way to stay motivated.

BENEFITS OF EXERCISE

For children as well as for adults, regular exercise means:

- Decreased depression and improved self-esteem
- Improved nutritional health
- Reduction of body fat
- Increased bone density
- Improved lung capacity, especially in patients with asthma
- Lowered risk for diabetes
- Stronger immune system to fight infection and disease such as cancers
- A longer life and a better quality of life
- More energy and improved thinking

Just do it.

Part VI
Helping Ourselves and Helping Each Other

Chapter 20

Organ Transplantation and Donation: Cultural Issues

H ypertension, renal disease, and diabetes are among the most common chronic diseases in the African–American population. When these diseases are left unchecked, or are diagnosed late and perhaps treated less effectively by a health care system that is not always sensitive to the special needs of African American patients, major organs fail.

From a public health perspective, an increased rate of organ failure means an increased demand for donor organs. Unfortunately, because viable (living) and cadaveric (no longer alive) African–American organ donors are in short supply, many African Americans who need organs won't be able to get them and will die. Successful transplants depend on close genetic matching, and race can play a role here. (For more on this subject, see below: "Transplant Problems Specific to African Americans.")

THE HEALTH CARE SYSTEM

The health care system is broken and in need of repair, especially when it comes to serving the health needs of African Americans, and it's important for us to understand this situation if we wish to improve the health of our community. Poor African Americans can't expect good health care. African Americans living in rural areas of the U.S. have limited access to doctors. Even African Americans who can afford to pay for health care are likely to run into prejudice, sometimes in the form of culturally insensitive, hasty, and careless diagnoses.

Many African Americans have paranoid feelings toward the health care system. These feelings are captured in a statement made by one of my patients, Ms. Brown, a sixty-year-old African American grandmother: "You can't trust them doctors." It's hard to fault her. Didn't the health care system first create this mistrust in the minds of many African American people? Didn't research improprieties, such as the Tuskegee Experiment, leave us with a bitter skepticism towards medical and scientific institutions?

SHARED RESPONSIBILITY

Having said that, the truth remains that African Americans must also share responsibility for our own health care. Few African Americans, especially in inner-city communities, know much about organ transplants or about how they save lives. And some believe that donating organs is in direct conflict with religious beliefs.

LEARNING THE FACTS ABOUT ORGAN TRANSPLANTATION

Since the inception of the organ transplantation registry in the U.S. in 1954, there have been fewer African–American organ donors than donors from other population groups. At the same time, the gap between donors and patients in the general population has steadily widened. Today, some 82,000 people await transplantation organs, and many of them die because of the shortage. African Americans are especially vulnerable to disease that may require organ transplants.

Thirty percent of all patients on dialysis are African Americans. Almost thirty percent of all patients with end-stage renal disease, who will eventually require dialysis, and of patients waiting for kidney transplants, are African Americans.

TRANSPLANT PROBLEMS SPECIFIC TO AFRICAN AMERICANS

Studies have identified certain genetic patterns in African Americans that differ from genetic patterns in White Americans. Genetic match-ups between organ donors and recipients of the same race lessen the likelihood of complications or even death as a result of the transplantation. The fact that African Americans do poorly after organ transplantation is probably due to genetic incompatibilities between White–American donors and African–American recipients.

WHY AFRICAN AMERICANS DON'T DONATE ORGANS

Why is it that only eleven percent of African Americans donate organs compared to thirty percent of White Americans? In 1982, the Howard University Hospital Transplant Center in Washington, DC conducted an in-depth study to identify problems in the African American community that limit participation in organ transplant programs. The study showed that in Washington, DC, with a seventy percent African–American population, eighty percent of donated cadaver organs were non-African American. Though the study focused only on kidney transplants, it identified these factors as helping to account for the shortage of African Americans willing to donate organs:

- Lack of information and knowledge about programs
- Religious beliefs and misperceptions
- Distrust of the medical community
- Limited access to medical care
- Negative reactions to White American organ procurement specialists

Some African Americans who would be willing to donate organs don't do so because they believe their organs will benefit only White American recipients.

The Howard study revealed several additional points. Many African Americans felt that the body should be kept intact for "life after death." They feared that if they carried a donor card and were treated at an inner-city clinic or emergency room, they might not receive proper care because doctors would be eager to pluck out their organs and give them to someone else. This skepticism about and fear of the White medical establishment has been caused by studies like the one conducted at Tuskegee, involving experiments conducted on unknowing African Americans many years ago.

As to the fear of White organ procurement specialists, just as African-Americans are reluctant to talk to them, perhaps these specialists also have problems talking to African Americans, especially during emotional and tragic times. Only five percent of organ procurement specialists are African American.

SUGGESTIONS FOR CHANGE

- Talk to a culturally sensitive family doctor about organ transplantation and get more information. You can also contact your local hospital for additional information. Teaching hospitals are especially receptive to organ donation.
- Organ procurement organizations must encourage African–American donation in a culturally sensitive way.
- Outreach to African–American communities by federal and local government and the medical establishment must provide information to dispel the myths associated with organ donation.

Chapter 21

Hospice and African Americans

'd seen something of the good work of Hospice when I visited patients who were dying. Patients on the regular wards were often surrounded by an atmosphere of gloom and doom. But when I visited dying patients on the Hospice ward, I'd find my patients surrounded by cheerful and loving staff who did everything they could to meet the patient's emotional as well as their physical needs and to bring calm and comfort to the loved ones as well.

When my own sister lay dying she was in Hospice care, and on the day she died my mood was gloomy. One of the Hospice staff noticed me, and soon I was in their family room, surrounded by several Hospice staff members. In that safe place, I let out the pain and grief I felt, and the kindness and understanding they showed me was overwhelming.

That was when I then realized what Hospice is all about. Hospice supports the natural dying process with respect and dignity. The emotional support they gave me was part of the genuine commitment they have for their patients.

WHAT IS HOSPICE CARE?

Hospice is a federally funded organization that consists of a team of doctors, nurses, lay staff, and volunteers who are skilled in pain management, symptom control, and bereavement assistance. Hospice services are a Medicare benefit and are offered to the dying person, family, and loved ones. Hospice staff makes the dying patient more comfortable with up-to-date supportive and palliative measures. ("Palliative" means "affording relief.") These services can be given at the hospital, in the patient's home, or in a nursing home. A recent Gallup poll showed that eighty-five percent of people would prefer to be in their homes with loved ones if they were terminally ill.

ELIGIBILITY CRITERIA FOR HOSPICE CARE

For you to get Medicare coverage for Hospice, your doctor must certify that the patient's expected prognosis is six months or less of life. Other criteria for eligibility include:

- Advanced dementia—meaning the patient cannot care for him- or herself or make decisions, and the need for feeding tubes or CPR is imminent
- Medical conditions of sufficient severity to require medical care within the past year
- Inability to walk without assistance
- Inability to dress or bathe properly without assistance
- Incontinence
- Inability to speak or communicate meaningfully

FAMILY CONCERNS WHEN A LOVED ONE IS ILL

Many African–American families overburden themselves with the care of the dying. The results can be devastating. Many people:

- Quit their jobs
- Become severally emotionally stressed

- Experience new economic pressures, especially when they have no health insurance
- Isolate themselves from social support
- Feel guilt that they may somehow have contributed to the illness
- Become fearful of the dying process

THE DYING PROCESS

In the final moments of dying, physical systems shut down. The process is predictable: fluid and food intake and urine output decrease, active consciousness is replaced by increased sleep patterns, and, as respiration decreases, it also becomes more labored.

The dying person becomes restless, begins to withdraw, and may no longer communicate clearly with loved ones. The dying person's disorientation at the time of last good-byes is very difficult for family and loved ones.

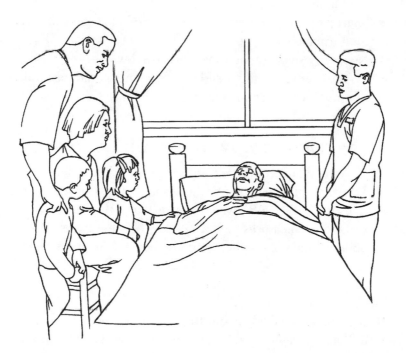

HOSPICE AND BEREAVEMENT

Hospice services don't end with the person's death. Hospice is also invaluable to bereaved families afterwards, by offering them comfort and guidance in the grief process itself, for a period as long as a year after the death.

SERVICES PROVIDED BY HOSPICE

Here is a complete list of services offered by the Medicare Hospice Benefit Organization:

- Visits by the multidisciplinary team to hospitals (Hospice may sometimes have their own wards or hospital floors), homes, and nursing homes
- Rental or purchase of durable medical equipment
- Payment for supplies ordered by the Hospice team
- Payment for drugs used in palliative care (in some instances, the family pays a minimal co-payment)
- Shared management with the doctor of all aspects of care for the terminally ill patient
- Necessary social services by staff social workers
- Counseling for dietary needs, bereavement, and pastoral care
- Physical, occupational, and speech therapy

PREPARING ADVANCED DIRECTIVES

Before they are ill, many people prepare advanced directives so hospitals and doctors will know their wishes. Some directives may indicate, "Do not resuscitate" (DNR), which means that if the patient becomes severely ill, heroic measures such as feeding or other tubes, or ventilation support should not be offered by the hospital or doctors.

The Living Will

The living will is a legal document that lists what you want done if you are so ill that you cannot speak for yourself. The document also provides information about assets and liabilities, specifies what course of action should be taken upon your death, and designates the person you want to represent you. Ask your doctor about the living will.

Organ Donation

If you want to donate your body to medical science, you must have all documents prepared and agreed upon by your family before the time of your death. Hospice can help you prepare these documents. (See the Chapter 20, "Organ Transplantation and Donation: Cultural Issues," for more information.)

In times of need, your doctor can put you in touch with your local Hospice.

Appendix I

Minority Health Resources

FEDERAL OFFICES

1. The Office of Minority Health Resource Center
   P.O. Box 37337
   Washington, DC 20013–7337
   1–800–444–6472
   The Office of Minority Health Resource Center can provide
   information resources on minority health. Documents from
   the center are free and can be obtained by calling the number
   listed above. Information can be obtained in English,
   Spanish, and Chinese.

2. Centers for Disease Control and Prevention (CDC)
   1600 Clifton Road, NE, Mail Stop D39
   Atlanta, GA 30333
   1–800–311–3435

3. Food and Drug Administration (FDA)
   Executive Director of Special Health Programs
   Office of Consumer Affairs
   Parklawn Building, Room 16–85

5600 Fishers Lane
Rockville, MD 20857
1–888–463–6332

4. National Institutes of Health (NIH)
Associate Director for Minority Programs
NIH Bldg. 31, Room 260
9000 Rockville Pike
Bethesda, MD 20892
FAX: 301–402–2517

5. **Substance Abuse and Mental Health Services
Administration**
Associate Administrator for Minority Concerns
Rockwall II, Room 9D-18
5600 Fishers Lane
Rockville, MD 20857
Substance Abuse: 301–443–0365
Mental Health: 301–443–1001

TEN US REGIONS OF THE PUBLIC HEALTH SERVICE: CONTACT THE OFFICE NEAREST TO YOU

1. **Public Health Service Region I**
Regional Program Consultant for Minority Health
John F. Kennedy Federal Building, Room 1826
Boston, MA 02203
617–565–1505
States: CT, MA, ME, NH, RI and VT

2. **Public Health Service Region II**
Regional Program Consultant for Minority Health
26 Federal Plaza, Room 3337
New York, NY 10278
212–264–1324
States: NJ, NY, PR and US Virgin Islands

3. **Public Health Service Region III**
Regional Minority Health Consultant
P.O. Box 13716, Mail Stop 14
3535 Market Street, Room 10200
Philadelphia, PA 19104
215–596–0487
States: DE, DC, MD, PA, VA, WV

4. **Public Health Service Region IV**
Regional Minority Health Consultant
101 Marietta Tower, Suite 1106
Atlanta, GA 30323
404–331–5917
States: AL, FL, GA, KY, MS, NC, SC, TN

5. **Public Health Service Region V**
Regional Minority Health Consultant
105 West Adams Street, Seventeenth Floor
Chicago, IL 60603
312–353–0718
States: IL, IN, MI, MN, OH, WI

6. **Public Health Service Region VI**
Regional Minority Health Consultant
1200 Main Tower Building, Room 1800
Dallas, TX 75202
214–767–3871
States: AR, LA, NM, OK, TX

7. **Public Health Service Region VII**
Regional Minority Health Consultant
601 East Twelfth Street, Room 501
Kansas City, MO 64106
816–426–2178
States : IA, KS, MO, NE

8. **Public Health Service Region VIII**
   Regional Minority Health Consultant
   1961 Stout Street, Room 498
   Denver, CO 80294
   303–844–2019
   States: CO, MT, ND, SD, UT, WV

9. **Public Health Service Region IX**
   Regional Minority Health Consultant
   50 United Nations Plaza, Room 327
   San Francisco, CA 94102
   415–556–3436
   States: AZ, CA, HI, NV, American Samoa, Guam, and Trust
   Territories of the Pacific Islands

10. **Public Health Service Region X**
    Regional Program Consultant for Minority Health
    2201 Sixth Avenue, Mail Stop RX-20
    Seattle, WA 98121
    206–615–2500
    States: AK, ID, OR, WA

STATE MINORITY HEALTH CONTACTS

These states have official offices for Minority Health. They are branches of the federal offices. If your state is not listed here, contact the federal office to determine your state's point of contact.

ALABAMA
Director
Minority Health Branch
Alabama Department of Public Health
11 South Union Street, Room 229
Montgomery, AL 36130–1701
205–613–5225

ARIZONA
Manager
Center for Minority Health, Room 005
Arizona Department of Health Services
1740 West Adams Street
Phoenix, AZ 85007
602–542–1025

ARKANSAS
Director
Office of Minority Health
Arkansas Department of Health
4815 West Markham Street-Slot 35
Little Rock, AR 72205
502–661–2193

CALIFORNIA
Chief
Office of Multicultural Health
California State Department of Health Services
601 North Seventh Street, MS-675
Sacramento, CA 95814
916–322–1519

DELAWARE
Minority Health Coordinator
Office of the Director
Delaware Health and Social Services
P.O. Box 637
Dover, DE 19903
302–739–4700

FLORIDA
Chairperson
Florida Commission on Minority Health
Florida A&M University

Ware-Rhaney Bldg., Room 103
Tallahassee, FL 32307
904–599–3817

GEORGIA
Director of Minority Health
Office of Policy and Planning
Division of Public Health
2 Peachtree Street, NW, Suite 203
Atlanta, GA 30302
404–657–2722

HAWAII
Administrator
Office of Hawaiian Health
State of Hawaii Department of Health
1250 Punch Bowl Street
Honolulu, HI 96813
808–586–4800

ILLINOIS
Director
Center for Minority Health
Illinois Department of Health
100 West Randolph, Suite 6–600
Chicago, IL 60601
312–814–5278

INDIANA
Director
Office of Special Populations
Indiana State Board of Health
1330 West Michigan Street, P.O. Box 1964
Indianapolis, IN 46206–1964
317–633–0100

LOUISIANA
Staff Director
Minority Health Affairs Council
State of Louisiana
Department of Health and Hospitals
P.O. Box 629
Baton Rouge, LA 70821–0629
504–342–9500

MASSACHUSETTS
Director
Office of Minority Health
Department of Public Health
150 Tremont Street, Tenth Floor
Boston, MA 02111
617–727–7099

MICHIGAN
Chief
Office of Minority Health
Michigan Department of Public Health
3423 North Logan, P.O. Box 30195
Lansing, MI 48909
517–335–9287

MINNESOTA
Director
Office of Minority Health
Minnesota Department of Health
717 South East Delaware Street
P.O. Box 9441
Minneapolis, MN 55440
612–623–5794

MISSOURI
Chief

Office of Minority Health
State Department of Health
1738 East Elm Street, P.O. Box 570
Jefferson City, MO 65102
314–751–6064

NEBRASKA
Administrator
Office of Minority Health
Nebraska Department of Health
P.O. Box 95007
Lincoln, NE 86509–5007
402–471–2337

NEW JERSEY
Director
Office of Minority Health
State of New Jersey Department of Health-CN360
Trenton, NJ 08625–0369
609–292–6962

NEW YORK
Director
Office of Minority Health
New York State Department of Health
Empire State Plaza-Corning Tower, Room 1417
Albany, NY 12237–0601
518–474–2180

NORTH CAROLINA
Executive Director
Office of Minority Health
Environmental Health/Natural Resources
P.O. Box 27687
Raleigh, NC 27611–7687
919–733–7081

OHIO
Executive Director
Commission on Minority Health
77 South High Street, Suite 745
Vern Riffe Government Center
Columbus, OH 43266–0377
614–466–4000

OREGON
Manager
Minority Health Programs
Department of Human Resources
800 N.E. Oregon Street, #21
Portland, OR 97232
503–731–4582

RHODE ISLAND
Minority Health Coordinator
Office of Health Policy and Planning
Rhode Island Department of Health
Three Capitol Hill, Cannon, Room 408
Providence, RI 02908–5097
401–277–2901

SOUTH CAROLINA
Director
Office of Minority Health
Health and Environmental Control
2600 Bull Street
Columbia, SC 29201
803–734–4972

TENNESSEE
Director, Minority Health
Tennessee Department of Health
Tower 312

8th Avenue North-11th Floor
Nashville, TN 37219
615–741–7308

TEXAS
Director
Office of Minority Health
Texas Department of Health
1100 West Forty-ninth Street
Austin, TX 78756–3179
512–458–7629

UTAH
Director
Ethnic Health Project
Department of Health
288 North 1460 West
Salt Lake City, UT 84116–0660
801–538–6129

VIRGINIA
Analyst for Minority Health
Office of the Commissioner
Virginia Department of Health
1500 East Main Street, Suite 213
Richmond, VA 23219
804–786–4891

U.S. VIRGIN ISLANDS
Acting Commissioner of Health
Office of the Commissioner
Virgin Islands Department of Health
48 Sugar Estate
Charlotte Amalie
U.S. Virgin Islands 00802
340–774–0117 or 340–773–6551

FEDERAL HEALTH INFORMATION CENTERS AND CLEARINGHOUSES

Listed below are clearinghouses for more information concerning the health and welfare of African Americans. These information centers are equipped to answer questions concerning the specific topics outlined.

AGING

Alzheimer's Disease Education and Referral Center (ADEAR)
P.O. Box 8250
Silver Spring, MD 20907–8250
301–495–3311

National Elder Care Institute on Health Promotion
601 E Street, NW, Fifth Floor
Washington, DC 20049
202–434–2200

National Center on Aging Information Center
P.O. Box 8057
Gaithersburg, MD 20898–8057
800–222–2225 or 800–222–4225 (TTY)

AIDS

CDC National AIDS Clearinghouse (NAC)
P.O. Box 6003
Rockville, MD 20850
800–458–5231 or 301–251–5160

ALCOHOL, DRUGS, SUBSTANCE ABUSE

CSAP National Clearinghouse for Alcohol and Drug Information (NCADI)
P.O. Box 2345
Rockville, MD 20847
800–729–6686 or 301–468–2600

CSAP National Resource Center for Prevention of Perinatal
Substance Abuse
9302 Lee Highway
Fairfax, VA 22031
703–218–5700

ALLERGY AND INFECTIOUS DISEASES
National Institute of Allergy and Infectious Diseases (NIAID)
Building 31, Room 7A32
900 Rockville Pike
Bethesda, MD 20892
301–496–5717

ARTHRITIS
National Arthritis and Musculoskeletal and
Skin Diseases Information Clearinghouse (NAMSIC)
9000 Rockville Pike, P.O. Box AMS
Bethesda, MD 20892
301–587–4352

BLINDNESS
National Library Service for the Blind and Physically Handicapped
(NLSBPH)
Library of Congress
1291 Taylor Road, NW
Washington, DC 20542
202–707–0712

CANCER
Cancer Information Service (CIS)/ National Cancer Institute (NCI)
Building 31, Room 10A16
9000 Rockville Pike
Bethesda, MD 20892
800–422–6237 or 301–469–5583

CHILD ABUSE
National Clearinghouse on Child Abuse and Neglect and
Family Violence Information
3998 Fairridge Drive, Suite 350
Fairfax, VA 22033
800–394–3366 or 703–385–7565

CHILDREN AND YOUTH WITH HANDICAPS
National Information Center for Handicapped Children and Youth
(NICHCY)
P.O. Box 1492
Washington, DC 20013
202–884–8200

CHRONIC DISEASE PREVENTION
Center for Disease Control and Prevention
Office of Public Enquiry
1600 Clifton Road, NE
Atlanta, GA 30333
404–639–3534

CONSUMER INFORMATION
Consumer Information Center
GSA, Room G142
Eighteenth & F Streets, NW
Washington, DC 20405
202–501–1794

Consumer Product Safety Commission Hotline (CPSC)
USCPSC
Washington, DC 20207
800–638–2772
800–638–8270 (AK, HI)
800–492–8104 (MD)

DEAFNESS
National Institute on Deafness and Other
Communication Disorders Clearinghouse (NIDCD)
1 Communications Drive
Bethesda, MD 20892
800–241–1044
800–241–1055 (TTY)

DENTAL RESEARCH
National Institute of Dental Research (NIDR)
Public Information Office
Building 31, Room 2C35
9000 Rockville Pike
Bethesda, MD 20892
301–496–4261

DIABETES
National Diabetes Information Clearinghouse (NDIC)
9000 Rockville Pike, P.O. Box NDIC
Bethesda, MD 20892
301–654–3327

DIGESTIVE DISEASES
National Digestive Diseases Information Clearinghouse (NDDIC)
9000 Rockville Pike, P.O. Box NDDIC
Bethesda, MD 20892
301–654–3810

DIRLINE
(Directory of Information Resources Online)
National Library of Medicine
8600 Rockville Pike
Bethesda, MD 20894
301–480–3537
http://www.nlm.nih.gov/

DISABILITIES
Clearinghouse on Disability Information
OSERS/Department of Education
Switzer Building, Room 3132
400 Maryland Avenue, SW
Washington, DC 20202–2524
202–205–8412

EYE HEALTH
National Eye Institute (NEI)
Building 31, Room 6A32
9000 Rockville Pike
Bethesda, MD 20892
301–496–5248

FAMILY LIFE
Family Life Information Exchange (FLIE)
P.O. Box 37299
Washington, DC 20013–7299
301–585–6636

FOOD AND NUTRITION
Food and Nutrition Information Center (FNIC)
National Agricultural Library, Room 304
1301 Baltimore Boulevard
Beltsville, MD 20705–2351
301–504–5719

HEALTH CARE POLICY AND RESEARCH
AHCPR Publications Clearinghouse
P.O. Box 8547
Silver Springs, MD 20907–8547
9295– or 301–495–3453

HEALTH PROMOTION AND DISEASE PREVENTION
ODPHP National Health Information Center (ONHIC)

P.O. Box 1133
Washington, DC 20013–1133
800–336–4797

HEART, LUNG AND BLOOD
NHLBI Education Programs Information Center
P.O. Box 30105
Bethesda, MD 20824–0105
301–251–1222

HUMAN SERVICES
Administration for Children and Families
370 L'Enfant Promenade, SW, Sixth Floor West
Washington, DC 20447
202–401–9215

KIDNEY AND UROLOGIC DISEASES
National Kidney and Urologic Diseases Information Clearinghouse
(NKUDIC)
9000 Rockville Pike, P.O. Box NKUDIC
Bethesda, MD 20892
301–654–4415

MATERNAL AND CHILD HEALTH
National Center for Education in Maternal and Child Health
Clearinghouse 8201 Greensboro Drive, Suite 600
McLean, VA 22102
703–821–8955, Ext. 254/255

MENTAL HEALTH
National Institute of Mental Health (NIMH)
Parklawn Building, Room 7C02
5600 Fishers Lane
Rockville, MD 20857
301–443–4513

MINORITY HEALTH
Office of Minority Health Resource Center (OMH-RC)
P.O. Box 37337
Washington, DC 20013–7337
6472–   or 301–587–1938

ORGAN TRANSPLANTATION
Health Resources and Services Administration (HRSA)
Division of Organ Transplantation
Parklawn Building, Room 7–18
5600 Fishers Lane
Rockville, MD 20857
301–443–7577

PHYSICAL FITNESS
President's Council on Physical Fitness and Sports
Market Square East Building, Suite 250
701 Pennsylvania Avenue, NW
Washington, DC 20004
202–272–3430

OPINION
National Second Surgical Opinion Hotline
200 Independence Avenue, SW
Washington, DC 20201
800–638–6833

SMOKING
Office on Smoking and Health (OSH)
Centers for Disease Control and Prevention MS K-50
4770 Buford Highway, NE
Atlanta, GA 30341
404–488–5707 (Public Information Center)

NATIONAL MINORITY ORGANIZATIONS

Listed below are National Minority Organization resources.

AFRICAN AMERICAN
National Black Women's Health Project
1237 Abernathy Boulevard, SW
Atlanta, GA 30310
404–758–9590

Association of Black Psychologists
821 Kennedy, NW
Washington, DC 20011
202–347–1895

National Medical Association
1012 Tenth Street, NW
Washington, DC 20001
202–393–6870

National Urban League, Inc. (NUL)
500 East Sixty-second Street
New York, NY 10021
212–310–9000

National Association of Black Social Workers, Inc. (NABSW)
15231 West McNichols
Detroit, MI 48235
313–862–6700

National Minority Health Association
P.O. Box 11876
Harrisburg, PA 17108–1876
717–761–1323

Black Congress on Health Law and Economics
1025 Connecticut Avenue, NW, Suite 610
Washington, DC 20036
202–659–4020

Sources of Additional Health Material for African Americans
American Association of Retired Persons
1909 K Street, NW
Washington, DC 20049
202–434–2277

American Cancer Society
3340 Peachtree Road NE
Atlanta, GA 30026
800–227–2345

American Diabetes Association
National Service Center
1660 Duke Street
Alexandria, VA 22314
703–549–1500

American Heart Association National Center
7320 Greenville Avenue
Dallas, TX 75231
214–373–6300

American Lung Association
1740 Broadway
New York, NY 10019–4374
800–LUNG-USA

CDC National AIDS Clearinghouse
P.O. Box 6003
Rockville, MD 20849–6003
800–458–5231

Institute on Black Chemical Dependency
2616 Nicollet Avenue South
Minneapolis, MN 55408
612–871–7878

March of Dimes Birth Defects Foundation
1275 Mamaroneck Avenue
White Plains, NY 10605
914–428–7100

Minority AIDS Project
5149 West Jefferson Boulevard
Los Angeles, CA 90016
213–936–4949

National Association for Equal Opportunity in Higher Education
Black Higher Education Center
Lovejoy Building
400 Twelfth Street, NE
Washington, DC 20002
202–543–9111

National Black Child Development Institute, Inc.
1023 Fifteenth Street, NW
Washington, DC 20005
202–387–1281

PersonalDoc.com
http://www.personaldoc.com
Web site for G. Edmond Smith, MD, MEd

Appendix II

Glossary

Adrenal glands Glands located on top of the kidneys that provide necessary hormones to your body

Aerobic exercise Exercise in which the body is able meet the muscles' need for oxygen or "air"; these exercises include brisk walking, jogging, swimming, and cycling

AIDS (Acquired immune deficiency syndrome) When a person is no longer able to fight infections; caused by the virus known as HIV

Algorithm Special method for solving a problem

Alleviate Relieve, get rid of

Anal fissures Ulcer of the anus which causes pain with bowel movements and sometimes bleeding

Anemia Below normal number of red blood cells

Angina Heaviness or pain in your chest; usually caused lack of blood supply to your heart

Angioplasty (balloon catheter) Procedure involving small balloon is inserted into a blood vessel to help widen it

Angiotensins Medication for controlling low blood pressure

Anorexia Loss of appetite

Anoscopy Visual examination of the anus using a tube-like instrument

Anti-inflammatory Something to help stop the redness, swelling, etc. of an injury or infection

Antibodies Found in white blood cells to help fight off infections

Arrhythmia Abnormal rhythm or rate of your heart beat

Arterioles Blood vessel that branches off an artery

Arteriosclerosis Thickening of the artery walls

Arthroscopic Examination of a joint through a steel tube that contains a tiny camera

Ascites Excess fluid in the space between the two layers that line the inside of that abdominal wall and outside of the abdominal organs; can be caused from congestive heart failure, liver disease, or cancer, among other things

Aspirate 1) To breathe in or 2) medical removal of fluid from a part of the body such as the knee

Asymptomatic Without symptoms

Atherosclerosis Fatty buildup in the blood vessels

Axilla Armpit

Bacteria Germs that can be treated with antibiotics

Barium enema X-ray of the large intestines involving a fluid inserted into the rectum

Benign prostatic hypertrophy (BPH) Enlarged prostate occurring normally in males over fifty

Beta blockers Medications used in treating chest pain, high blood pressure, or irregular heart beats

Biopsy Test involving removal of sample cells and examination of them under a microscope

Bradypnea Slow breathing

Bronchioles Small branches of the air passageways leading from the windpipe to the lungs

Bronchitis Inflammation in the airways that connect the windpipe to the lungs that results in a cough

Bronchodilation Widening of the air passages

Bruits Sounds made in the heart, arteries, or veins when the blood flows at an abnormal speed

BUN Blood test that tells how your kidneys are functioning

Bursitis Pain and swelling of a small sac that is found near joints; a person may have shoulder, knee, or other joint pain

Calcium Mineral needed for the functioning of your body's cells, muscles, and nerves; it is what the teeth and bones are made of; found in food like milk, cheese, eggs, fish, green vegetables, and fruit

Capitation Fixed amount of money paid on a monthly basis to an HMO or to an individual health provider for the full medical care of a patient

Cardiovascular Relating to the heart, blood vessels (arteries and veins), and circulation

Caries Tooth decay

Carotid artery One of four arteries in the neck and head that supply the blood to the brain

Case manager Health professional (nurse, doctor, social worker) affiliated with a health plan who is responsible for coordinating the medical care of a patient enrolled in a managed care plan

CAT or CT scan Computer-aided X-ray scan that provides clearer and more detailed information than just an X-ray (C=computerized, A = axial, T= tomography)

Catheterization Procedure involving tube inserted into a part of the body; in cardiac catheterization a tube is inserted into the heart so the doctor can make a diagnosis; in urinary catheterization, a tube is inserted into the bladder to help drain the urine

Cecum Beginning of the large intestine where it is the widest; the appendix comes off of this part

Cerebral Related to the brain

Cervical spine Neck bones

Chemzyme Plus Routine blood test

Chlamydia Bacterial infection that can be transmitted sexually

Cholecystectomy Removal of the gallbladder

Cholesterol Fat found in your body; too much can lead to heart disease

Cholesterol (LDL, HDL) Types of fat; LDL is known as bad cholesterol, that can cause heart disease; HDL is known as good cholesterol, that can help prevent heart disease

Chromosomes Parts of a cell responsible for heredity and genetic information

Chronic obstructive pulmonary disease (COPD) Long-term lung disease which is a combination of bronchitis and emphysema; there is not enough airflow into or out of the lungs

Co–insurance Amount of money paid out-of- pocket by plan members for medical services; co–insurance payments usually constitute a fixed percentage of the total cost of a medical service covered by the plan, for example, if a health plan pays eighty percent of a physician's bill, the remaining twenty percent that the member pays is referred to as co–insurance

Colitis Inflammation of the colon causing diarrhea

Colon Intestines

Colonoscopy Visual examination of the colon using a long, flexible tube

Colposcopy Visual inspection of a woman's cervix (neck of the uterus) and vagina

Complete blood count

(CBC) Blood test that tells the numbers of red and white blood cells

Congenital A term meaning "present at birth"

Congestive heart failure

(CHF) Condition that occurs when the heart has a hard time pumping blood around to the rest of the body; symptoms include shortness of breath and swelling of the feet and legs; treatable with medication

Conjunctivitis Inflammation of the white of the eye that causes redness, discomfort, and a discharge; often know as "pink eye"

Co-payment Amount of money (always a flat fee) paid by plan members up front and out-of-pocket for specific medical services at the time they are rendered; most managed care co-payments are between $0–$15 per visit or per prescription

Cornea Front part of the tough outer shell of the eyeball that helps focus light rays onto retina and provides a protective cover for the eye

Coronary arteries Arteries that supply blood to the heart

Cranial nerves Group of twelve nerves that come from the brain, some of which provide the senses (vision, hearing, taste, etc.)

Creatinine Blood tests to determine kidney function

Crohn's disease A disease of the gastrointestinal tract

Cushing's disease A disorder caused by too many steroids in your blood; some symptoms are a red and round face, large trunk and small arms and legs

Cystitis Inflammation of the bladder

Depression Symptoms include: chronic sadness, appetite changes, sleep disturbances

Dermatology The study of skin diseases

Diabetes A disease marked by high blood sugar; causes excessive urination, constant thirst and hunger

Diastolic pressure Bottom number in your blood pressure; is considered high if over 90

Digital rectal exam Procedure in which physician inserts a gloved, lubricated finger into the rectum to feel for abnormalities such as an enlarged prostate or tumor

Diphtheria An uncommon disease caused by bacteria that causes a sore throat and fever and sometimes more serious complications; babies are immunized in their first year with the DPT vaccine

Diuretics Drugs that help remove excess water from the body through urination

Dyspnea Shortness of breath, difficulty breathing

Dysuria Painful urination

Echocardiogram A painless procedure that allows the doctor to get a picture of the heart and its valves and the way they are working

Ectopic pregnancy Pregnancy that develops outside of the uterus, usually in one of the fallopian tubes

Eczema An inflammation of the skin that causes itching

Edema Swelling in feet, ankles, and legs

Electrocardiogram (EKG, ECG) A record of electrical impulses of the heart that helps the doctor in diagnosing heart disorders

Emphysema A lung disease caused by cigarette smoking that causes shortness of breath

Endometriosis A condition that occurs when pieces of the lining of the uterus are found in other places; leads to heavy bleeding and sometimes pain during menstruation

Endometrium The lining of the uterus

Endoscopy Visual examination of a body cavity with a tube-like instrument

Enzymes Proteins in the blood that regulate the rate of chemical reactions in the body; measuring enzyme levels helps diagnose organ disorders

Esophagitis Inflammation of the esophagus

Esophagus The tube that takes food from your mouth to your stomach

Etiology Cause

Extrinsic asthma Asthma triggered by an allergy

Formulary Health plan's list of approved prescription medications for which it will reimburse members or pay directly

Gallstones Lumps of matter found in the gallbladder or bile ducts

Gastroesophageal reflux disease (GERD) Condition in which stomach acid backs up into the esophagus

Gastrointestinal Having to do with the stomach and intestines

Gatekeeper physician Primary care physician who directs the medical care of HMO members; HMOs require that each enrollee be assigned to a primary care physician; this physician is referred to as the "gatekeeper"

Genes Parts of the cells that you inherit from your parents; these determine your hair and eye color as well as other more complicated things that make your body function in a certain way

Gingivitis Inflammation of the gums caused by too much plaque, which contains bacteria, mucus, food particles, and other irritants

Glaucoma Condition that occurs when pressure of the fluid in the eye is too high; can be detected on routine eye examination and treated with eye drops; if not detected and treated, can lead to blindness

Glucose Sugar, the body's chief source of energy

Hamstrings Group of muscles found at the back of the thigh that help to bend the knee

Hard palate Roof of your mouth

Health maintenance organization (HMO) Health plans that contract with medical groups to provide a full range of health services for their enrollees for a fixed, prepaid, per member fee

Health plan HMO or traditional health insurance plan that covers a set range of health services

Heart valves Structures at the exit of the four heart chambers that allow the blood to flow out but not back in

Hematuria Blood in the urine

Hemoglobin A1C (HbA1c) Blood test to determine the presence of diabetes

Hemorrhagic stroke Condition that occurs when blood vessels that supply the brain rupture, causing decreased brain function or even death

Hemorrhoids Veins that stick out in the lining of the anus

Hereditary When traits and/or disorders are passed to you through your genes (see genetics)

Herniated disc A painful disorder of the spine; pain usually occurs in the lower back

Herpes An infection caused by a virus: type 1: fever blisters; type 2: genital ulcer disease

Hiatal hernia A condition in which part of the stomach goes up into the chest through an opening in the diaphragm, causing heartburn

HIV (Human immunodeficiency virus) A virus that destroys the immune system and eventually leads to AIDS

Homeostasis The way your body keeps things normal (for example, to keep your body temperature normal when it is hot out, you sweat)

Hormones Chemicals that are produced by glands or organs; these chemicals have many functions, including metabolism, growth, and sexual development

Human papilloma virus (HPV) A sexually transmitted disease in which warts form on the genital areas

Hyperglycemia A condition in which there is too much sugar in the blood

Hypertension High blood pressure

Hyperventilation Breathing too quickly

Hypoglycemia A condition in which there is too little sugar in the blood

Hypothalamus The part of the brain that regulates body temperature, breathing rate, emotions

Hypoventilation Breathing too slowly

Immune system System that protects the body from harmful infections

Immunizations Required "shots" that help prevent diseases, such as measles, mumps, tetanus

Inflammation Redness, pain, heat, swelling, or loss of function that occurs as a reaction to an injury, infection, irritation, etc.

Insulin A hormone produced by the pancreas that is used to absorb sugar in the body

iItegumentary Having to do with the skin

Intrinsic asthma Asthma triggered by stress or anxiety

Iron A mineral needed for the formation of red blood cells; good sources of iron are found in liver, eggs, fish, green leafy vegetables, and beans

Irritable Bowel Syndrome (IBS) Colon problems with abdominal pain, altered bowel movements, and bloating

Ischemia Condition in which there is not enough blood supply to an organ or tissue

Jaundice Yellowing of the skin and whites of the eyes

Laryngitis Inflammation of the voice box that leads to hoarseness

Lesion An abnormality in any part of the body; may be a wound, infection, tumor, abscess

Ligaments Elastic tissue found in joints

Lipids Fats

Lumbar spine Part of the back between the lowest pair of ribs and the top of the pelvis

Lymph nodes Glands found in places throughout the body that help in fighting infection

Lymphocytes White blood cells that fight infections

Magnesium An element needed for the formation of bones and teeth; this can be found in green leafy vegetables, nuts, whole grains, soybeans, milk, and seafood

Mammogram X-ray of the breasts used for early detection of breast cancer

Mass A large lump

Mastalgia Painful breasts

Measles A disease caused by a virus that causes rash and fever; not seen very often now because of required measles immunization

Medicaid Federal/state health insurance program for low-income Americans; Medicaid also foots the bill for nursing home care for the indigent elderly

Medicare Federal health insurance program for older Americans and the disabled

Metabolic disorders A disorder caused by a defect in a gene or too much or too little of a hormone; diabetes and Cushing's disease are two examples of metabolic disorders

Metabolism Chemical processes that take place in your body—as, for example, burning up of sugar to make energy

Metastatic disease A tumor that has spread to another place in the body

Mortality Death rate (usually the number of deaths per 100,000)

MRI (Magnetic Resonance Imaging) While the patient lies inside a big cylinder, images of the blood vessels and internal organs are produced by magnetic and radio waves

Mucosa Soft, pink, skin-like layer that lines parts of the body - like throat, eyelids, and urinary tract

Murmur An abnormal sound of the blood flowing through the heart

Myocardial infarction Heart attack

Nausea Feeling sick in your stomach: feeling the need to vomit

Nebulizer A device used to administer a drug that is to be given through a face mask; commonly used to treat asthma

Nephrosclerosis Constriction of the blood vessels to the kidney; caused by high blood pressure and leading to the shrinking and hardening of the kidney

Obesity Too much body fat; a person who weighs more than twenty percent over what would be considered his or her maximum ideal weight

Occlusion Blockage of a passage

Ophthalmologist A doctor who specializes in eye care

Ophthalmoscope Instrument used to examine the inside of the eye

Optometrist A specialist trained to examine the eyes and prescribe glasses or contact lenses, but not drugs

Oral candidiasis White splotches in the mouth

Osteoporosis Condition that occurs when bone becomes brittle and breaks easily

Otitis media Inflammation of the middle ear

Overflow incontinence Over-extended bladder that can cause frequent leakage

Pap smear A test to detect changes in the cells of the cervix (the neck of the uterus)

Papilledema Swelling of the nerve to the eye visible through an ophthalmoscope

Parasites Organisms that live in or on another living thing—such as worms and lice

Pathology The study of disease

Pelvic exam Examination of a woman's external and internal genitalia

Peptic ulcer disease An ulcer that is found in the stomach or beginning of small intestine

Perforation A hole made in an organ or tissue by a disease or injury

Periodontal disease A disorder to the tissues surrounding and supporting the teeth

Peripheral vascular disease Narrowing of the blood vessels in the legs

Pertussis An infectious disease also known as whooping cough; babies are immunized against this disease

Phosphate Essential part of the diet found in cereals, dairy products, eggs, and meat, necessary for the structure of bones and teeth

Pleura Thin membrane that covers the lungs

Pleuritic chest pain Pain with deep breathing

PMS (Premenstrual syndrome) A variety of physical and emotional symptoms that happen a week or two before menstruation

Pneumonia Inflammation of the lungs caused by a viral or bacterial infection

Polio An infectious disease that leads to paralysis; rare in the United States because of required immunization

Polyp A growth that comes out of any mucous membrane, the soft, pink lining of parts of the body (see mucosa)

Potassium Mineral that helps maintain normal heart rhythm, regulates the body's water balance, and is responsible for the contraction of muscles. Potassium is found in lean meat, whole grains, green leafy vegetables, beans, and many fruits (especially bananas and oranges)

Preventative care Measures such as routine physical exams, diagnostic tests (for example, Pap smears) immunizations, etc. that help prevent and detect disease and harmful medical conditions at early stages

Prostate An organ in men that sits under the bladder; produces secretions that are part of the ejaculatory fluid; often becomes enlarged after the age of fifty

Prostatitis A urinary tract infection; symptoms include fever and painful urination

Pulmonary embolism Blood clot in the lung

Pulse Heart rate examined by feeling one of the arteries in the wrist

Pyelonephritis A kidney infection

Quadriceps Muscles in front of the thigh that allow straightening of the knee

Radiological Having to do with X-rays

Respiration Breathing rate

Retina The light-sensitive membrane at the back of the eye; a disorder of the retina affects vision

Reyes syndrome A rare disease that occurs in children and causes brain and liver damage after a cold, chicken pox, or flu; aspirin is thought to be a cause, so doctors recommend giving children Tylenol® instead

Sclera The white outer coat of the eye which protects the inner structures from injury

Sedentary Not much activity, sitting around a lot

Seizures A sudden episode of uncontrolled electrical activity in the brain that leads to twitching, jerking, or sometimes loss of consciousness

Septum Thin dividing wall between parts of the body such as the wall that separates the nostrils

Sickle cell disease (SCD) An inherited blood disease that causes fatigue, headaches, shortness of breath, and bone pain

Sigmoidoscopy Examination of the rectum and last part of the large intestine through a tube-like instrument

Skeletal Having to do with the bones

Sleep Apnea Condition in which breathing stops for ten seconds or longer while a person is asleep

Sodium Mineral that regulates the body's water balance; Ssodium is a salt found in table salt, processed foods, cheese, breads, cereals, smoked meats, pickles, and snack foods

Soft palate Floor of your mouth

Somatization Physical symptoms for which no cause can be found; caused from anxiety or depression

Sputum Substance that is coughed up

Stenosis Narrowing of a duct or blood vessel

Stress incontinence Wetting your pants when sneezing, coughing, or laughing

Stress test Fitness test done when someone has chest pain, shortness of breath, or palpitations during exercise; test tells if there is heart disease

Stricture Narrowing of a duct

Stroke Damage to part of the brain, caused frequently by high blood pressure; symptoms include weakness on one side of the body, sometimes difficulty in talking

Symptoms Complaints you have (like pain)

Systolic pressure Top number of your blood pressure; may be considered high if it is over 140

Tachypnea Fast rate of breathing

Tendonitis Inflammation of a cord that joins muscle to bone or muscle to muscle

Tendons Cords that join muscle to bone or muscle to muscle

Tetanus A serious disease caused from a wound infection; DPT vaccination prevents this disease; recommended immunization booster every ten years

Thoracic cavity Chest cavity

Thorax The chest

Thrombus Blood clot

Thyroid gland A gland found in front of the neck that helps regulate your body's metabolism

Tinnitus Ringing in the ears

Trachea Windpipe

Triglycerides A form of fat

Tuberculosis An infectious disease in the lungs; symptoms are coughing, shortness of breath, fever, sweating

Ulcer An open sore that can be found on the skin, in the mouth, in the stomach, etc.

Ulcerative colitis Inflammation of the lining of the colon, causing diarrhea, pain, bleeding, fever, and generally feeling "bad"

Ultrasound A painless test that uses sound waves to help a doctor view a part of the body

Upper GI A test that involves swallowing a liquid and then having X-rays done so the doctor can view the top part of the digestive tract (throat, stomach, small bowel)

Urethritis Inflammation of the canal the leads from the bladder to outside of the body

Urge incontinence Sudden urge to urinate

Urinalysis

Urinary incontinence Involuntary loss of urine (wetting your pants)

Uterine fibroid Benign tumor in the uterus

Utilization reviews Various methods devised by health plans to measure the amount and appropriateness of health services used by its members; these checks can occur before, during, or after services have been received by the patient

Vaginalis/vaginosis An inflammation in the vagina

Vasoconstriction Narrowing of the blood vessels

Vertigo Dizziness, balance problems

Vesicle A blister filled with fluid

Virus An infection that cannot be treated with antibiotics - an example is the common cold; some viral infections are prevented with immunizations (polio, measles, mumps, rabies, etc.)

Vital signs Temperature, pulse, respiration, and blood pressure

Index

osteoporosis, 189–193
  diagnosis, 191
  hormone replacement therapy
    (HRT), 192
  risk factors, 190–191
  treatment, 191–193
  what is, 189–190

pap smear, 45, 183–184. *See also*
    pelvic exam
  follow-up tests if abnormal,
    185–186
  reading the results, 183–184
  treatment of abnormalities
    revealed by, 184
  what is, 183
pelvic exam, 45, 182–183. *See
    also* pap smear
pelvic inflammatory disease
    (PID), 111, 113
physical exam by doctor, 29–42
  lab tests, 42–44
  routine procedures, 44–46
  vital signs monitored, 30–33
pink eye (conjunctivitis), 35, 165
pleurisy, 39–40
pneumonia, 39, 40. *See also* com-
    munity-acquired pneumonia
  and HIV/AIDS, 122
polio, immunization to prevent,
    162, 164
Post Traumatic Stress Disorder
    (PTSD), 97
pregnancy, teenage, 174–177
  solutions, 176–177
primary care doctors, 15–16
prostate cancer, 86–91

African American men and, 6,
    91
early detection, importance of,
    6, 89
  PSA test, 84, 89
  screening guidelines, 84
  rectal exam, 45–46, 84, 89
  risk factors, 90
  signs and symptoms, 89–90
protein, 238–239
pulmonary embolism (blood clot
    in a major vessel), 40
pulse, measuring, 32

radiation therapy, for cancer, 85,
    96
rage. *See* anger and rage
rectal exam, 45–46, 84
renal failure. *See* kidney disease
respiration rate, measuring, 33
rubella (German measles),
    immunization, 162, 165

safe sex, 101–102
scleritis (eye disorder), 35
self-reflection, stages of, 233
sexually transmitted diseases
    (STDs), 99–124
  chlamydia, 109–111
  drug/alcohol use and, 102
  genital herpes, 107–109
  genital warts, 106–107
  gonorrhea, 111–114
  HIV/AIDS, 116–124
  how do you get, 99–100
  questions your doctor might
    ask, 102–103